National Safety Council®

INJURY FACTS ™

2000 Edition

Formerly **ACCIDENT FACTS**®

2000

The National Safety Council, chartered by an act of Congress, is a nongovernmental, not-for-profit, public service organization devoted solely to educating and influencing society to adopt safety, health, and environmental policies, practices, and procedures that prevent and mitigate human suffering and economic losses arising from preventable causes.

Injury Facts™, the Council's annual statistical report on unintentional injuries and their characteristics and costs, was prepared by:

Research and Statistics Department
Mei-Li Lin, Director
Alan F. Hoskin, Manager
Lee W. Brendel
Kevin T. Fearn
Kathleen T. Porretta, Production Manager

Work injury and illness incidence rates and fleet accident rates of reporters to the National Safety Council were prepared by:

Motivation Programs
Jean Adams, Administrator
Mary Drinkwine
Molly Holt

The Environmental Health section was prepared by:

Joseph A. Davis, Ph.D
Bud Ward

Questions or comments about the content of *Injury Facts*™ should be directed to the Research and Statistics Department, National Safety Council, 1121 Spring Lake Drive, Itasca, IL 60143, or telephone 630-775-2322, or fax 630-285-0242, or E-mail rssdept@nsc.org.

For price and ordering information, write Customer Relations, National Safety Council, 1121 Spring Lake Drive, Itasca, IL 60143, or telephone 1-800-621-7619, or fax 630-285-0797.

Acknowledgments
The information presented in *Injury Facts*™ was made possible by the cooperation of many organizations and individuals, including state vital and health statistics authorities, state traffic authorities, state workers' compensation authorities, state and local safety councils, trade associations, Bureau of the Census, Bureau of Labor Statistics, Consumer Product Safety Commission, Federal Highway Administration, Federal Railroad Administration, National Center for Health Statistics, National Fire Protection Association, National Highway Traffic Safety Administration, National Transportation Safety Board, National Weather Service, Mine Safety and Health Administration, Statistics Canada, and World Health Organization. Specific contributions are acknowledged in footnotes and source notes throughout the book.

Visit the National Safety Council on the World Wide Web at
http://www.nsc.org

Suggested citation: National Safety Council. (2000). *Injury Facts*™, *2000 Edition.* Itasca, IL: Author.

Library of Congress Catalog Card Number: 99-74142

Printed in U.S.A.   ISBN 0-87912-230-7   NSC Press Product No. 02300-0000

TABLE OF CONTENTS

FOREWORD

Summary and Trends

Unintentional-injury deaths increased 4% in 1999 compared to the revised 1998 total. Unintentional-injury deaths were estimated to total 96,900 in 1999 and 93,200 in 1998. The 1999 estimate is only 1% higher than the 1997 final count of 95,644. The 1999 figure is 12% greater than the 1992 total of 86,777 (the lowest annual total since 1924) but 17% below the 1969 peak of 116,385 deaths.

The death rate in 1999 was 35.5 per 100,000 population—4% greater than the lowest rate on record, which was 34.0 in 1992.

According to the latest final data (1997), unintentional injuries continued to be the fifth leading cause of death, exceeded only by heart disease, cancer, stroke, and chronic obstructive pulmonary diseases. Preliminary data for 1998, however, indicate that unintentional injuries may have moved to sixth place with pneumonia and influenza moving into fifth place.

Nonfatal injuries also affect millions of Americans. In 1997, about 2.5 million people were hospitalized for injuries; about 35.1 million people were treated in hospital emergency departments; and about 81.7 million visits to physicians' offices were due to injuries. In 1996, about 54.3 million people—nearly one in five—sought medical attention or suffered at least one day of activity restriction because of an injury.

The economic impact of these fatal and nonfatal unintentional injuries amounted to $469.0 billion in 1999. This is equivalent to about $1,700 per capita, or about $4,600 per household. These are costs that every individual and household pays whether directly out of pocket, through higher prices for goods and services, or through higher taxes.

The graph on the opposite page shows the overall trends in unintentional-injury deaths, resident population, and death rates over most of the 20th century. Deaths generally increased from the early part of the century through the 1960s. Deaths declined from 1969 to a low point in 1992 and then began to rise again. The resident population of the United States increased steadily with the exception of a few years during World War II when about 12 million military personnel served overseas. The population death rate has shown a long-term downward trend with some random variation and micro-trends superimposed. For example, the steady growth in unintentional-injury deaths during the 1960s, which led to the creation of several federal safety agencies, is clearly visible.

Changes in the 2000 Edition

Eight pages have been added to this edition to provide more usable information to readers. The Environmental Health section has been expanded to six pages to cover more subjects within that field. A new section of State Data has been added to make the book more useful at the local level. It includes the top five causes of unintentional-injury death in each state as well as recent trends in deaths and rates in each state.

Because we have now entered both a new decade and a new century, several special articles look back at the trends in unintentional-injury deaths and rates over the 1990s and the 20th century.

Also look for new or updated data on...

- Workplace violence
- Forklifts
- Back injuries
- Workplace health promotion
- Highway work zones
- Heat wave–related deaths
- Carbon monoxide poisoning
- Agricultural work fatalities by state
- Work injury and illness incidence rates

UNINTENTIONAL-INJURY DEATHS, DEATH RATES, AND POPULATION, UNITED STATES, 1900–1999

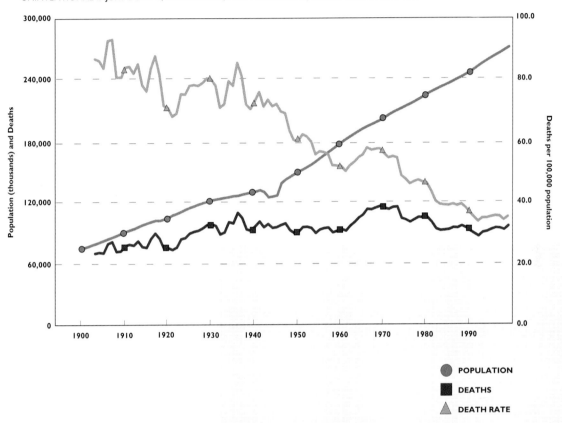

ALL UNINTENTIONAL INJURIES

ALL UNINTENTIONAL INJURIES, 1999

Unintentional-injury deaths were up 4% in 1999 compared to 1998 following a decrease in 1998. The 1999 death total was 96,900, the highest annual total since 1988.

The population death rate for all unintentional injuries increased slightly. The 1999 death rate of 35.5 per 100,000 population was 3% higher than the 1998 revised rate of 34.5. The 1992 rate, 34.0, was the lowest on record.

Comparing 1999 to 1998, home and public deaths increased, while work was virtually unchanged and motor-vehicle deaths declined slightly. The population death rate in the motor-vehicle class declined, work was unchanged, and home and public increased.

The motor-vehicle death total decreased slightly in 1999—the third decrease in a row. The motor-vehicle death rate per 100,000,000 vehicle-miles was 1.54 in 1999, down 3% from the 1998 revised rate of 1.59.

ALL UNINTENTIONAL INJURIES, 1999

Class	1999 Deaths	Change from 1998	Deaths per 100,000 Persons	Disabling Injuries[a]
All Classes[b]	**96,900**	**+4%**	**35.5**	**20,800,000**
Motor-vehicle	41,300	-1%	15.1	2,200,000
Public nonwork	*38,900*			*2,100,000*
Work	*2,200*			*100,000*
Home	*200*			*([c])*
Work	5,100	([d])	1.9	3,800,000
Nonmotor-vehicle	*2,900*			*3,700,000*
Motor-vehicle	*2,200*			*100,000*
Home	28,800	+5%	10.6	6,900,000
Nonmotor-vehicle	*28,600*			*6,900,000*
Motor-vehicle	*200*			*([c])*
Public	24,100	+13%	8.8	8,000,000

Source: National Safety Council estimates (rounded) based on data from the National Center for Health Statistics, Bureau of Labor Statistics, state departments of health, state traffic authorities, and state industrial commissions. The National Safety Council adopted the Bureau of Labor Statistics' Census of Fatal Occupational Injuries count for work-related unintentional injuries retroactive to 1992 data. See the Glossary for definitions and the Technical Appendix for revised estimating procedures.

[a] Disabling beyond the day of injury. Injuries are not reported on a national basis, so the totals shown are approximations based on ratios of disabling injuries to deaths developed each year by the National Safety Council. The totals are the best estimates for the current year. They should not, however, be compared with totals shown in previous editions of this book to indicate year-to-year changes or trends. See the Glossary for definitions and the Technical Appendix for estimating procedures.

[b] Deaths and injuries above for the four separate classes add to more than the All Classes figures due to rounding and because some deaths and injuries are included in more than one class. For example, 2,200 work deaths involved motor vehicles in transport and are in both the work and motor-vehicle totals and 200 motor-vehicle deaths occurred on home premises and are in both home and motor-vehicle. The total of such duplication amounted to about 2,400 deaths and 100,000 injuries in 1999.

[c] Less than 10,000.

[d] Change less than 0.5%.

UNINTENTIONAL-INJURY DEATHS BY CLASS, UNITED STATES, 1995–1999

Motor-Vehicle

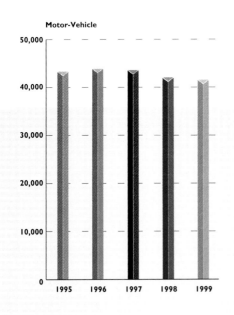

Work

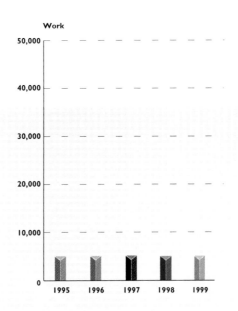

Home

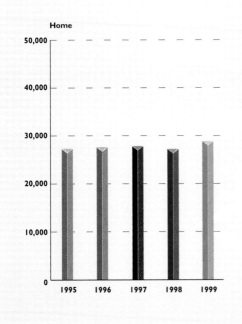

Public

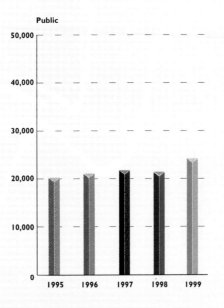

COSTS OF UNINTENTIONAL INJURIES BY CLASS, 1999

The total cost of unintentional injuries in 1999, $469.0 billion, includes estimates of economic costs of fatal and nonfatal unintentional injuries together with employer costs, vehicle damage costs, and fire losses. Wage and productivity losses, medical expenses, administrative expenses, and employer costs are included in all four classes of injuries. Cost components unique to each class are identified below.

Motor-vehicle costs include property damage from motor-vehicle accidents. Work costs include the value of property damage in on-the-job motor-vehicle accidents and fires. Home and public costs include estimated fire losses, but do not include other property damage costs.

Besides the estimated $469.0 billion in economic losses from unintentional injuries in 1999, lost quality of life from those injuries is valued at an additional $1,091.4 billion, making the comprehensive cost $1,560.4 billion in 1999.

Cost estimating procedures were revised extensively for the 1993 edition of *Accident Facts*®. New components were added, new benchmarks adopted, and a new discount rate assumed (see the Technical Appendix). In general, cost estimates are not comparable from year to year. As additional or more precise data become available, they are used from that point forward. Previously estimated figures are not revised.

CERTAIN COSTS OF UNINTENTIONAL INJURIES BY CLASS, 1999 ($ BILLIONS)

Cost	Total[a]	Motor-Vehicle	Work	Home	Public Nonmotor-Vehicle
Total	**$469.0**	**$181.5**	**$122.6**	**$101.7**	**$78.4**
Wage and productivity losses	245.6	66.1	63.9	66.7	52.5
Medical expenses	77.4	20.1	19.9	21.8	16.7
Administrative expenses[b]	77.6	53.3	23.5	4.6	4.3
Motor-vehicle damage	40.2	40.2	2.0	(c)	(c)
Employer cost	20.0	1.8	11.0	4.2	3.4
Fire loss	8.2	(c)	2.3	4.4	1.5

Source: National Safety Council estimates. See the Technical Appendix.
[a] *Duplication between work and motor-vehicle, which amounted to $15.2 billion, was eliminated from the total.*
[b] *Home and public insurance administration costs may include costs of administering medical treatment claims for some motor-vehicle injuries filed through health insurance plans.*
[c] *Not included, see comments above.*

COST OF UNINTENTIONAL INJURIES BY CLASS, 1999

TOTAL COST $469.0 BILLION

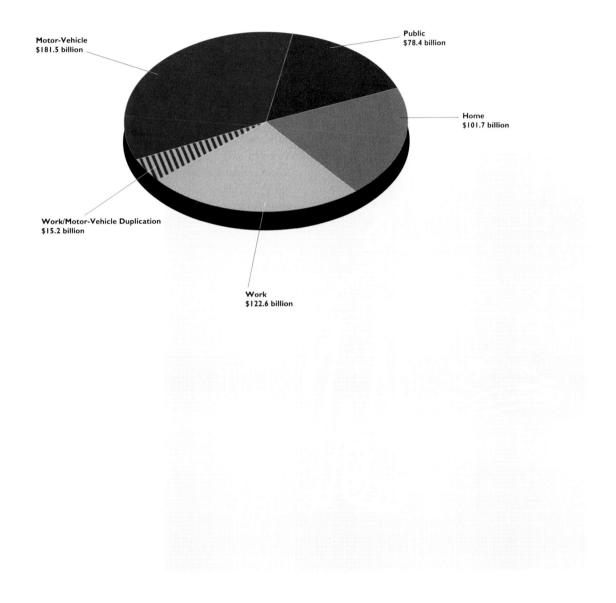

Motor-Vehicle
$181.5 billion

Public
$78.4 billion

Home
$101.7 billion

Work/Motor-Vehicle Duplication
$15.2 billion

Work
$122.6 billion

COSTS OF UNINTENTIONAL INJURIES BY COMPONENT

Wage and Productivity Losses
A person's contribution to the wealth of the nation usually is measured in terms of wages and household production. The total of wages and fringe benefits together with an estimate of the replacement-cost value of household services provides an estimate of this lost productivity. Also included is travel delay for motor-vehicle accidents.

Medical Expenses
Doctor fees, hospital charges, the cost of medicines, future medical costs, and ambulance, helicopter, and other emergency medical services are included.

Administrative Expenses
Includes the administrative cost of public and private insurance, and police and legal costs. Private insurance administrative costs are the difference between premiums paid to insurance companies and claims paid out by them. It is their cost of doing business and is a part of the cost total. Claims paid by insurance companies are not identified separately, as every claim is compensation for losses such as wages, medical expenses, property damage, etc.

Motor-Vehicle Damage
Includes the value of property damage to vehicles from motor-vehicle accidents. The cost of normal wear and tear to vehicles is not included.

Employer Costs
This is an estimate of the uninsured costs incurred by employers, representing the dollar value of time lost by uninjured workers. It includes time spent investigating and reporting injuries, giving first aid, hiring and training of replacement workers, and the extra cost of overtime for uninjured workers.

Fire Loss
Includes losses from both structure fires and nonstructure fires such as vehicles, outside storage, crops, and timber.

Work–Motor-Vehicle Duplication
The cost of motor-vehicle accidents that involve persons in the course of their work is included in both classes but the duplication is eliminated from the total. The duplication in 1999 amounted to $15.2 billion and was made up of $3.6 billion in wage and productivity losses, $1.1 billion in medical expenses, $8.1 billion in administrative expenses, $2.0 billion in vehicle damage, and $0.4 billion in uninsured employer costs.

TOTAL COST $469.0 BILLION

Medical Expenses
$77.4 billion

Wage and Productivity Losses
$245.6 billion

Administrative Expenses
$77.6 billion

Motor-Vehicle Damage
$40.2 billion

Employer Costs
$20.0 billion

Fire Losses
$8.2 billion

COST EQUIVALENTS

The costs of unintentional injuries are immense—billions of dollars. Since figures this large can be difficult to comprehend, it is sometimes useful to reduce the numbers to a more understandable scale by relating them to quantities encountered in daily life.

The table below shows how the costs of unintentional injuries compare to common quantities such as taxes, profits reported by major petroleum companies, or stock dividends.

COST EQUIVALENTS

The Cost of ...	Is Equivalent to ...
...All Injuries (\$469.0 billion)	...53 cents of every dollar paid in 1999 federal personal income taxes, **or** ...51 cents of every dollar spent on food in the United States in 1999.
...Motor-Vehicle Crashes (\$181.5 billion)	...purchasing 714 gallons of gasoline for each registered vehicle in the United States, **or** ...more than 16 times greater than the combined profits reported by ExxonMobil, Texaco, and Chevron in 1999.
...Work Injuries (\$122.6 billion)	...34 cents of every dollar of 1999 corporate dividends to stockholders, **or** ...15 cents of every dollar of 1999 pre-tax corporate profits, **or** ...exceeds the combined profits reported by the top 17 Fortune 500 companies in 1999.
...Home Injuries (\$101.7 billion)	...a \$76,200 rebate on each new single-family home built in 1999, **or** ...43 cents of every dollar of property taxes paid in 1999.
...Public Injuries (\$78.4 billion)	...an \$8.8 million grant to each public library in the United States, **or** ...a \$93,200 bonus for each police officer and firefighter.

Source: National Safety Council estimates.

DEATHS DUE TO UNINTENTIONAL INJURIES, 1999

TYPE OF EVENT AND AGE OF VICTIM

All Unintentional Injuries

The term "unintentional" covers most deaths from injury and poisoning. Excluded are homicides (including legal intervention), suicides, deaths for which none of these categories can be determined, and war deaths.

	Total	Change from 1998	Death Rate[a]
Deaths	96,900	+4%	35.5

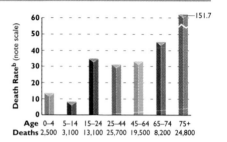

Motor-Vehicle Accidents

Includes deaths involving mechanically or electrically powered highway-transport vehicles in motion (except those on rails), both on and off the highway or street.

	Total	Change from 1998	Death Rate[a]
Deaths	41,300	−1%	15.1

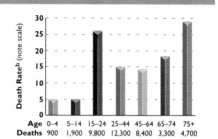

Falls

Includes deaths from falls from one level to another or on the same level. Excludes falls in or from transport vehicles, or while boarding or alighting from them.

	Total	Change from 1998	Death Rate[a]
Deaths	17,100	+6%	6.3

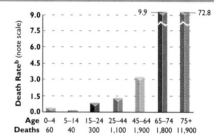

Poisoning by Solids and Liquids

Includes deaths from drugs, medicines, mushrooms, and shellfish, as well as commonly recognized poisons. Excludes poisonings from spoiled foods, salmonella, etc., which are classified as disease deaths.

	Total	Change from 1998	Death Rate[a]
Deaths	10,500	+13%	3.8

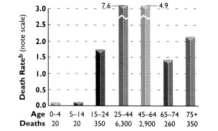

Drowning

Includes all drownings (work and nonwork) in boat accidents and those resulting from swimming, playing in the water, or falling in. Excludes drownings in floods and other cataclysms, which are classified to the cataclysm.

	Total	Change from 1998	Death Rate[a]
Deaths	4,000	−5%	1.5

See footnotes on page 9.

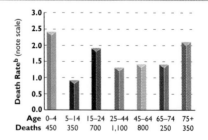

Suffocation by Ingested Object

Includes deaths from unintentional ingestion or inhalation of food or other objects, resulting in the obstruction of respiratory passages.

	Total	Change from 1998	Death Rate[a]
Deaths	3,200	–6%	1.2

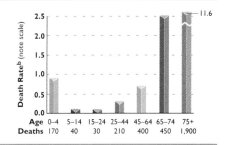

Age	0–4	5–14	15–24	25–44	45–64	65–74	75+
Deaths	170	40	30	210	400	450	1,900

Fires, Burns, and Deaths Associated with Fires

Includes deaths from fires, burns, and injuries in conflagrations—such as asphyxiation, falls, and struck by falling objects. Excludes burns from hot objects or liquids.

	Total	Change from 1998	Death Rate[a]
Deaths	3,100	+3%	1.1

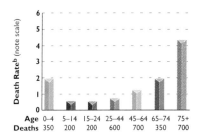

Age	0–4	5–14	15–24	25–44	45–64	65–74	75+
Deaths	350	200	200	600	700	350	700

Firearms

Includes unintentional deaths from firearms injuries principally in recreational activities or on home premises. Excludes deaths from explosive material or in war operations.

	Total	Change from 1998	Death Rate[a]
Deaths	700	–13%	0.3

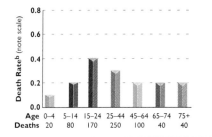

Age	0–4	5–14	15–24	25–44	45–64	65–74	75+
Deaths	20	80	170	250	100	40	40

Poisoning by Gases and Vapors

Mostly carbon monoxide due to incomplete combustion, involving cooking and heating equipment and standing motor vehicles. Excludes deaths in conflagrations, or associated with transport vehicles in motion.

	Total	Change from 1998	Death Rate[a]
Deaths	500	–17%	0.2

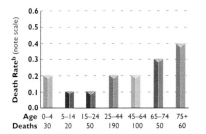

Age	0–4	5–14	15–24	25–44	45–64	65–74	75+
Deaths	30	20	50	190	100	50	60

All Other Types

Most important types included are: medical and surgical complications and misadventures, machinery, air transport, water transport (except drownings), mechanical suffocation, and excessive cold.

	Total	Change from 1998	Death Rate[a]
Deaths	16,500	+18%	6.0

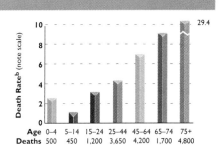

Age	0–4	5–14	15–24	25–44	45–64	65–74	75+
Deaths	500	450	1,200	3,650	4,200	1,700	4,800

[a]Deaths per 100,000 population.
[b]Deaths per 100,000 population in each age group.

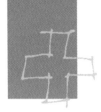

LEADING CAUSES OF DEATH

Unintentional injuries are the leading cause of death among persons in age groups from 1 to 34. Among persons of all ages, unintentional injuries are the fifth leading cause of death. For children in the 5 to 14 year age group, unintentional injuries claim nearly three and one-half times as many lives as the next leading cause of death, accounting for more than 41% of the 8,061 total deaths of these persons in 1997. Nearly 60% of the victims in this age group are males.

DEATHS AND DEATH RATES BY AGE AND SEX, 1997

Cause	Number of Deaths			Death Rates[a]		
	Total	Male	Female	Total	Male	Female
All Ages						
All Causes	**2,314,245**	**1,154,039**	**1,160,206**	**864.3**	**882.6**	**847.0**
Heart disease	726,974	356,598	370,376	271.5	272.7	270.4
Cancer	539,577	281,110	258,467	201.5	215.0	188.7
Stroke (cerebrovascular disease)	159,791	62,564	97,227	59.7	47.8	71.0
Chronic obstructive pulmonary disease	109,029	55,984	53,045	40.7	42.8	38.7
Unintentional Injuries	**95,644**	**61,963**	**33,681**	**35.7**	**47.4**	**24.6**
Motor-vehicle	43,458	28,770	14,688	16.2	22.0	10.7
Falls	15,447	7,705	7,742	5.8	5.9	5.7
Poison (solid, liquid)	9,587	7,176	2,411	3.6	5.5	1.8
Drowning	4,051	3,261	790	1.5	2.5	0.6
Fires, burns	3,490	2,086	1,404	1.3	1.6	1.0
All other unintentional injuries	19,611	12,965	6,646	7.3	9.9	4.9
Pneumonia and influenza	86,449	39,284	47,165	32.3	30.0	34.4
Diabetes mellitus	62,636	28,187	34,449	23.4	21.6	25.1
Suicide	30,535	24,492	6,043	11.4	18.7	4.4
Nephritis and nephrosis	25,331	12,140	13,191	9.5	9.3	9.6
Chronic liver disease, cirrhosis	25,183	16,266	8,917	9.4	12.4	6.5
Septicemia	22,401	9,656	12,745	8.4	7.4	9.3
Homicide and legal intervention	19,846	15,449	4,397	7.4	11.8	3.2
Atherosclerosis	16,735	6,269	10,466	6.3	4.8	7.6
Human immunodeficiency virus infection	16,516	12,892	3,624	6.2	9.9	2.6
Certain conditions originating in perinatal period	13,092	7,398	5,694	4.9	5.7	4.2
Under 1 Year						
All Causes	**28,045**	**15,788**	**12,257**	**741.9**	**818.0**	**662.9**
Certain conditions originating in perinatal period	12,935	7,308	5,627	342.2	378.7	304.3
Congenital anomalies	6,178	3,266	2,912	163.4	169.2	157.5
Sudden infant death syndrome	2,997	1,815	1,182	79.3	94.0	63.9
Unintentional Injuries	**765**	**430**	**335**	**20.2**	**22.3**	**18.1**
Mechanical suffocation	303	176	127	8.0	9.1	6.9
Motor-vehicle	165	84	81	4.4	4.4	4.4
Ingestion of food, object	76	48	28	2.0	2.5	1.5
Drowning	60	34	26	1.6	1.8	1.4
Fires, burns	51	28	23	1.3	1.5	1.2
All other unintentional injuries	110	60	50	2.9	3.1	2.7
Heart disease	690	398	292	18.3	20.6	15.8
Pneumonia and influenza	421	257	164	11.1	13.3	8.9
Homicide and legal intervention	317	182	135	8.4	9.4	7.3
Stroke (cerebrovascular disease)	269	150	119	7.1	7.8	6.4
Septicemia	196	119	77	5.2	6.2	4.2
Nephritis and nephrosis	136	81	55	3.6	4.2	3.0
Cancer	102	52	50	2.7	2.7	2.7
Meningitis	97	40	57	2.6	2.1	3.1
Hernia	77	49	28	2.0	2.5	1.5
Benign neoplasms	63	31	32	1.7	1.6	1.7
Chronic obstructive pulmonary disease	50	32	18	1.3	1.7	1.0
Anemias	25	11	14	0.7	0.6	0.8
1 to 4 Years						
All Causes	**5,501**	**3,121**	**2,380**	**35.9**	**39.8**	**31.8**
Unintentional Injuries	**2,005**	**1,192**	**813**	**13.1**	**15.2**	**10.9**
Motor-vehicle	768	419	349	5.0	5.3	4.7
Drowning	456	306	150	3.0	3.9	2.0
Fires, burns	348	196	152	2.3	2.5	2.0
Ingestion of food, object	71	43	28	0.5	0.5	0.4
Mechanical suffocation	71	47	24	0.5	0.6	0.3
All other unintentional injuries	291	181	110	1.9	2.3	1.5
Congenital anomalies	589	317	272	3.8	4.0	3.6
Cancer	438	240	198	2.9	3.1	2.6
Homicide and legal intervention	375	209	166	2.4	2.7	2.2
Heart disease	212	119	93	1.4	1.5	1.2
Pneumonia and influenza	180	89	91	1.2	1.1	1.2
Certain conditions originating in perinatal period	75	46	29	0.5	0.6	0.4
Septicemia	73	38	35	0.5	0.5	0.5
Stroke (cerebrovascular disease)	56	36	20	0.4	0.5	0.3
Human immunodeficiency virus infection	54	25	29	0.4	0.3	0.4

See source and footnote on page 12.

DEATHS AND DEATH RATES BY AGE AND SEX, 1997, Cont.

Cause	Number of Deaths			Death Rates[a]		
	Total	Male	Female	Total	Male	Female
5 to 14 Years						
All Causes	**8,061**	**4,763**	**3,298**	**20.8**	**24.0**	**17.4**
Unintentional injuries	**3,371**	**2,110**	**1,261**	**8.7**	**10.6**	**6.7**
Motor-vehicle	1,967	1,154	813	5.1	5.8	4.3
Drowning	449	326	123	1.2	1.6	0.6
Fires, burns	277	150	127	0.7	0.8	0.7
Firearms	122	107	15	0.3	0.5	0.1
Mechanical suffocation	100	87	13	0.3	0.4	0.1
All other unintentional injuries	456	286	170	1.2	1.4	0.9
Cancer	1,030	560	470	2.7	2.8	2.5
Homicide and legal intervention	457	295	162	1.2	1.5	0.9
Congenital anomalies	447	232	215	1.2	1.2	1.1
Heart disease	313	180	133	0.8	0.9	0.7
Suicide	307	233	74	0.8	1.2	0.4
Pneumonia and influenza	141	71	70	0.4	0.4	0.4
Chronic obstructive pulmonary diseases	129	71	58	0.3	0.4	0.3
Human immunodeficiency virus infection	102	63	39	0.3	0.3	0.2
Benign neoplasms	76	30	46	0.2	0.2	0.2
15 to 24 Years						
All Causes	**31,544**	**23,312**	**8,232**	**86.1**	**124.4**	**46.0**
Unintentional injuries	**13,367**	**9,791**	**3,576**	**36.5**	**52.3**	**20.0**
Motor-vehicle	10,208	7,167	3,041	27.9	38.3	17.0
Drowning	665	598	67	1.8	3.2	0.4
Poison (solid, liquid)	658	523	135	1.8	2.8	0.8
Firearms	300	282	18	0.8	1.5	0.1
Falls	269	231	38	0.7	1.2	0.2
All other unintentional injuries	1,267	990	277	3.5	5.3	1.5
Homicide and legal intervention	6,146	5,302	844	16.8	28.3	4.7
Suicide	4,186	3,559	627	11.4	19.0	3.5
Cancer	1,645	981	664	4.5	5.2	3.7
Heart disease	1,098	674	424	3.0	3.6	2.4
Congenital anomalies	420	241	179	1.1	1.3	1.0
Human immunodeficiency virus infection	276	145	131	0.8	0.8	0.7
Pneumonia and influenza	220	119	101	0.6	0.6	0.6
Chronic obstructive pulmonary disease	201	135	66	0.5	0.7	0.4
Stroke (cerebrovascular disease)	188	106	82	0.5	0.6	0.5
25 to 34 Years						
All Causes	**45,538**	**31,707**	**13,831**	**115.2**	**161.3**	**69.6**
Unintentional injuries	**12,598**	**9,590**	**3,008**	**31.9**	**48.8**	**15.1**
Motor-vehicle	7,500	5,447	2,053	19.0	27.7	10.3
Poison (solid, liquid)	2,102	1,648	454	5.3	8.4	2.3
Drowning	631	568	63	1.6	2.9	0.3
Falls	366	315	51	0.9	1.6	0.3
Fires, burns	288	196	92	0.7	1.0	0.5
All other unintentional injuries	1,711	1,416	295	4.3	7.2	1.5
Suicide	5,672	4,684	988	14.3	23.8	5.0
Homicide and legal intervention	5,075	4,068	1,007	12.8	20.7	5.1
Cancer	4,607	2,284	2,323	11.7	11.6	11.7
Human immunodeficiency virus infection	3,993	2,991	1,002	10.1	15.2	5.0
Heart disease	3,286	2,145	1,141	8.3	10.9	5.7
Stroke (cerebrovascular disease)	678	335	343	1.7	1.7	1.7
Diabetes mellitus	620	325	295	1.6	1.7	1.5
Pneumonia and influenza	534	313	221	1.4	1.6	1.1
Chronic liver disease, cirrhosis	518	339	179	1.3	1.7	0.9
35 to 44 Years						
All Causes	**89,408**	**58,141**	**31,267**	**203.2**	**266.3**	**141.0**
Cancer	17,099	7,557	9,542	38.9	34.6	43.0
Unintentional injuries	**14,531**	**10,822**	**3,709**	**33.0**	**49.6**	**16.7**
Motor-vehicle	6,667	4,642	2,025	15.2	21.3	9.1
Poison (solid, liquid)	3,870	2,979	891	8.8	13.6	4.0
Falls	656	530	126	1.5	2.4	0.6
Drowning	602	508	94	1.4	2.3	0.4
Fires, burns	409	286	123	0.9	1.3	0.6
All other unintentional injuries	2,327	1,877	450	5.3	8.6	2.0
Heart disease	13,227	9,569	3,658	30.1	43.8	16.5
Human immunodeficiency virus infection	7,073	5,578	1,495	16.1	25.5	6.7
Suicide	6,730	5,223	1,507	15.3	23.9	6.8
Homicide and legal intervention	3,677	2,735	942	8.4	12.5	4.2
Chronic liver disease, cirrhosis	3,509	2,464	1,045	8.0	11.3	4.7
Stroke (cerebrovascular disease)	2,787	1,419	1,368	6.3	6.5	6.2
Diabetes mellitus	1,858	1,158	700	4.2	5.3	3.2
Pneumonia and influenza	1,394	851	543	3.2	3.9	2.4

See source and footnote on page 12.

DEATHS AND DEATH RATES BY AGE AND SEX, 1997, Cont.

Cause	Number of Deaths			Death Rates[a]		
	Total	Male	Female	Total	Male	Female
45 to 54 Years						
All Causes	**144,882**	**90,587**	**54,295**	**430.9**	**551.4**	**315.8**
Cancer	45,429	22,709	22,720	135.1	138.2	132.2
Heart disease	35,277	25,954	9,323	104.9	158.0	54.2
Unintentional injuries	**10,416**	**7,594**	**2,822**	**31.0**	**46.2**	**16.4**
Motor-vehicle	4,805	3,274	1,531	14.3	19.9	8.9
Poison (solid, liquid)	1,897	1,448	449	5.6	8.8	2.6
Falls	746	574	172	2.2	3.5	1.0
Drowning	422	352	70	1.3	2.1	0.4
Fires, burns	369	250	119	1.1	1.5	0.7
All other unintentional injuries	2,177	1,696	481	6.5	10.3	2.8
Stroke (cerebrovascular disease)	5,695	3,160	2,535	16.9	19.2	14.7
Chronic liver disease, cirrhosis	5,622	4,198	1,424	16.7	25.6	8.3
Suicide	4,948	3,697	1,251	14.7	22.5	7.3
Diabetes mellitus	4,335	2,442	1,893	12.9	14.9	11.0
Human immunodeficiency virus infection	3,513	2,862	651	10.4	17.4	3.8
Chronic obstructive pulmonary disease	2,838	1,443	1,395	8.4	8.8	8.1
Pneumonia and influenza	2,233	1,375	858	6.6	8.4	5.0
55 to 64 Years						
All Causes	**231,993**	**138,876**	**93,117**	**1,063.4**	**1,337.4**	**814.5**
Cancer	86,314	47,110	39,204	395.6	453.7	342.9
Heart disease	65,958	45,158	20,800	302.3	434.9	181.9
Stroke (cerebrovascular disease)	9,676	5,342	4,334	44.4	51.4	37.9
Chronic obstructive pulmonary disease	10,109	5,247	4,862	46.3	50.5	42.5
Diabetes mellitus	8,370	4,213	4,157	38.4	40.6	36.4
Unintentional injuries	**7,105**	**4,817**	**2,288**	**32.6**	**46.4**	**20.0**
Motor-vehicle	3,329	2,101	1,228	15.3	20.2	10.7
Falls	841	605	236	3.9	5.8	2.1
Poison (solid, liquid)	452	293	159	2.1	2.8	1.4
Fires, burns	355	219	136	1.6	2.1	1.2
Surgical, medical complications	347	183	164	1.6	1.8	1.4
All other unintentional injuries	1,516	1,193	323	6.9	11.5	2.8
Chronic liver disease, cirrhosis	5,254	3,655	1,599	24.1	35.2	14.0
Pneumonia and influenza	3,759	2,194	1,565	17.2	21.1	13.7
Suicide	2,946	2,331	615	13.5	22.4	5.4
Human immunodeficiency virus infection	1,065	882	183	4.9	8.5	1.6
65 to 74 Years						
All Causes	**464,274**	**263,875**	**200,399**	**2,505.8**	**3,185.0**	**1,956.3**
Cancer	156,746	87,515	69,231	846.0	1,056.3	675.8
Heart disease	139,416	85,257	54,159	752.5	1,029.2	528.7
Chronic obstructive pulmonary disease	30,569	16,643	13,926	165.0	200.9	135.9
Stroke (cerebrovascular disease)	24,944	12,663	12,281	134.6	152.9	119.9
Diabetes mellitus	16,311	8,030	8,281	88.0	96.9	80.8
Pneumonia and influenza	10,535	6,147	4,388	56.9	74.2	42.8
Unintentional injuries	**8,578**	**5,213**	**3,365**	**46.3**	**62.9**	**32.8**
Motor-vehicle	3,370	1,955	1,415	18.2	23.6	13.8
Falls	1,840	1,097	743	9.9	13.2	7.3
Surgical, medical complications	659	357	302	3.6	4.3	2.9
Ingestion of food, object	480	272	208	2.6	3.3	2.0
Fires, burns	405	250	155	2.2	3.0	1.5
All other unintentional injuries	1,824	1,282	542	9.8	15.5	5.3
Chronic liver disease, cirrhosis	5,805	3,448	2,357	31.3	41.6	23.0
Nephritis and nephrosis	4,729	2,525	2,204	25.5	30.5	21.5
Septicemia	4,179	2,190	1,989	22.6	26.4	19.4
75 Years and Over						
All Causes	**1,264,999**	**523,869**	**741,130**	**8,073.3**	**9,061.9**	**7,495.2**
Heart disease	467,497	187,144	280,353	2,983.6	3,237.2	2,835.3
Cancer	226,167	112,102	114,065	1,443.4	1,939.1	1,153.6
Stroke (cerebrovascular disease)	115,422	39,309	76,113	736.6	680.0	769.8
Pneumonia and influenza	67,032	27,868	39,164	427.8	482.1	396.1
Chronic obstructive pulmonary disease	63,849	31,781	32,068	407.5	549.7	324.3
Diabetes mellitus	30,980	11,938	19,042	197.7	206.5	192.6
Unintentional injuries	**22,908**	**10,404**	**12,504**	**146.2**	**180.0**	**126.5**
Falls	10,614	4,280	6,334	67.7	74.0	64.1
Motor-vehicle	4,679	2,527	2,152	29.9	43.7	21.8
Ingestion of food, object	1,876	826	1,050	12.0	14.3	10.6
Surgical, medical complications	1,443	603	840	9.2	10.4	8.5
Fires, burns	791	379	412	5.0	6.6	4.2
All other unintentional injuries	3,505	1,789	1,716	22.4	30.9	17.4
Alzheimer's Disease	20,846	6,302	14,544	133.0	109.0	147.1
Nephritis and nephrosis	17,058	7,631	9,427	108.9	132.0	95.3
Atherosclerosis	13,949	4,615	9,334	89.0	79.8	94.4

Source: Deaths are latest figures from National Center for Health Statistics. Rates are National Safety Council calculations. The All Causes total for each age group includes deaths not shown separately.
[a]Deaths per 100,000 population in each age group.

LEADING CAUSES OF DEATH BY AGE GROUP, UNITED STATES, 1997

Rank	All Ages	Under 1	1–4	5–14	15–24	25–44	45–64	65 & Over
					Age Group			
1	Heart disease 726,974	Congenital anomalies 6,178	Unintentional injuries 2,005	Unintentional injuries 3,371	Unintentional injuries 13,367	Unintentional injuries 27,129	Malignant neoplasms 131,743	Heart disease 606,913
2	Malignant neoplasms 539,577	Short gestation[a] 3,925	Congenital anomalies 589	Malignant neoplasms 1,030	Homicide 6,146	Malignant neoplasms 21,706	Heart disease 101,235	Malignant neoplasms 382,913
3	Cerebrovascular diseases 159,791	SIDS[b] 2,991	Malignant neoplasms 438	Homicide 457	Suicide 4,186	Heart disease 16,513	Unintentional injuries 17,521	Cerebrovascular diseases 140,366
4	COPD[d] 109,029	Respiratory distress[a] 1,301	Homicide 375	Congenital anomalies 447	Malignant neoplasms 1,645	Suicide 12,402	Cerebrovascular diseases 15,371	COPD[c] 94,411
5	Unintentional injuries 95,644	Maternal complications[a] 1,244	Heart disease 212	Heart disease 313	Heart disease 1,098	HIV[d] 11,066	COPD[d] 12,947	Pneumonia & Influenza 77,561
6	Pneumonia & Influenza 86,449	Placenta, cord, membranes[a] 960	Pneumonia & Influenza 180	Suicide 307	Congenital anomalies 420	Homicide 8,752	Diabetes mellitus 12,705	Diabetes mellitus 47,289
7	Diabetes mellitus 62,636	Perinatal infections[a] 777	Perinatal conditions 75	Pneumonia & Influenza 141	HIV[d] 276	Liver disease 4,024	Liver disease 10,875	Unintentional injuries 31,386
8	Suicide 30,535	Unintentional injuries 765	Septicemia 73	COPD[c] 129	Pneumonia & Influenza 220	Cerebrovascular diseases 3,465	Suicide 7,894	Alzheimer's disease 22,154
9	Nephritis[e] 25,331	Intrauterine hypoxia[a] 452	Benign neoplasms 65	HIV[d] 102	COPD[c] 201	Diabetes mellitus 2,478	Pneumonia & Influenza 5,992	Nephritis[e] 21,787
10	Liver disease 25,175	Pneumonia & Influenza 421	Cerebrovascular diseases 56	Benign neoplasms[f] 76	Cerebrovascular diseases 188	Pneumonia & Influenza 1,928	HIV[d] 4,578	Septicemia 18,079

Source: Hoyert, D.L., Kochanek, K.D., & Murphy, S.L. (1999). Deaths: Final Data for 1997. National Vital Statistics Reports, 47(19). Hyattsville, MD: National Center for Health Statistics.
[a] Included in "Certain conditions originating in perinatal period" on p. 10.
[b] Sudden infant death syndrome.
[c] Chronic obstructive pulmonary disease.
[d] Human immunodeficiency virus infection.
[e] Including nephrotic syndrome and nephrosis.
[f] Tied with cerebrovascular diseases.

LEADING CAUSES OF DEATH BY AGE, 1997

Heart disease, cancer, stroke, chronic obstructive pulmonary disease, and unintentional injuries were the leading causes of death in the United States in 1997. The graph below depicts the number of deaths attributed to these causes by single-year ages.

Unintentional injuries were the leading cause of death of individuals aged 1 to 38 in 1997. The pattern of 1997 unintentional-injury fatalities shows that a substantial increase in fatalities occurred to persons between ages 15 and 21, rising from 726 for 15-year-olds to 1,525 for 21-year-olds. This trend can be attributed to the sharp increase in motor-vehicle deaths for persons of the same age range. Persons age 19 fell victim to the most unintentional-injury fatalities with motor-vehicle crashes accounting for a majority of the death total. Fatalities gradually decreased and remained relatively stable thereafter with the exception of a slight increase in unintentional-injury deaths for persons between ages 30 and 42. From ages 1 to 33, deaths from motor-vehicle crashes alone exceeded those for any other cause.

Heart disease, the leading cause of death overall, was also the leading cause of death of persons aged 74 and over in 1997. Heart disease fatalities peaked at 25,146 for persons 83 years of age. Cancer, the second leading cause of death overall, was the leading cause of death of persons from aged 39 to 73 in 1997. Cancer deaths peaked at 18,152 for individuals aged 75. Human immunodeficiency virus (HIV) deaths peaked at 783 for persons aged 40, compared to the high in 1996 of 1,508 for persons of age 37.

The third leading cause of death in the United States in 1997 was stroke, which was the second leading cause of death of persons aged 91 and over. Stroke deaths peaked at 6,552 for persons age 86. The next leading cause of death was chronic obstructive pulmonary disease, which was the third leading cause of death of persons aged 59 to 75. Chronic obstructive pulmonary disease deaths reached a high at 4,399 deaths for persons 79 years of age.

Source: National Safety Council tabulations of National Center for Health Statistics data. ICD codes are 390–398, 402, 404–429 for heart disease; 140–208 for cancer; 430–438 for stroke; 490–496 for chronic obstructive pulmonary disease; E800–E949 for unintentional injuries; E810–E825 for motor-vehicle fatalities.

LEADING CAUSES OF DEATH BY AGE, UNITED STATES, 1997

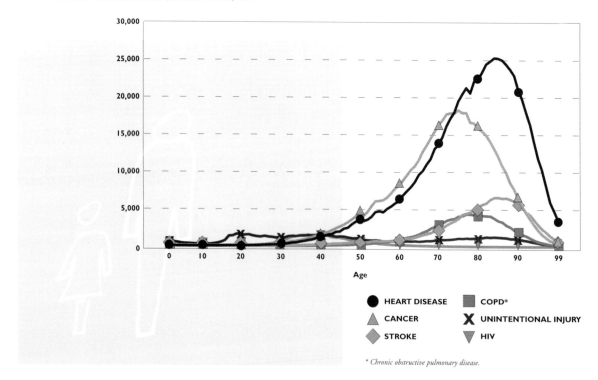

* Chronic obstructive pulmonary disease.

LEADING CAUSES OF UNINTENTIONAL-INJURY DEATH BY AGE, 1997

Motor-vehicle accidents, falls, poisoning by solids and liquids, drownings, and fires and burns were the leading causes of unintentional-injury death in the United States in 1997. The graph below depicts the number of deaths attributed to these causes by single-year ages.

Motor-vehicle accidents were the leading cause of unintentional-injury death overall and the leading cause of unintentional-injury death from age 1 to 77 in 1997. The distribution of 1997 motor-vehicle fatalities shows a sharp increase for persons aged 13 to 18, rising from 229 for 13-year-olds to 1,274 for 18-year-olds. The greatest number of motor-vehicle fatalities occurred to persons aged 18 in 1997.

The second leading cause of unintentional-injury death overall in 1997 was falls. Falls were the leading cause of unintentional-injury death of persons aged 78 and over;

deaths resulting from falls peaked at 607 for individuals age 87. Poisoning by solids and liquids was the third leading cause of unintentional-injury death in the United States in 1997. Solid and liquid poisoning fatalities reached a high of 430 for 39-year-old individuals and were the second leading cause of unintentional-injury death for persons aged 19 to 54.

Drownings were the fourth leading cause of unintentional-injury death in 1997. Drowning fatalities reached a high of 162 for 1-year-olds and were the second leading cause of unintentional-injury death for 1- and 2-year-olds and again for those aged 8 to 18. The fifth leading cause of unintentional-injury death was fires and burns, which peaked at 105 for 3-year-olds.

Source: National Safety Council tabulations of National Center for Health Statistics data. ICD codes are E810–E825 for motor-vehicle; E880–E888 for falls; E850–E866 for solid and liquid poisonings; E890–E899 for fires; E910 for drownings.

LEADING CAUSES OF UNINTENTIONAL-INJURY DEATH BY AGE, UNITED STATES, 1997

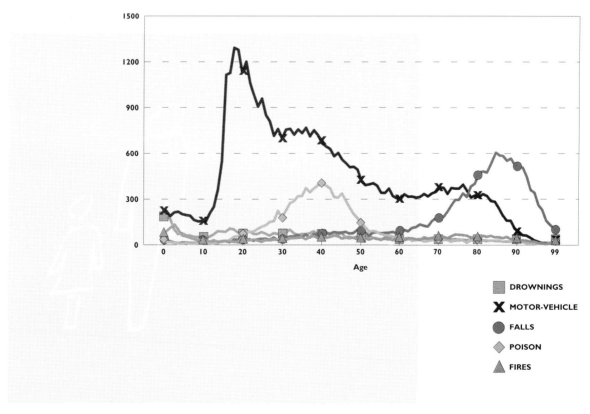

ALL DEATHS DUE TO INJURY

ALL DEATHS DUE TO INJURY, UNITED STATES, 1995–1997

Type of Accident or Manner of Injury	1997[a]	1996	1995
Total Deaths Due to Injuries, E800–E999[b]	**149,691**	**150,298**	**150,809**
All Accidental Deaths, E800–E949	**95,644**	**94,948**	**93,320**
Transport Accidents, E800–E848	**45,798**	**46,224**	**45,805**
Railway, E800–E807	527	565	569
Motor-vehicle, E810–E825	43,458	43,649	43,363
Other road vehicle, E826–E829	220	202	211
Water transport, E830–E838	758	675	762
Drowning (excluded from drowning below), E830, E832	*490*	*471*	*560*
Other water transport, E831, E833–E838	*268*	*204*	*202*
Air and space transport, E840–E845	734	1,061	851
Vehicle accidents not elsewhere classifiable, E846–E848	101	72	49
Poisoning by solids and liquids (see also page 132), E850–E866	9,587	8,872	8,461
Drugs, medicaments and biologicals, E850–E858	9,099	8,431	8,000
Analgesics, antipyretics, and antirheumatics, E850	*2,813*	*2,490*	*2,508*
Barbiturates, E851	*24*	*19*	*10*
Other sedatives and hypnotics, E852	*9*	*15*	*12*
Tranquilizers, E853	*94*	*82*	*72*
Other psychotropic agents, E854	*393*	*344*	*373*
Other drugs acting on central and autonomic nervous system, E855	*1,336*	*1,411*	*1,156*
Antibiotics, E856	*48*	*47*	*26*
Anti-infectives, E857	*8*	*6*	*8*
Other drugs, E858	*4,374*	*4,017*	*3,835*
Poisoning by other solids and liquids, E860–E866	488	441	461
Alcohol, E860	*342*	*308*	*318*
Cleansing, polishing agents, disinfectants, paints, varnishes, E861	*14*	*10*	*10*
Petroleum products, other solvents and their vapors, E862	*46*	*50*	*57*
Agricultural, horticultural chemical, pharmaceutical preparations, E863	*12*	*16*	*9*
Corrosives and caustics, E864	*8*	*9*	*10*
Foodstuffs and poisonous plants, E865	*11*	*6*	*7*
Other and unspecified solids and liquids, E866	*55*	*42*	*50*
Poisoning by gases and vapors (see also page 132), E867–E869	576	638	611
Gas distributed by pipeline, E867	13	23	27
Other utility gas and other carbon monoxide, E868	459	502	506
Motor-vehicle exhaust gas, E868.2	*208*	*219*	*234*
Others, not motor-vehicle exhaust gas, E868.0, E868.1, E868.3–E868.9	*251*	*283*	*272*
Other gases and vapors, E869	104	113	78
Complications, misadventures of surgical, medical care, E870–E879	3,043	2,919	2,712
Falls, E880–E888	**15,447**	**14,986**	**13,986**
Fall on or from stairs or steps, E880	1,295	1,239	1,241
Fall on or from ladders or scaffolding, E881	368	369	352
Fall from or out of building or other structure, E882	549	444	467
Fall into hole or other opening in surface, E883	70	88	94
Other fall from one level to another, E884	1,106	1,129	1,145
Fall on same level from slipping, tripping, or stumbling, E885	726	688	491
Fall on same level from collision, pushing, or shoving, E886	4	3	8
Fracture, cause unspecified, E887	3,589	3,694	3,503
Other and unspecified fall, E888	7,740	7,332	6,685
Fire and flames, E890–E899	**3,490**	**3,741**	**3,761**
Conflagration, E890–E892	2,927	3,165	3,205
Ignition of clothing, E893	165	160	151
Ignition of highly inflammable material, E894	52	54	46
Other and unspecified fire and flames, E895–E899	346	362	359
Natural and environmental factors, E900–E909	**1,316**	**1,550**	**1,821**
Excessive heat, E900	182	249	716
Excessive cold, E901	501	685	553
Hunger, thirst, exposure, and neglect, E904	224	224	203
Poisoning by and toxic reaction to venomous animals, plants, E905	68	68	81
Venomous snakes, lizards, and spiders, E905.0, E905.1	*12*	*13*	*16*
Hornets, wasps, and bees, E905.3	*43*	*45*	*59*
Other and unspecified animals, plants, E905.2, E905.4–E905.9	*13*	*10*	*6*
Other injury caused by animals, E906	102	107	78
Dog bite, E906.0	*19*	*23*	*18*
Other and unspecified injury by animal, E906.1–E906.9	*83*	*84*	*60*
Lightning, E907	58	63	76
Cataclysmic storms, and floods resulting from storms, E908	136	93	74
Cataclysmic earth surface movements and eruptions, E909	20	42	25
Other natural and environmental factors, E902, E903	25	19	15
Other accidents, E910–E928	**14,935**	**14,639**	**14,866**
Drowning, submersion (excluding water transport drownings above), E910	3,561	3,488	3,790
During sport or recreation, E910.0–E910.2	*648*	*645*	*822*
In bathtub, E910.4	*329*	*330*	*281*
Other, unspecified drowning, submersion, E910.3, E910.8, E910.9	*2,584*	*2,513*	*2,687*
Inhalation and ingestion of food, E911	1,095	1,126	1,088
Inhalation and ingestion of other object, E912	2,180	2,080	2,097

See source and footnotes on page 17.

ALL DEATHS DUE TO INJURY, UNITED STATES, 1995–1997, Cont.

Type of Accident or Manner of Injury	1997[a]	1996	1995
Mechanical suffocation, E913	1,145	1,114	1,062
In bed or cradle, E913.0	236	219	207
By plastic bag, E913.1	44	40	37
Due to lack of air (in refrigerator, other enclosed space), E913.2	21	15	14
By falling earth (noncataclysmic cave-in), E913.3	54	57	59
Other and unspecified mechanical suffocation, E913.8, E913.9	790	783	745
Struck by falling object, E916	727	732	656
Struck against or by objects or persons, E917	247	171	198
Caught in or between objects, E918	85	71	90
Machinery, E919	1,055	926	986
Agricultural machines, E919.0	530	496	514
Lifting machines and appliances, E919.2	119	115	141
Earth moving, scraping, and other excavating machines, E919.7	85	73	106
Other, unspecified machinery, E919.1, E919.3–E919.6, E919.8, E919.9	321	242	225
Cutting or piercing instruments or objects, E920	104	97	118
Firearm missile, E922	981	1,134	1,225
Handgun, E922.0	161	187	233
Shotgun (automatic), E922.1	84	93	116
Hunting rifle, E922.2	65	50	64
Other and unspecified firearm missile, E922.3–E922.9	671	804	812
Explosive material, E923	149	130	170
Fireworks, E923.0	8	9	2
Explosive gases, E923.2	57	49	62
Other and unspecified explosive material, E923.1, E923.8, E923.9	84	72	106
Hot substance or object, corrosive material and steam, E924	111	104	97
Electric current, E925	488	482	559
Domestic wiring and appliances, E925.0	53	66	88
Generating plants, distribution stations, transmission lines, E925.1	139	135	158
Industrial wiring, appliances, and electrical machinery, E925.2	27	15	26
Other and unspecified electric current, E925.8, E925.9	269	266	287
Radiation, E926	0	0	0
Other and unspecified, E914, E915, E921, E927, E928	3,007	2,984	2,730
Late effects (deaths more than one year after accident), E929	1,204	1,126	1,091
Adverse effects of drugs in therapeutic use, E930–E949	248	253	206
All Suicide Deaths, E950–E959	**30,535**	**30,903**	**31,284**
Poisoning by solid and liquid, E950	3,310	3,073	3,052
Poisoning by gases and vapors, E951, E952	1,818	2,007	2,095
Motor-vehicle exhaust gas, E952.0	1,367	1,508	1,659
Other and unspecified gases and vapors, E951, E952.1–E952.9	451	499	436
Hanging, strangulation, and suffocation, E953	5,413	5,330	5,217
Drowning, E954	384	361	410
Firearms, E955.0–E955.4	17,566	18,166	18,503
Handgun, E955.0	3,519	3,675	3,700
Shotgun, E955.1	2,214	2,293	2,391
Hunting rifle, E955.2	865	945	971
Other and unspecified firearm, E955.3, E955.4	10,968	11,253	11,441
Cutting and piercing instruments, E956	499	435	454
Jumping from high places, E957	600	645	713
Other, unspecified suicide and late effects, E955.5, E955.9, E958, E959	945	886	840
All Homicide Deaths, E960–E969	**19,491**	**20,634**	**22,552**
Assault by hanging and strangulation, E963	724	762	841
Assault by firearm, E965.0–E965.4	13,252	14,037	15,551
Handgun, E965.0	1,307	1,256	1,405
Shotgun, E965.1	734	827	972
Hunting rifle, E965.2	163	138	159
Other and unspecified firearm, E965.3, E965.4	11,048	11,816	13,015
Assault by cutting and piercing instrument, E966	2,246	2,619	2,780
Child battering and other maltreatment, E967	177	242	275
Other, unspecified assault and late effects, E960–E962, E964, E965.5–E965.9, E968, E969	3,092	2,974	3,105
Legal Intervention, E970–E978	**355**	**337**	**343**
Undetermined Whether Accidentally or Purposely Inflicted, E980–E989	**3,657**	**3,463**	**3,301**
Poisoning by solid and liquid, E980	2,254	1,910	1,931
Poisoning by gases and vapors, E981, E982	77	118	107
Motor-vehicle exhaust gas, E982.0	41	61	67
Other and unspecified gases and vapors, E981, E982.1–E982.9	36	57	40
Drowning, E984	231	242	244
Firearms, E985.0–E985.4	367	413	394
Other, unspecified undetermined deaths and late effects, E983, E985.5–E989	728	780	625
Deaths from Operations of War, E990–E999	**9**	**13**	**9**

Source: National Center for Health Statistics. Deaths are classified on the basis of the Ninth Revision of "The International Classification of Diseases" (ICD), which became effective in 1979.
[a]*Latest official figures.*
[b]*Numbers following titles refer to External Cause of Injury and Poisoning classifications in the ICD.*

DEATHS BY AGE, SEX, AND TYPE

Of the 95,644 unintentional-injury deaths in 1997, males accounted for 65% of all deaths. For women, the percentage was highest in the 75 and over age group. By type of accident, men accounted for 87% of all firearm deaths, about seven times higher than the deaths for women.

UNINTENTIONAL-INJURY DEATHS BY AGE, SEX, AND TYPE, UNITED STATES, 1997[a]

Age & Sex	All Types[b]	Motor-Vehicle	Falls	Fires, Burns[c]	Drowning[d]	Ingest. of Food, Object	Firearms	Poison (Solid, Liquid)	Poison by Gas	% Male, All Types
All Ages	**95,644**	**43,458**	**15,477**	**3,490**	**4,051**	**3,275**	**981**	**9,587**	**576**	**65%**
Under 5	2,770	933	62	399	516	147	20	22	17	59%
5 to 14	3,371	1,967	53	277	449	38	122	19	23	63%
15 to 24	13,367	10,208	269	197	665	42	300	658	72	73%
25 to 44	27,129	14,167	1,022	697	1,233	262	295	5,972	199	75%
45 to 64	17,521	8,134	1,587	724	687	430	154	2,349	137	71%
65 to 74	8,578	3,370	1,840	405	218	480	51	220	51	61%
75 & over	22,908	4,679	10,614	791	283	1,876	39	347	77	45%
Male	**61,963**	**28,770**	**7,705**	**2,086**	**3,261**	**1,676**	**856**	**7,176**	**446**	
Female	**33,681**	**14,688**	**7,742**	**1,404**	**790**	**1,599**	**125**	**2,411**	**130**	
Percent male	65%	66%	50%	60%	80%	51%	87%	75%	77%	

See source and footnotes on page 19.

UNINTENTIONAL-INJURY DEATH RATES BY TYPE AND SEX, UNITED STATES, 1997

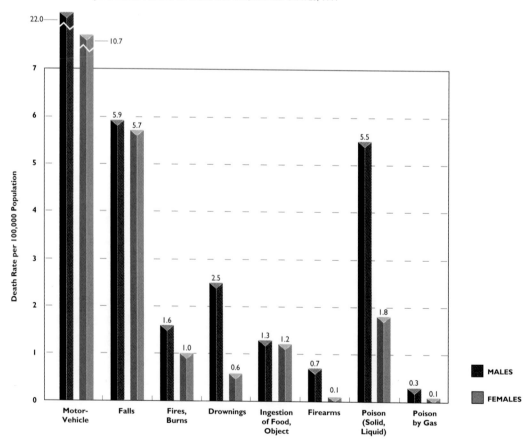

UNINTENTIONAL-INJURY DEATHS BY MONTH AND TYPE, 1997[a]

Month	All Types[b]	Motor-Vehicle	Falls	Fires, Burns[c]	Drowning[d]	Ingest. of Food, Object	Firearms	Poison (Solid, Liquid)	Poison by Gas	All Other Types
All Months	95,644	43,458	15,447	3,490	4,051	3,275	981	9,587	576	14,779
January	8,040	3,334	1,473	462	156	337	87	739	89	1,363
February	6,741	2,915	1,172	364	158	252	73	682	61	1,064
March	7,609	3,218	1,297	323	284	305	74	806	52	1,250
April	7,374	3,311	1,247	289	267	267	62	733	39	1,159
May	8,382	3,906	1,284	286	415	280	68	877	44	1,222
June	8,148	3,774	1,204	193	659	233	80	751	18	1,236
July	8,872	3,997	1,268	184	734	256	91	859	37	1,446
August	8,623	4,108	1,276	171	537	242	71	897	27	1,294
September	7,614	3,598	1,230	166	316	237	82	780	24	1,181
October	8,061	3,841	1,262	254	235	271	86	843	41	1,228
November	7,802	3,693	1,268	332	150	255	107	800	67	1,130
December	8,378	3,763	1,466	466	140	340	100	820	77	1,206
Average	7,970	3,622	1,287	291	338	273	82	799	48	1,232

Source: National Safety Council tabulations of National Center for Health Statistics mortality data.
[a]*Latest official figures.*
[b]*Includes some deaths not shown separately.*
[c]*Includes deaths resulting from conflagration regardless of nature of injury.*
[d]*Includes drowning in water transport.*

UNINTENTIONAL-INJURY DEATHS BY MONTH, UNITED STATES, 1997

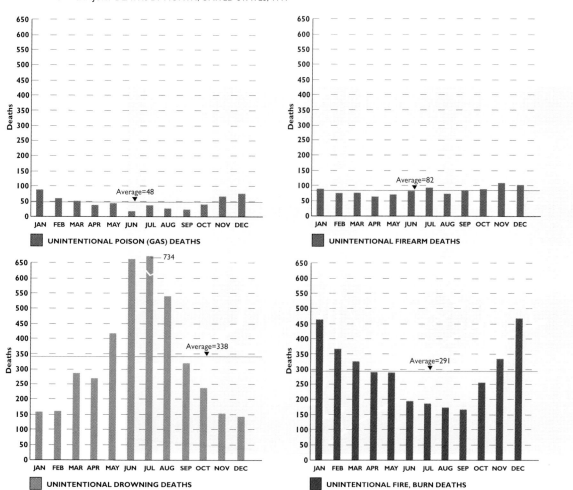

UNINTENTIONAL POISON (GAS) DEATHS

UNINTENTIONAL FIREARM DEATHS

UNINTENTIONAL DROWNING DEATHS

UNINTENTIONAL FIRE, BURN DEATHS

See page 86 for motor-vehicle deaths by month.

One in five Americans was injured in 1996.

THE NATIONAL HEALTH INTERVIEW SURVEY

The National Health Interview Survey, conducted by the U.S. Public Health Service, is a continuous, personal-interview sampling of households to obtain information about the health status of household members, including injuries experienced during the two weeks prior to the interview. Responsible family members residing in the household supplied the information found in the survey. Of the nation's 99,627,000 households in 1996, 24,371 households containing 63,402 persons were interviewed. See below for definitions and comparability with other injury figures published in *Injury Facts*™.

ESTIMATED NUMBER OF PERSONS INJURED, RESTRICTED ACTIVITY DAYS, AND BED DAYS, 1996[a]

Class or Place	Persons Injured		Restricted Activity Days		Bed Days	
	Number	Rate[b]	Number	Rate[b]	Number	Rate[b]
All Episodes:[c]	**54,278,000**	**20.5**	**598,208,000**	**226.4**	**189,685,000**	**71.8**
Moving Motor Vehicle:	**3,206,000**	**1.2**	**101,398,000**	**38.4**	**31,434,000**	**11.9**
Traffic	*3,059,000*	*1.2*	*95,260,000*	*36.0*	*31,300,000*	*11.8*
Work:[d]	**7,583,000**	**3.9**	**175,696,000**	**91.1**	**42,153,000**	**21.9**
Place of Accident:						
Home	17,189,000	6.5	147,676,000	55.9	45,064,000	17.1
Street, highway	5,837,000	2.2	133,850,000	50.7	49,721,000	18.8
Industrial Place	5,825,000	2.2	114,462,000	43.3	26,395,000	10.0
Other	13,835,000	5.2	154,809,000	58.6	45,794,000	17.3

NUMBER OF EPISODES OF PERSONS INJURED BY AGE, 1996[a]

Class or Place	Average Annual Number of Persons Injured						
	All Ages	Under 5 Years	5–17 Years	18–24 Years	25–44 Years	45–64 Years	65 Years & Over
All Episodes:[c]	**54,278,000**	**4,498,000**	**10,819,000**	**6,874,000**	**19,378,000**	**7,393,000**	**5,316,000**
Moving Motor Vehicle:	**3,206,000**	**(e)**	**492,000**	**719,000**	**1,336,000**	**659,000**	**(e)**
Traffic	*3,059,000*	*(e)*	*345,000*	*719,000*	*1,336,000*	*659,000*	*(e)*
Work:[d]	**7,583,000**	**(e)**	**(e)**	**1,338,000**	**5,337,000**	**908,000**	**(e)**
Place of Accident:							
Home	17,189,000	2,194,000	2,823,000	1,418,000	5,241,000	2,977,000	2,536,000
Street, highway	5,837,000	(e)	1,201,000	1,270,000	2,462,000	904,000	(e)
Industrial Place	5,825,000	(e)	156,000	1,422,000	3,502,000	634,000	112,000
Other	13,835,000	245,000	5,339,000	1,746,000	4,918,000	1,342,000	245,000

Source: Adams, P.F., Hendershot, G.E., & Marano, M.A. (1999, October). Current estimates from the National Health Interview Survey, 1996. Vital and Health Statistics, Series 10 (No. 200). Hyattsville, MD: National Center for Health Statistics.

[a] *Latest official figures.*
[b] *Per 100 persons per year.*
[c] *Estimates are calculated for three separate characteristics: whether in a moving vehicle, whether at work, and by place of accident. The "all episodes" estimate includes cases unclassified for one or more of these characteristics. For this reason, and because there is duplication among categories, individual estimates do not add to the "all episodes" total.*
[d] *Work includes employed persons 18 years of age and over only. Home includes yard, buildings, and sidewalks on the property as well as inside the house. Industrial place does not include business or professional offices, farms or other nonindustrial work locations.*
[e] *Not available, not applicable, or quantity zero.*

Injury Definitions

National Health Interview Survey Definitions. The National Health Interview Survey (NHIS) figures include injuries due to intentional violence as well as unintentional injuries. An injury is included in the NHIS totals if (1) it is *medically attended* or (2) it causes one-half day or more of *restricted activity*. A *medically attended* injury is one for which a physician has been consulted (in person or by telephone) for examination, diagnosis, treatment, or advice. *Restricted activity* is defined as one or more of the following types: bed day (person stayed in bed more than half a day); work-loss day (person missed more than half a day from job or business); school-loss day (currently enrolled 5-17-year-old student missed more than half a day of school); cut down day (person cuts down for more than half a day on the things he or she usually does).

National Safety Council definition of injury. A disabling injury is defined as one that results in death, some degree of permanent impairment, or renders the injured person unable to effectively perform their regular duties or activities for a full day beyond the day of the injury. This definition applies to all unintentional injuries. All injury totals labeled "disabling injuries" in *Injury Facts*™ are based on this definition. Some *rates* in the Work section are based on OSHA definitions of recordable cases (see Glossary).

Numerical differences between NHIS and National Safety Council injury totals are due mainly to the duration of disability. The Council's injury estimating procedure was revised for the 1993 edition of *Accident Facts*®. See the Technical Appendix for more information.

The graph below shows the population death rate trends for the principal types of unintentional injuries from 1910 to the present. See also page 31 for the trends in death rates for all unintentional injuries and the four classes.

Motor-vehicle death rates increased rapidly prior to World War II, then exhibited a sharp dip and recovery during and immediately after the war, a rapid rise during the 1960s, a sharp drop in the early 1970s associated with the oil embargo, and then generally decreased.

Deaths rates due to **falls** decreased sharply in the late 1910s then rose steadily through World War II and declined to a plateau from the mid-1950s through the mid-1960s, then declined again through the late 1980s. Since then rates have risen again.

Death rates for **fires and burns, drowning, gas and vapor poisonings, and firearms** show similar trends. All have decreased uniformly over the century to record low levels.

Deaths rates due to **solid and liquid poisonings** decreased steadily from the early part of the 20th century through the late 1960s and have increased steadily since then. Much of this increase can be attributed to the rise in unintentional overdoses of illegal drugs.

UNINTENTIONAL-INJURY DEATH RATE TRENDS BY EVENT, UNITED STATES, 1910–1999

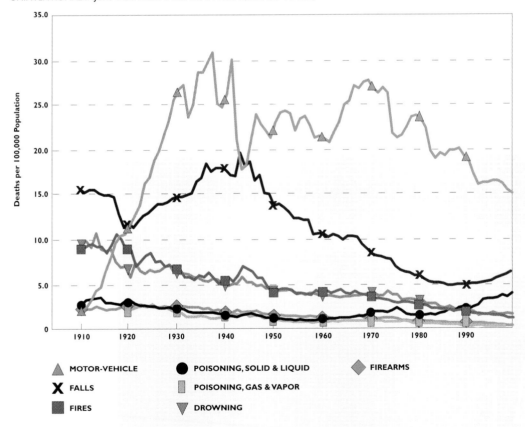

PRINCIPAL CLASSES BY STATE

The states listed below participate in the Accidental Death Summary reporting system. Reports from these states are used to make current year estimates. See the Technical Appendix for more information.

The estimated total number of unintentional-injury deaths for 1999 increased 4% from 1998. The number of unintentional-injury deaths in the Motor-Vehicle class showed a decrease of 1%, while the Work class

exhibited an increase of less than 0.5%. The estimates for the Home and Public Nonmotor-Vehicle classes showed increases of 5% and 13%, respectively. The population death rate for the Total class increased 3%, while the rate for the Motor-Vehicle class declined by 3%. The rates for the Home and Public Nonmotor-Vehicle classes increased 5% and 11%, respectively, while the rate for the Work class remained unchanged.

PRINCIPAL CLASSES OF UNINTENTIONAL-INJURY DEATHS BY STATE, 1999

State	Total[a]		Motor-Vehicle[b]		Work[c]		Home		Public Nonmotor-Vehicle		Unclassified[d]	
	Deaths	Rate[e]	Deaths	Rate[e]	Deaths	Rate[e]	Deaths	Rate[e]	Deaths	Rate[e]	Deaths	Rate[e]
Total U.S.	**96,900**	**35.5**	**41,300**	**15.1**	**5,100**	**1.9**	**28,800**	**10.6**	**24,100**	**8.8**	**—**	**—**
Arizona	2,422	50.7	1,099	23.0	24	0.5	683	14.3	587	12.3	27	0.6
Delaware (11 mos.)	209	30.3	92	13.3	2	0.3	75	10.9	33	4.8	7	1.0
Florida	5,759	38.1	2,254	14.8	250	1.7	1,187	7.9	2,068	13.7	—	—
Hawaii	309	26.1	106	8.9	5	0.4	76	6.4	120	10.1	2	0.2
Idaho	579	46.3	298	23.8	23	1.8	132	10.5	115	9.2	11	0.9
Kansas	1,024	38.6	511	19.3	55	2.1	196	7.4	262	9.9	—	—
Missouri	2,627	48.0	1,225	22.4	80	1.5	715	13.1	586	10.7	21	0.4
Montana	466	52.8	183	20.7	33	3.7	72	8.2	178	20.2	—	—
New Jersey (9 mos.)	1,451	23.8	477	7.8	67	1.1	503	8.2	404	6.6	—	—
New Mexico	1,033	59.4	500	28.7	18	1.0	286	16.4	226	13.0	3	0.2
South Carolina	1,874	48.2	906	23.3	—	—	—	—	—	—	968	24.9

Source: Provisional reports of vital statistics registrars; deaths are by place of occurrence. U.S. totals are National Safety Council estimates.
[a] *The all-class total may not equal the sum of the separate class totals because Motor-Vehicle and other transportation deaths occurring to persons in the course of their employment are included in the Work death totals as well as the Motor-Vehicle and Public Nonmotor-Vehicle totals.*
[b] *Differences between the figures given and those on pages 94 and 95 are due in most cases to the inclusion of nontraffic deaths in this table.*
[c] *Work death totals may be too low where incomplete information on death certificates results in the deaths being included in Public or Unclassified. The Work totals may include some cases that are not compensable. For compensable cases only, see page 51.*
[d] *Includes late effects (deaths occurring more than one year after the accident).*
[e] *Deaths per 100,000 population, adjusted to annual basis where less than 12 months were reported.*

UNINTENTIONAL-INJURY DEATH
RATES BY STATE

DEATH RATES PER 100,000 POPULATION BY STATE, 1999

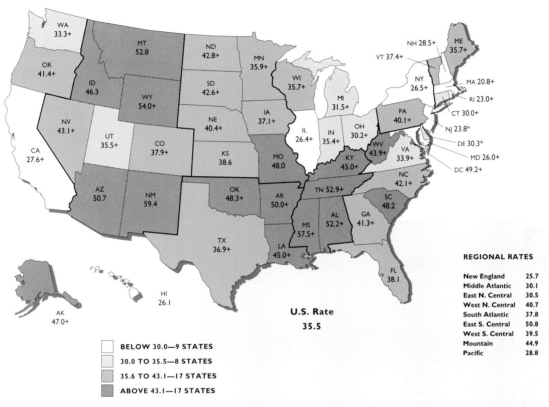

WA 33.3+
MT 52.8
ND 42.8+
MN 35.9+
NH 28.5+
ME 35.7+
VT 37.4+
OR 41.4+
ID 46.3
WY 54.0+
SD 42.6+
WI 35.7+
MI 31.5+
NY 26.5+
MA 20.8+
RI 23.0+
CT 30.0+
PA 40.1+
NJ 23.8*
DE 30.3*
MD 26.0+
DC 49.2+
NV 43.1+
NE 40.4+
IA 37.1+
IL 26.4+
IN 35.4+
OH 30.2+
WV 43.9+
VA 33.9+
CA 27.6+
UT 35.5+
CO 37.9+
KS 38.6
MO 48.0
KY 45.0+
NC 42.1+
AZ 50.7
NM 59.4
OK 48.3+
AR 50.0+
TN 52.9+
SC 48.2
AL 52.2+
GA 41.3+
TX 36.9+
MS 57.5+
LA 45.0+
FL 38.1
AK 47.0+
HI 26.1

U.S. Rate
35.5

BELOW 30.0—9 STATES
30.0 TO 35.5—8 STATES
35.6 TO 43.1—17 STATES
ABOVE 43.1—17 STATES

REGIONAL RATES

New England	25.7
Middle Atlantic	30.1
East N. Central	30.5
West N. Central	40.7
South Atlantic	37.8
East S. Central	50.8
West S. Central	39.5
Mountain	44.9
Pacific	28.8

Source: Rates estimated by the National Safety Council based on data from State Health Departments, National Center for Health Statistics, and U.S. Census Bureau.
* 1997 National Center for Health Statistics.
* Partly estimated.

MAJOR DISASTERS, 1999

Disasters are front-page news even though the lives lost in the United States are relatively few when compared to the day-to-day life losses from ordinary injuries. The National Safety Council tracks major disasters resulting in unintentional-injury deaths. Listed below are the three major U.S. disasters taking 25 or more lives during 1999.

Type and Location	No. of Deaths	Date of Disaster
Heat wave in the Midwest	232	July 22–31, 1999
Hurricane Floyd, North Carolina and other states	78	Sept. 14–18, 1999
Tornadoes in Oklahoma, Kansas, Texas, and Tennessee	54	May 3, 1999

Source: National Climatic Data Center.

LARGEST U.S. DISASTERS, 1980–1999

Year	Date	Type and Location	No. of Deaths
		Air Transportation	
1996	July 17	Crash of scheduled plane near East Moriches, N.Y.	230
1987	August 16	Crash of scheduled plane in Detroit, Mich.	156
1982	July 9	Crash of scheduled plane in Kenner, La.	154
1985	August 2	Crash of scheduled plane in Ft. Worth/Dallas, Texas Airport	135
1994	September 8	Crash of scheduled plane in Aliquippa, Pa.	132
1989	July 19	Crash of scheduled plane in Sioux City, Iowa	112
1996	May 11	Crash of scheduled plane near Miami, Fla.	110
1986	August 31	Two-plane collision over Los Angeles, Calif.	82
1982	January 13	Crash of scheduled plane in Washington, D.C.	78
1990	January 25	Crash of scheduled plane in Cove Neck, N.Y.	73
1994	October 31	Crash of scheduled plane in Indiana	68
1994	July 2	Crash of scheduled plane in Charlotte, N.C.	37
		Weather	
1995	July 11–27	Heat wave in Chicago, Ill.	465
1993	March 12–15	Severe snowstorm in Eastern States	270
1999	July 22–31	Heat wave in the Midwest	232
1998	May–July	Drought and heat wave in South and Southeast	200[a]
1996	January	Snowstorm and floods in Appalachians, Mid-Atlantic, and Northeast	187
1996	January–February	Cold wave in eastern two-thirds of the U.S.	100[a]
1993	June–July	Heat wave in Southeast	100[a]
1998	January 5	Winter storm and flooding in South and East	90[a]
1999	September 14–18	Hurricane Floyd, North Carolina and other states	78
1985	May 31	Storm and tornadoes in Pennsylvania and Ohio	74
1997	March	Tornadoes and flooding in South and Southeast	67
1985	November 4–5	Floods in W.Va., Va., Pa., and East Coast	65
1984	March 28–29	Storm and tornadoes in N.C., S.C., and East Coast	62
1999	May 3	Tornadoes in Oklahoma, Kansas, Texas, and Tennessee	54
1994	March 27	Tornado in Southeast	47
1998	February 22	Tornadoes across central Florida	42
1996	September 5	Hurricane Fran in North Carolina and Virginia	36
1998	April 8	Tornado in central Alabama	34
1997	May 27	Tornadoes in Texas	29
1994	July 4–17	Floods in Georgia	28
		Work	
1987	April 24	Collapse of apartment building under construction in Bridgeport, Conn.	28
1982	March 19	Military plane exploded and crashed near Chicago, Ill.	27
1984	December 21	Mine fire in Orangeville, Utah	27
1991	September 3	Fire at food processing plant in Hamlet, N.C.	25
		Other Disasters	
1981	July 17	Collapse of aerial walkways in Kansas City, Mo., hotel	113
1980	November 21	Hotel fire in Las Vegas, Nevada	84
1994	January 17	Earthquake in San Andreas Fault, Calif.	61
1989	October 17	Earthquake in San Francisco, Calif., and surrounding area	61
1980	May 18	Volcanic eruption of Mount St. Helens, Wash.	61
1993	September 22	Bridge collapse under train, Mobile, Ala.	47
1980	May 9	Collision of ship with bridge near Tampa Bay, Fla.	35
1981	October 26	Boat capsized near Hillsboro Beach, Fla.	33
1981	January 9	Fire in rest home for aged in Keansburg, N.J.	31

Source: National Safety Council, Accident Facts, *1980–1998 editions, and* Injury Facts, *1999 edition.*
[a] *Final death toll undetermined.*

While you make a 10-minute safety speech, 2 persons will be killed and about 396 will suffer a disabling injury. Costs will amount to $8,920,000. On the average, there are 11 unintentional-injury deaths and about 2,370 disabling injuries every hour during the year.

Deaths and disabling injuries by class occurred in the nation at the following rates in 1999:

DEATHS AND DISABLING INJURIES BY CLASS, 1999

| Class | Severity | One Every— | Number per ... | | | 1999 Total |
			Hour	Day	Week	
All	Deaths	5 minutes	11	265	1,860	96,900
	Injuries	2 seconds	2,370	57,000	400,000	20,800,000
Motor-Vehicle	Deaths	13 minutes	5	113	790	41,300
	Injuries	14 seconds	250	6,000	42,300	2,200,000
Work	Deaths	103 minutes	1	14	100	5,100
	Injuries	8 seconds	430	10,400	73,100	3,800,000
Workers Off-the-Job	Deaths	13 minutes	5	111	780	40,600
	Injuries	5 seconds	750	18,100	126,900	6,600,000
Home	Deaths	18 minutes	3	79	550	28,800
	Injuries	5 seconds	790	18,900	132,700	6,900,000
Public Nonmotor-Vehicle	Deaths	22 minutes	3	66	460	24,100
	Injuries	4 seconds	910	21,900	153,800	8,000,000

Source: National Safety Council estimates.

DEATHS EVERY HOUR . . .

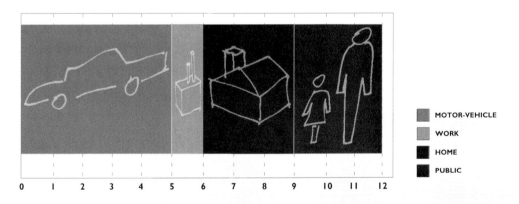

MOTOR-VEHICLE
WORK
HOME
PUBLIC

AN UNINTENTIONAL-INJURY DEATH EVERY FIVE MINUTES . . .

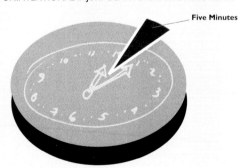

Five Minutes

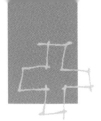

About 35.1 million visits to hospital emergency departments in 1997 were due to injuries.

INJURY-RELATED HOSPITAL EMERGENCY DEPARTMENT VISITS, 1997

About 37% of all hospital emergency department visits in the United States were injury related, according to information from the 1997 National Hospital Ambulatory Medical Care Survey conducted for the National Center for Health Statistics. There were approximately 94.9 million visits made to emergency departments, of which about 35.1 million were injury related. This resulted in an annual rate of about 35.6 emergency department visits per 100 persons, of which about 13.2 visits per 100 persons were injury related.

Males had a higher rate of injury-related visits than females. For males, about 14.8 visits per 100 persons were recorded; for females the rate was 11.6 per 100 persons. Those aged 15 to 24 had the highest rate of injury-related visits for males, and those aged 75 and over had the highest rate for females.

Falls and struck against or struck accidentally by objects or persons were the leading causes of injury-related emergency department visits, accounting for about 18% and 14% of the total, respectively. In total, about 6.4 million visits to emergency departments were made in

1997 due to accidental falls, and about 4.8 million due to being struck against or struck accidentally by objects or persons. The next leading types were motor-vehicle accidents with 4.6 million visits (13% of the total), and accidents caused by cutting or piercing instruments, which accounted for about 2.8 million visits (8% of the total).

Slightly over 28% of all injuries resulting in emergency department visits occurred at home, the most common place of injury. Street or highway was the place of injury for about 15% of the total, recreation/sport area accounted for just over 6%, and industrial place accounted for about 6%. Other public building was the place of injury for 3% of the total, while school accounted for 2%. However, 40% of all injuries resulting in emergency department visits occurred in an "other or unknown place."

The table and charts on these pages show totals, rates, and percent distributions of injury-related visits to hospital emergency departments in 1997 by age, sex, cause of injury, and place of injury.

NUMBER AND PERCENT DISTRIBUTION OF EMERGENCY DEPARTMENT VISITS BY CAUSE OF INJURY, UNITED STATES, 1997

Cause of Injury and E-Code[a]	Number of Visits (000)	%
All Injury-Related Visits	**35,111**	**100.0%**
Unintentional Injuries, E800–869, E880–E929	**27,953**	**79.6%**
Accidental Falls, E880–E888	6,383	18.2%
Striking Against or Struck Accidentally by Objects or Persons, E916–E917	4,806	13.7%
Total Motor Vehicle Accidents, E810–E825	4,574	13.0%
Motor vehicle traffic, E810–E819	4,277	12.2%
Motor vehicle, nontraffic, E820–E825(.0, .5, .7, .9)	297	0.8%
Accidents Caused by Cutting or Piercing Instruments, E920	2,786	7.9%
Overexertion, E927	1,406	4.0%
Accidents Due to Natural and Environmental Factors, E900–E909, E928.0–E928.2	1,201	3.4%
Accidents Caused by Fire and Flames, Hot Substances or Object, Caustic or Corrosive Material, and Steam, E890–E899, E924	695	2.0%
Accidental Poisoning by Drugs, Medicinal Substances, Biologicals, Other Solid and Liquid Substances, Gases and Vapors, E850–E869	522	1.5%
Pedalcycle, Nontraffic and Other, E800–E807(.3), E820–E825(.6), E826.1, E826.9	500	1.4%
Machinery, E919	471	1.3%

Cause of Injury and E-Code[a]	Number of Visits (000)	%
Other Transportation, E800–807(.0–.2, .8–.9), E826(.0, .2–.8), E827–E829, E831, E833–E845	152	0.4%
Other Mechanism[b], E830, E832, E846–E848, E910–E915, E918, E921–E923, E925–E926, E929.0–E929.5, E929.8	2,054	5.9%
Mechanism Unspecified, E887, E928.9, E929.8, E929.9	2,403	6.8%
Intentional Injuries, E950–E959, E960–E969, E970–E978, E990–E999	**2,157**	**6.1%**
Assault, E960–E969	1,686	4.8%
Unarmed Fight or Brawl and Striking by Blunt or Thrown Object, E960.0, E968.2	945	2.7%
Assault by Cutting and Piercing Instrument, E966	129	0.4%
Assault by Other and Unspecified Mechanism[c], E960.1, E962–964, E965.0–E965.9, E967–E968.1, E968.3–E969.9	611	1.7%
Self-inflicted Injury, E950–E959	401	1.1%
Poisoning by Solid or Liquid Substances, Gases or Vapors, E950–E952	252	0.7%
Other and Unspecified Mechanism[d], E954–E955, E957–E959	149	0.4%
Other Causes of Violence, E970–E978, E990–E999	70	0.2%
Adverse Effects of Medical Treatment, E870–E879, E930–E949	**1,186**	**3.4%**
Other and Unknown[e]	**3,815**	**10.9%**

Source: Nourjah, P. (1999). National Hospital Ambulatory Medical Care Survey: 1997 Emergency Department Summary (Advanced data, Number 304, May 6, 1999). Hyattsville, MD: National Center for Health Statistics.

Note: Sum of parts may not add to total due to rounding.

[a] Based on the International Classification of Diseases, 9th Revision, Clinical Modification (ICD-9-CM).

[b] Includes drowning, suffocation, firearm, and other mechanism.

[c] Includes assault by firearms and explosives, and other mechanism.

[d] Includes injury by cutting and piercing instrument, and other and unspecified mechanism.

[e] Includes all other major E-code categories where the estimate was too low to be reliable and uncodable, illegible, and blank E-codes.

NUMBER AND PERCENT DISTRIBUTION OF EMERGENCY DEPARTMENT VISITS BY PLACE OF INJURY AND AGE, UNITED STATES, 1997

Place of Injury	All Ages		Under 18		18–64 Years		65 Years & Over	
	Number of Visits (000)	%	Number of Visits (000)	%	Number of Visits (000)	%	Number of Visits (000)	%
Total	35,111	100.0	9,854	100.0	21,582	100.0	3,674	100.0
Home	9,980	28.4	3,525	35.8	4,833	22.4	1,623	44.2
Street or Highway	5,180	14.8	1,095	11.1	3,751	17.4	334	9.1
Recreation/Sport Area	2,209	6.3	1,113	11.3	1,053	4.9	(a)	(a)
Industrial Place	1,991	5.7	(a)	(a)	1,861	8.6	(a)	(a)
Other Public Building	995	2.8	176	1.8	708	3.3	111	3.0
School	689	2.0	545	5.5	144	0.7	(a)	(a)
Other/Unknown[b]	14,067	40.1	3,310	33.6	9,233	42.8	1,524	41.5

Source: Nourjah, P. (1999). National Hospital Ambulatory Medical Care Survey: 1997 Emergency Department Summary (Advanced data, Number 304, May 6, 1999). Hyattsville, MD: National Center for Health Statistics.
Note: Sum of parts may not add to total due to rounding.
[a]*Estimate did not meet standard of reliability or precision.*
[b]*"Other" and "unknown" combined due to processing error.*

RATE OF INJURY-RELATED VISITS TO EMERGENCY DEPARTMENTS BY PATIENT AGE AND SEX, 1997

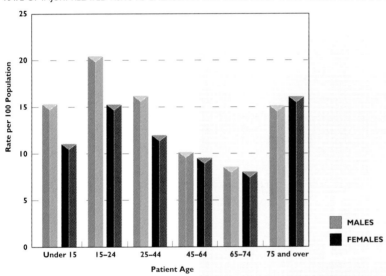

DISTRIBUTION OF EMERGENCY DEPARTMENT VISITS BY PLACE OF INJURY AND AGE, UNITED STATES, 1997

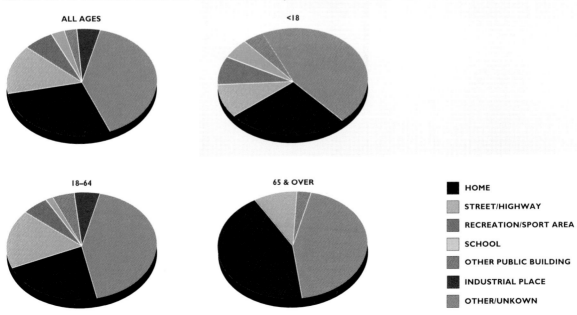

CHILDREN AND YOUTHS

For children and youths aged 1 to 24 years, unintentional injuries are the leading cause of death, accounting for more than 41% of the 45,106 total deaths of these persons in 1997. Overall, motor-vehicle accidents were the leading cause of unintentional-injury deaths for this age group, followed by drowning, and fires and burns.

While unintentional-injury deaths decrease fairly steadily for those aged 1 to 10, they increase markedly for teenagers—from 349 for those age 12 to 1,555 for those age 18. Motor-vehicle accidents account for most of this increase.

For infants under 1 year of age, unintentional injuries are the fourth leading cause of death, following certain conditions originating in the perinatal period, congenital anomalies, and sudden infant death syndrome (see page 10). Although unintentional injuries only account for 3% of deaths for those under age 1, the number of unintentional-injury deaths for this age is greater than that for any other age less than 16.

According to a 1998 report by the National Center for Health Statistics, the ambulatory health care service visit rate among infants under 1 year of age was four times the rate among school-age children 5–14 years of age. Injury visits accounted for 15% of the total visits by school-age children.

Source: National Center for Health Statistics. (1998). Ambulatory health care visits by children: principal diagnosis and place of visit, 1993–95. Hyattsville, MD: Author.

UNINTENTIONAL-INJURY DEATHS BY EVENT, AGES 0–24, UNITED STATES, 1997

| Age | Population (000) | Unintentional-Injury Deaths | | | | | | | | | |
		All	Rates[a]	Motor-Vehicle	Drowning[b]	Fires	Firearms	Poison (Solid, Liquid)	Falls	Mechanical Suffocation	All Other
Under 1 year	3,780	865	22.9	187	85	61	0	23	17	304	188
1-24 years	90,781	18,743	20.6	12,943	1,570	822	442	693	371	275	1,627
1 year	3,740	593	15.9	197	162	76	1	8	14	39	96
2 years	3,792	525	13.8	174	134	97	7	4	15	11	83
3 years	3,838	500	13.0	204	104	105	6	3	12	14	52
4 years	3,948	387	9.8	193	56	70	6	1	8	7	46
5 years	4,024	377	9.4	177	61	67	7	1	6	8	50
6 years	4,047	325	8.0	174	51	34	5	2	5	10	44
7 years	4,031	304	7.5	192	32	34	5	1	8	5	27
8 years	3,733	271	7.3	153	46	29	5	3	4	3	28
9 years	3,913	257	6.6	154	44	14	6	0	5	11	23
10 years	3,877	295	7.6	176	30	34	6	2	6	10	31
11 years	3,820	272	7.1	167	35	11	10	1	2	13	33
12 years	3,810	349	9.2	197	40	24	20	3	5	19	41
13 years	3,738	387	10.4	229	49	18	26	2	5	14	44
14 years	3,844	534	13.9	348	61	12	32	4	7	7	63
15 years	3,887	726	18.7	516	61	15	30	10	14	16	64
16 years	3,832	1,237	32.3	1,019	62	14	28	19	10	13	72
17 years	3,931	1,495	38.0	1,202	75	22	47	36	23	5	85
18 years	3,692	1,555	42.1	1,274	69	14	28	64	25	11	70
19 years	3,798	1,590	41.9	1,202	82	21	31	84	34	10	126
20 years	3,742	1,430	38.2	1,101	56	21	33	75	25	11	108
21 years	3,509	1,525	43.5	1,171	59	21	29	83	42	9	111
22 years	3,444	1,345	39.1	987	75	21	19	89	38	11	105
23 years	3,327	1,297	39.0	922	56	21	36	91	34	14	123
24 years	3,462	1,167	33.7	814	70	27	19	107	24	4	102

Source: National Safety Council tabulations of National Center for Health Statistics mortality data.
[a] Deaths per 100,000 population in each age group.
[b] Includes transport drownings.

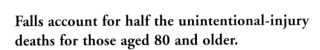

Falls account for half the unintentional-injury deaths for those aged 80 and older.

More than 76,000 adults aged 25 and older died as a result of unintentional injuries in 1997, with motor vehicles accounting for about 40% of these deaths. Data for five year age groups indicate that motor-vehicle accidents are the most common type of unintentional-injury death through age 79. Poisoning by solids and liquids is the second most common type for age groups 25 through 54, and falls are the second most common type from age 55 through age 79, at which point it becomes the primary cause of fatal injury for those aged 80 and older. Falls account for more than half the unintentional-injury deaths of those in this age group.

Death rates per 100,000 population are relatively stable for those aged 25–49, averaging 32.4. Death rates increase with age for each group beginning with age 60. The average death rate for those aged 85 and older is more than 11 times higher than the average rate for those aged 25–49. All age groups older than 65 have death rates higher than the all-ages rate of 35.7.

UNINTENTIONAL-INJURY DEATHS BY EVENT, AGES 25 AND OLDER, UNITED STATES, 1997

| Age Group | Population (000) | Unintentional-Injury Deaths | | Motor-Vehicle | Falls | Poisoning by | | Suffocation by Ingestion | Fires, Burns | Surgical & Medical Mis-adventures[b] | Drowning[c] | All Other |
		Number	Rate[a]			Solids, Liquids	Gases, Vapors					
25–29	18,812	6,141	32.6	3,943	153	808	43	50	124	28	298	694
30–34	20,732	6,457	31.1	3,557	213	1,294	42	47	164	31	333	776
35–39	22,629	7,341	32.4	3,527	282	1,916	44	72	187	73	307	933
40–44	21,376	7,190	33.6	3,140	374	1,954	70	93	222	71	295	971
45–49	18,465	5,938	32.2	2,643	392	1,327	49	97	186	121	244	879
50–54	15,157	4,478	29.5	2,162	354	570	38	94	183	141	178	758
55–59	11,755	3,680	31.3	1,776	368	290	25	112	174	136	133	666
60–64	10,062	3,425	34.0	1,553	473	162	25	127	181	211	132	561
65–69	9,775	3,841	39.3	1,596	706	128	29	198	193	291	104	596
70–74	8,753	4,737	54.1	1,774	1,134	92	22	282	212	368	114	739
75–79	7,086	5,792	81.7	1,840	1,779	111	28	408	256	479	108	783
80–84	4,664	6,313	135.4	1,552	2,624	102	27	476	236	412	80	804
85–89	2,480	5,668	228.5	962	2,933	74	13	483	183	313	47	660
90–94	1,080	3,451	319.5	262	2,179	32	7	345	78	162	19	367
95–99	305	1,310	429.5	32	906	9	0	132	23	64	4	140
100 and over	54	274	507.4	9	189	2	0	32	5	13	0	24
25 and over	173,185	76,036	43.9	30,328	15,059	8,871	462	3,048	2,607	2,914	2,396	10,351
35 and over	133,641	63,438	47.5	22,828	14,693	6,769	377	2,951	2,319	2,855	1,765	8,881
45 and over	89,636	48,907	54.6	16,161	14,037	2,899	263	2,786	1,910	2,711	1,163	6,977
55 and over	56,014	38,491	68.7	11,356	13,291	1,002	176	2,595	1,541	2,449	741	5,340
65 and over	34,197	31,386	91.8	8,027	12,450	550	126	2,356	1,186	2,102	476	4,113
75 and over	15,669	22,808	145.6	4,657	10,610	330	75	1,876	781	1,443	258	2,778

Source: National Safety Council tabulations of National Center for Health Statistics mortality data.
[a]*Deaths per 100,000 population in each age group.*
[b]*Surgical and medical complications and misadventures.*
[c]*Includes transport drownings.*

TRENDS IN UNINTENTIONAL-INJURY DEATH RATES

Between 1912 and 1999, unintentional-injury deaths per 100,000 population were reduced 55% (after adjusting for the classification change in 1948) from 82.5 to 35.5. The reduction in the overall rate during a period when the nation's population nearly tripled has resulted in more than 4,300,000 fewer people being killed due to unintentional injuries than there would have been if the rate had not been reduced.

Age-adjusted rates, which eliminate the effect of shifts in the age distribution of the population, have decreased 63% from 1912 to 1999. The adjusted rates, which are shown in the graph on the opposite page, are standardized to the 1940 age distribution of the U.S. population. The break in the lines at 1948 shows the estimated effect of changes in the International Classification of Diseases. The break in the lines at 1992 resulted from the adoption of the Bureau of Labor Statistics Census of Fatal Occupational Injuries for work-related deaths.

The table below shows the change in the age distribution of the population since 1910. Note that

the age groups shown are slightly different from the standard age groups used elsewhere in *Injury Facts*™.

The age-adjusted death rate for all unintentional injuries increased and decreased significantly several times during the period from 1910 to 1940. Since 1940, there have been some setbacks, such as in the early 1960s, but the overall trend has been positive. The age-adjusted death rates for unintentional-injury deaths in the work and home classes have declined fairly steadily since they became available in the late 1920s. The rates in the public class declined for three decades, rose in the 1960s and then continued declining. The age-adjusted motor-vehicle death rate rose steadily from 1910 to the late 1930s as the automobile became more widely used. A sharp drop in use occurred during World War II and a sharp rise in rates occurred in the 1960s, with death rates reflecting economic cycles and a long-term downward trend since then.

UNITED STATES POPULATION, SELECTED YEARS

Year	All Ages	0–13	14–24	25–44	45–64	65 & Older
Number (in thousands)						
1910	92,407	27,806	20,024	27,037	13,555	3,985
1940	132,122	30,521	26,454	39,868	26,249	9,031
1999	272,691	54,545	41,665	82,749	59,191	34,540
Percent						
1910	100.0	30.1	21.7	29.3	14.7	4.3
1940	100.0	23.1	20.0	30.2	19.9	6.8
1999	100.0	20.0	15.3	30.3	21.7	12.7

Source: For 1910 and 1940: U. S. Bureau of the Census. (1960). Historical Statistics of the United States, Colonial Times to 1957. Washington, DC: U.S. Government Printing Office. For 1999: Population Estimates Program, Population Division. (Internet Release Date: June 28, 2000). Resident Population Estimates of the United States by Age and Sex: April 1, 1990 to July 1, 1999, with Short-Term Projection to May 1, 2000. Washington, DC: U. S. Bureau of the Census. http://www.census.gov/population/estimates/nation/intfile2-1.txt

AGE-ADJUSTED DEATH RATES BY CLASS OF INJURY, UNITED STATES, 1910–1999

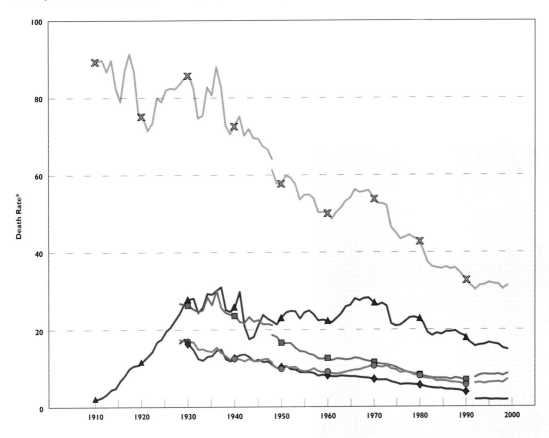

Deaths per 100,000 population, adjusted to 1940 age distribution. The break at 1948 shows the estimated effect of classification changes. The break at 1992 is due to the adoption of the Bureau of Labor Statistics' Census of Fatal Occupational Injuries for work-related deaths.

✕ **ALL**

▲ **MOTOR-VEHICLE**

■ **HOME**

● **PUBLIC**

◆ **WORK**

PRINCIPAL CLASSES OF UNINTENTIONAL-INJURY DEATHS

PRINCIPAL CLASSES OF UNINTENTIONAL-INJURY DEATHS, UNITED STATES, 1903–1999

Year	Total[a] Deaths	Rate[b]	Motor-Vehicle Deaths	Rate[b]	Work Deaths	Rate[b]	Home Deaths	Rate[b]	Public Nonmotor-Vehicle Deaths	Rate[b]
1903	70,600	87.2	(c)	–	(c)	–	(c)	–	(c)	–
1904	71,500	86.6	(c)	–	(c)	–	(c)	–	(c)	–
1905	70,900	84.2	(c)	–	(c)	–	(c)	–	(c)	–
1906	80,000	93.2	400	0.5	(c)	–	(c)	–	(c)	–
1907	81,900	93.6	700	0.8	(c)	–	(c)	–	(c)	–
1908	72,300	81.2	800	0.9	(c)	–	(c)	–	(c)	–
1909	72,700	80.1	1,300	1.4	(c)	–	(c)	–	(c)	–
1910	77,900	84.4	1,900	2.0	(c)	–	(c)	–	(c)	–
1911	79,300	84.7	2,300	2.5	(c)	–	(c)	–	(c)	–
1912	78,400	82.5	3,100	3.3	(c)	–	(c)	–	(c)	–
1913	82,500	85.5	4,200	4.4	(c)	–	(c)	–	(c)	–
1914	77,000	78.6	4,700	4.8	(c)	–	(c)	–	(c)	–
1915	76,200	76.7	6,600	6.6	(c)	–	(c)	–	(c)	–
1916	84,800	84.1	8,200	8.1	(c)	–	(c)	–	(c)	–
1917	90,100	88.2	10,200	10.0	(c)	–	(c)	–	(c)	–
1918	85,100	82.1	10,700	10.3	(c)	–	(c)	–	(c)	–
1919	75,500	71.9	11,200	10.7	(c)	–	(c)	–	(c)	–
1920	75,900	71.2	12,500	11.7	(c)	–	(c)	–	(c)	–
1921	74,000	68.4	13,900	12.9	(c)	–	(c)	–	(c)	–
1922	76,300	69.4	15,300	13.9	(c)	–	(c)	–	(c)	–
1923	84,400	75.7	18,400	16.5	(c)	–	(c)	–	(c)	–
1924	85,600	75.6	19,400	17.1	(c)	–	(c)	–	(c)	–
1925	90,000	78.4	21,900	19.1	(c)	–	(c)	–	(c)	–
1926	91,700	78.7	23,400	20.1	(c)	–	(c)	–	(c)	–
1927	92,700	78.4	25,800	21.8	(c)	–	(c)	–	(c)	–
1928	95,000	79.3	28,000	23.4	19,000	15.8	30,000	24.9	21,000	17.4
1929	98,200	80.8	31,200	25.7	20,000	16.4	30,000	24.6	20,000	16.4
1930	99,100	80.5	32,900	26.7	19,000	15.4	30,000	24.4	20,000	16.3
1931	97,300	78.5	33,700	27.2	17,500	14.1	29,000	23.4	20,000	16.1
1932	89,000	71.3	29,500	23.6	15,000	12.0	29,000	23.2	18,000	14.4
1933	90,932	72.4	31,363	25.0	14,500	11.6	29,500	23.6	18,500	14.7
1934	100,977	79.9	36,101	28.6	16,000	12.7	34,000	26.9	18,000	14.2
1935	99,773	78.4	36,369	28.6	16,500	13.0	32,000	25.2	18,000	14.2
1936	110,052	85.9	38,089	29.7	18,500	14.5	37,000	28.9	19,500	15.2
1937	105,205	81.7	39,643	30.8	19,000	14.8	32,000	24.8	18,000	14.0
1938	93,805	72.3	32,582	25.1	16,000	12.3	31,000	23.9	17,000	13.1
1939	92,623	70.8	32,386	24.7	15,500	11.8	31,000	23.7	16,000	12.2
1940	96,885	73.4	34,501	26.1	17,000	12.9	31,500	23.9	16,500	12.5
1941	101,513	76.3	39,969	30.0	18,000	13.5	30,000	22.5	16,500	12.4
1942	95,889	71.6	28,309	21.1	18,000	13.4	30,500	22.8	16,000	12.0
1943	99,038	73.8	23,823	17.8	17,500	13.0	33,500	25.0	17,000	12.7
1944	95,237	71.7	24,282	18.3	16,000	12.0	32,500	24.5	16,000	12.0
1945	95,918	72.4	28,076	21.2	16,500	12.5	33,500	25.3	16,000	12.1
1946	98,033	70.0	33,411	23.9	16,500	11.8	33,000	23.6	17,500	12.5
1947	99,579	69.4	32,697	22.8	17,000	11.9	34,500	24.1	18,000	12.6
1948 (5th Rev.)[d]	98,001	67.1	32,259	22.1	16,000	11.0	35,000	24.0	17,000	11.6
1948 (6th Rev.)[d]	93,000	63.7	32,259	22.1	16,000	11.0	31,000	21.2	16,000	11.0
1949	90,106	60.6	31,701	21.3	15,000	10.1	31,000	20.9	15,000	10.1
1950	91,249	60.3	34,763	23.0	15,500	10.2	29,000	19.2	15,000	9.9
1951	95,871	62.5	36,996	24.1	16,000	10.4	30,000	19.6	16,000	10.4
1952	96,172	61.8	37,794	24.3	15,000	9.6	30,500	19.6	16,000	10.3
1953	95,032	60.1	37,955	24.0	15,000	9.5	29,000	18.3	16,500	10.4
1954	90,032	55.9	35,586	22.1	14,000	8.7	28,000	17.4	15,500	9.6
1955	93,443	56.9	38,426	23.4	14,200	8.6	28,500	17.3	15,500	9.4
1956	94,780	56.6	39,628	23.7	14,300	8.5	28,000	16.7	16,000	9.6
1957	95,307	55.9	38,702	22.7	14,200	8.3	28,000	16.4	17,500	10.3
1958	90,604	52.3	36,981	21.3	13,300	7.7	26,500	15.3	16,500	9.5
1959	92,080	52.2	37,910	21.5	13,800	7.8	27,000	15.3	16,500	9.3
1960	93,806	52.1	38,137	21.2	13,800	7.7	28,000	15.6	17,000	9.4
1961	92,249	50.4	38,091	20.8	13,500	7.4	27,000	14.8	16,500	9.0
1962	97,139	52.3	40,804	22.0	13,700	7.4	28,500	15.3	17,000	9.2
1963	100,669	53.4	43,564	23.1	14,200	7.5	28,500	15.1	17,500	9.3
1964	105,000	54.9	47,700	25.0	14,200	7.4	28,000	14.6	18,500	9.7
1965	108,004	55.8	49,163	25.4	14,100	7.3	28,500	14.7	19,500	10.1
1966	113,563	58.1	53,041	27.1	14,500	7.4	29,500	15.1	20,000	10.2
1967	113,169	57.3	52,924	26.8	14,200	7.2	29,000	14.7	20,500	10.4
1968	114,864	57.6	54,862	27.5	14,300	7.2	28,000	14.0	21,500	10.8
1969	116,385	57.8	55,791	27.7	14,300	7.1	27,500	13.7	22,500	11.2
1970	114,638	56.2	54,633	26.8	13,800	6.8	27,000	13.2	23,500	11.5
1971	113,439	54.8	54,381	26.3	13,700	6.6	26,500	12.8	23,500	11.4
1972	115,448	55.2	56,278	26.9	14,000	6.7	26,500	12.7	23,500	11.2
1973	115,821	54.8	55,511	26.3	14,300	6.8	26,500	12.5	24,500	11.6

See source and footnotes on page 33.

PRINCIPAL CLASSES OF UNINTENTIONAL-INJURY DEATHS, UNITED STATES, 1903–1999, Cont.

Year	Total[a] Deaths	Total[a] Rate[b]	Motor-Vehicle Deaths	Motor-Vehicle Rate[b]	Work Deaths	Work Rate[b]	Home Deaths	Home Rate[b]	Public Nonmotor-Vehicle Deaths	Public Nonmotor-Vehicle Rate[b]
1974	104,622	49.0	46,402	21.8	13,500	6.3	26,000	12.2	23,000	10.8
1975	103,030	47.8	45,853	21.3	13,000	6.0	25,000	11.6	23,000	10.6
1976	100,761	46.3	47,038	21.6	12,500	5.7	24,000	11.0	21,500	10.0
1977	103,202	47.0	49,510	22.5	12,900	5.9	23,200	10.6	22,200	10.1
1978	105,561	47.5	52,411	23.6	13,100	5.9	22,800	10.3	22,000	9.9
1979	105,312	46.9	53,524	23.8	13,000	5.8	22,500	10.0	21,000	9.4
1980	105,718	46.5	53,172	23.4	13,200	5.8	22,800	10.0	21,300	9.4
1981	100,704	43.9	51,385	22.4	12,500	5.4	21,700	9.5	19,800	8.6
1982	94,082	40.6	45,779	19.8	11,900	5.1	21,200	9.2	19,500	8.4
1983	92,488	39.6	44,452	19.0	11,700	5.0	21,200	9.1	19,400	8.3
1984	92,911	39.4	46,263	19.6	11,500	4.9	21,200	9.0	18,300	7.8
1985	93,457	39.3	45,901	19.3	11,500	4.8	21,600	9.1	18,800	7.9
1986	95,277	39.7	47,865	19.9	11,100	4.6	21,700	9.0	18,700	7.8
1987	95,020	39.2	48,290	19.9	11,300	4.7	21,400	8.8	18,400	7.6
1988	97,100	39.7	49,078	20.1	11,000	4.5	22,700	9.3	18,400	7.5
1989	95,028	38.5	47,575	19.3	10,900	4.4	22,500	9.1	18,200	7.4
1990	91,983	36.9	46,814	18.8	10,100	4.0	21,500	8.6	17,400	7.0
1991	89,347	35.4	43,536	17.3	9,800	3.9	22,100	8.8	17,600	7.0
1992	86,777	34.0	40,982	16.1	4,968[e]	1.9[e]	24,000[e]	9.4[e]	19,000[e]	7.4[e]
1993	90,523	35.1	41,893	16.3	5,035	2.0	26,100	10.1	19,700	7.6
1994	91,437	35.1	42,524	16.3	5,338	2.1	26,300	10.1	19,600	7.5
1995	93,320	35.5	43,363	16.5	5,018	1.9	27,200	10.3	20,100	7.6
1996	94,948	35.8	43,649	16.5	5,058	1.9	27,500	10.4	21,000	7.9
1997[f]	95,644	35.7	43,458	16.2	5,162	1.9	27,700	10.3	21,700	8.1
1998[f]	93,200	34.5	41,800	15.5	5,094	1.9	27,300	10.1	21,400	7.9
1999[g]	96,900	35.5	41,300	15.1	5,100	1.9	28,800	10.6	24,100	8.8
Changes										
1989 to 1999	+2%	–8%	–13%	–22%	[h]	[h]	[h]	[h]	[h]	[h]
1998 to 1999	+4%	+3%	–1%	–3%	[i]	0%	+5%	+5%	+13%	+11%

Source: Total and motor-vehicle deaths, 1903–1932 based on National Center for Health Statistics death registration states; 1933–1948 (5th Rev.), 1949–1963, 1965–1997 are NCHS totals for the U.S. Work deaths for 1992–1998 are from the Bureau of Labor Statistics, Census of Fatal Occupational Injuries. All other figures are National Safety Council estimates.
[a] *Duplications between Motor-Vehicle, Work, and Home are eliminated in the Total column.*
[b] *Rates are deaths per 100,000 population.*
[c] *Data insufficient to estimate yearly totals.*
[d] *In 1948 a revision was made in the International Classification of Diseases. The first figures for 1948 are comparable with those for earlier years, the second with those for later years.*
[e] *Adoption of the Census of Fatal Occupational Injuries figure for the Work class necessitated adjustments to the Home and Public classes. See the Technical Appendix for details.*
[f] *Revised.*
[g] *Preliminary.*
[h] *Comparison not valid for 1989–1999 because of change in estimating procedure (see footnote "e").*
[i] *Change less than 0.5%.*

UNINTENTIONAL-INJURY DEATHS BY CLASS, UNITED STATES, 1999

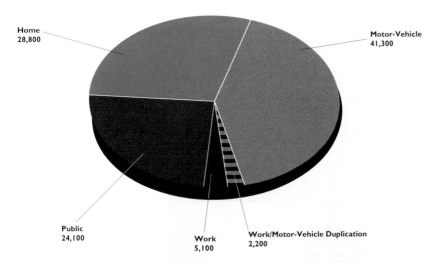

Home
28,800

Motor-Vehicle
41,300

Public
24,100

Work
5,100

Work/Motor-Vehicle Duplication
2,200

UNINTENTIONAL-INJURY DEATHS BY AGE, UNITED STATES, 1903–1999

Year	All Ages	Under 5 Years	5–14 Years	15–24 Years	25–44 Years	45–64 Years	65–74 Years	75 Years & Over[a]
1903	70,600	9,400	8,200	10,300	20,100	12,600	10,000	
1904	71,500	9,700	9,000	10,500	19,900	12,500	9,900	
1905	70,900	9,800	8,400	10,600	19,600	12,600	9,900	
1906	80,000	10,000	8,400	13,000	24,000	13,600	11,000	
1907	81,900	10,500	8,300	13,400	24,900	14,700	10,100	
1908	72,300	10,100	7,600	11,300	20,500	13,100	9,700	
1909	72,700	9,900	7,400	10,700	21,000	13,300	10,400	
1910	77,900	9,900	7,400	11,900	23,600	14,100	11,000	
1911	79,300	11,000	7,500	11,400	22,400	15,100	11,900	
1912	78,400	10,600	7,900	11,500	22,200	14,700	11,500	
1913	82,500	9,800	7,400	12,200	24,500	16,500	12,100	
1914	77,000	10,600	7,900	11,000	21,400	14,300	11,800	
1915	76,200	10,300	8,200	10,800	20,500	14,300	12,100	
1916	84,800	11,600	9,100	7,700	24,900	17,800	13,700	
1917	90,100	11,600	9,700	11,700	24,400	18,500	14,200	
1918	85,100	10,600	10,100	10,600	21,900	17,700	14,200	
1919	75,500	10,100	10,000	10,200	18,600	13,800	12,800	
1920	75,900	10,200	9,900	10,400	18,100	13,900	13,400	
1921	74,000	9,600	9,500	9,800	18,000	13,900	13,200	
1922	76,300	9,700	9,500	10,000	18,700	14,500	13,900	
1923	84,400	9,900	9,800	11,000	21,500	16,900	15,300	
1924	85,600	10,200	9,900	11,900	20,900	16,800	15,900	
1925	90,000	9,700	10,000	12,400	22,200	18,700	17,000	
1926	91,700	9,500	9,900	12,600	22,700	19,200	17,800	
1927	92,700	9,200	9,900	12,900	22,900	19,700	18,100	
1928	95,000	8,900	9,800	13,100	23,300	20,600	19,300	
1929	98,200	8,600	9,800	14,000	24,300	21,500	20,000	
1930	99,100	8,200	9,100	14,000	24,300	22,200	21,300	
1931	97,300	7,800	8,700	13,500	23,100	22,500	21,700	
1932	89,000	7,100	8,100	12,000	20,500	20,100	21,200	
1933	90,932	6,948	8,195	12,225	21,005	20,819	21,740	
1934	100,977	7,034	8,272	13,274	23,288	24,197	24,912	
1935	99,773	6,971	7,808	13,168	23,411	23,457	24,958	
1936	110,052	7,471	7,866	13,701	24,990	26,535	29,489	
1937	105,205	6,969	7,704	14,302	23,955	24,743	27,532	
1938	93,805	6,646	6,593	12,129	20,464	21,689	26,284	
1939	92,628	6,668	6,378	12,066	20,164	20,842	26,505	
1940	96,885	6,851	6,466	12,763	21,166	21,840	27,799	
1941	101,513	7,052	6,702	14,346	22,983	22,509	27,921	
1942	95,889	7,220	6,340	13,732	21,141	20,764	26,692	
1943	99,038	8,039	6,636	15,278	20,212	20,109	28,764	
1944	95,237	7,912	6,704	14,750	19,115	19,097	27,659	
1945	95,918	7,741	6,836	12,446	19,393	20,097	29,405	
1946	98,033	7,949	6,545	13,366	20,705	20,249	29,219	
1947	99,579	8,219	6,069	13,166	21,155	20,513	30,457	
1948 (5th Rev.)[b]	98,001	8,387	5,859	12,595	20,274	19,809	31,077	
1948 (6th Rev.)[b]	93,000	8,350	5,850	12,600	20,300	19,300	9,800	16,800
1949	90,106	8,469	5,539	11,522	19,432	18,302	9,924	16,918
1950	91,249	8,389	5,519	12,119	20,663	18,665	9,750	16,144
1951	95,871	8,769	5,892	12,366	22,363	19,610	10,218	16,653
1952	96,172	8,871	5,980	12,787	21,950	19,892	10,026	16,667
1953	95,032	8,678	6,136	12,837	21,422	19,479	9,927	16,553
1954	90,032	8,380	5,939	11,801	20,023	18,299	9,652	15,938
1955	93,443	8,099	6,099	12,742	29,911	19,199	9,929	16,464
1956	94,780	8,173	6,319	13,545	20,986	19,207	10,160	16,393
1957	95,307	8,423	6,454	12,973	20,949	19,495	10,076	16,937
1958	90,604	8,789	6,514	12,744	19,658	18,095	9,431	15,373
1959	92,080	8,748	6,511	13,269	19,666	18,937	9,475	15,474
1960	93,806	8,950	6,836	13,457	19,600	19,385	9,689	15,829
1961	92,249	8,622	6,717	13,431	19,273	19,134	9,452	15,620
1962	97,139	8,705	6,751	14,557	19,955	20,335	10,149	16,687
1963	100,669	8,688	6,962	15,889	20,529	21,262	10,194	17,145
1964	100,500	8,670	7,400	17,420	22,080	22,100	10,400	16,930
1965	108,004	8,586	7,391	18,688	22,228	22,900	10,430	17,781
1966	113,563	8,507	7,958	21,030	23,134	24,022	10,706	18,206
1967	113,169	7,825	7,874	21,645	23,255	23,826	10,645	18,099
1968	114,864	7,263	8,369	23,012	23,684	23,896	10,961	17,679
1969	116,385	6,973	8,186	24,668	24,410	24,192	10,643	17,313
1970	114,638	6,594	8,203	24,336	23,979	24,164	10,644	16,718
1971	113,439	6,496	8,143	24,733	23,535	23,240	10,494	16,798
1972	115,448	6,142	8,242	25,762	23,852	23,658	10,446	17,346
1973	115,821	6,037	8,102	26,550	24,750	23,059	10,243	17,080

See source and footnotes on page 35.

UNINTENTIONAL-INJURY DEATHS BY AGE, UNITED STATES, 1903–1999, Cont.

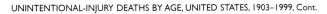

Year	All Ages	Under 5 Years	5–14 Years	15–24 Years	25–44 Years	45–64 Years	65–74 Years	75 Years & Over[a]
1974	104,622	5,335	7,037	24,200	22,547	20,334	9,323	15,846
1975	103,030	4,948	6,818	24,121	22,877	19,643	9,220	15,403
1976	100,761	4,692	6,308	24,316	22,399	19,000	8,823	15,223
1977	103,202	4,470	6,305	25,619	23,460	19,167	9,006	15,175
1978	105,561	4,766	6,118	26,622	25,024	18,774	9,072	15,185
1979	105,312	4,429	5,689	26,574	26,097	18,346	9,013	15,164
1980	105,718	4,479	5,224	26,206	26,722	18,140	8,997	15,950
1981	100,704	4,130	4,866	23,582	26,928	17,339	8,639	15,220
1982	94,082	4,108	4,504	21,306	25,135	15,907	8,224	14,898
1983	92,488	3,999	4,321	19,756	24,996	15,444	8,336	15,636
1984	92,911	3,652	4,198	19,801	25,498	15,273	8,424	16,065
1985	93,457	3,746	4,252	19,161	25,940	15,251	8,583	16,524
1986	95,277	3,843	4,226	19,975	27,201	14,733	8,499	16,800
1987	95,020	3,871	4,198	18,695	27,484	14,807	8,686	17,279
1988	97,100	3,794	4,215	18,507	28,279	15,177	8,971	18,157
1989	95,028	3,770	4,090	16,738	28,429	15,046	8,812	18,143
1990	91,983	3,496	3,650	16,241	27,663	14,607	8,405	17,921
1991	89,347	3,626	3,660	15,278	26,526	13,693	8,137	18,427
1992	86,777	3,286	3,388	13,662	25,808	13,882	8,165	18,586
1993	90,523	3,488	3,466	13,966	27,277	14,434	8,125	19,767
1994	91,437	3,406	3,508	13,898	27,012	15,200	8,279	20,134
1995	93,320	3,067	3,544	13,842	27,660	16,004	8,400	20,803
1996	94,948	2,951	3,433	13,809	27,092	16,717	8,780	22,166
1997[c]	94,644	2,770	3,371	13,367	27,129	17,521	8,578	22,908
1998[c]	93,200	2,400	3,200	13,000	25,700	17,700	8,700	22,500
1999[d]	96,900	2,500	3,100	13,100	25,700	19,500	8,200	24,800
Changes								
1989 to 1999	+2%	–34%	–24%	–22%	–10%	+30%	–7%	+37%
1998 to 1999	+4%	+4%	–3%	+1%	0%	+10%	–6%	+10%

Source: 1903 to 1932 based on National Center for Health Statistics data for registration states; 1933-1948 (5th Rev.), 1949-1963, 1965-1997 are NCHS totals. All other figures are National Safety Council estimates. See Technical Appendix for comparability.
[a] Includes "age unknown." In 1997, these deaths numbered 100.
[b] In 1948, a revision was made in the International Classification of Diseases. The first figures for 1948 are comparable with those for earlier years, the second with those for later years.
[c] Revised.
[d] Preliminary.

CHANGES IN UNINTENTIONAL-INJURY DEATHS BY AGE, UNITED STATES, 1989, 1998, 1999

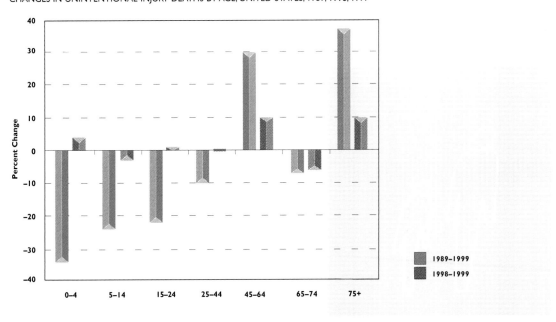

UNINTENTIONAL-INJURY DEATH RATES BY AGE

UNINTENTIONAL-INJURY DEATH RATES[a] BY AGE, UNITED STATES, 1903–1999

Year	Index	All Ages	Under 5 Years	5–14 Years	15–24 Years	25–44 Years	45–64 Years	65–74 Years	75 Years & Over[b]
1903	98.7	87.2	98.7	46.8	65.0	87.4	111.7		299.8
1904	103.2	86.6	99.1	50.9	64.9	84.6	108.1		290.0
1905	98.2	84.2	98.6	47.0	64.1	81.4	106.2		282.5
1906	114.5	93.2	99.1	46.5	77.1	97.3	111.7		306.0
1907	114.4	93.6	102.7	45.5	78.0	98.8	117.8		274.2
1908	100.0	81.2	97.5	41.2	64.4	79.5	102.2		256.7
1909	97.0	80.1	94.2	39.6	59.9	79.6	101.0		268.2
1910	103.1	84.4	92.8	39.1	65.3	87.3	104.0		276.0
1911	103.6	84.7	101.9	39.3	62.1	81.4	108.7		292.1
1912	100.0	82.5	97.1	40.5	62.3	79.2	103.2		275.8
1913	103.4	85.5	88.4	37.4	65.2	85.6	112.5		281.7
1914	95.1	78.6	94.3	38.9	58.5	73.2	94.6		268.1
1915	91.1	76.7	90.8	39.7	57.3	69.0	92.4		268.8
1916	100.6	84.1	101.4	43.3	40.8	82.5	112.1		297.6
1917	105.4	88.2	108.4	45.3	62.1	79.8	113.8		301.2
1918	100.1	82.1	91.0	46.5	58.7	72.2	106.3		294.2
1919	87.2	71.9	87.2	45.9	55.3	60.1	81.8		262.0
1920	86.3	71.2	87.4	44.9	55.5	56.9	85.6		289.5
1921	82.5	68.4	80.8	42.4	51.4	55.5	79.4		259.8
1922	84.7	69.4	80.6	41.5	51.4	57.1	81.4		265.1
1923	92.2	75.7	82.0	42.4	55.6	64.5	92.6		282.8
1924	91.1	75.6	82.9	42.4	58.6	61.7	90.2		283.5
1925	94.6	78.4	78.6	42.3	59.7	64.7	97.8		293.9
1926	95.1	78.7	77.9	41.4	59.9	65.4	98.2		298.7
1927	94.8	78.4	75.9	41.0	60.2	65.2	98.0		295.4
1928	91.4	79.3	74.4	40.4	59.9	65.6	99.9		306.2
1929	98.1	80.8	73.3	40.0	63.1	67.7	102.1		308.9
1930	97.9	80.5	71.8	36.9	62.3	67.0	102.9		317.9
1931	95.1	78.5	69.9	35.2	59.7	63.0	102.1		313.3
1932	86.1	71.3	65.1	32.8	52.7	55.6	89.3		296.9
1933	86.9	72.4	65.5	33.4	53.6	56.3	90.8		295.3
1934	95.4	79.9	68.1	33.9	57.8	61.8	103.3		328.5
1935	93.0	78.4	68.5	32.2	56.9	61.6	98.0		319.8
1936	101.5	85.9	74.4	32.9	58.8	65.3	108.6		367.4
1937	95.5	81.7	69.6	32.7	60.9	62.1	99.3		333.4
1938	84.0	72.3	65.3	28.5	51.3	52.5	85.4		308.9
1939	81.4	70.8	62.9	28.2	50.7	51.2	81.0		300.0
1940	84.1	73.4	64.8	28.8	53.5	53.2	83.4		305.7
1941	86.7	76.3	65.0	29.7	60.9	57.2	84.8		297.4
1942	81.0	71.6	63.9	27.9	59.8	52.4	77.1		275.5
1943	82.9	73.8	66.9	29.0	69.7	50.3	73.6		287.8
1944	80.2	71.7	63.2	29.1	72.9	48.9	68.9		268.6
1945	80.0	72.4	59.8	29.5	64.5	50.5	71.6		277.6
1946	77.8	70.0	60.2	28.1	61.7	48.8	70.9		267.9
1947	76.9	69.4	57.4	25.8	59.6	49.0	70.6		270.7
1948 (5th Rev.)[c]	73.9	67.1	56.3	24.6	56.8	46.2	66.8		267.4
1948 (6th Rev.)[c]	70.4	63.7	56.0	24.5	56.8	46.2	65.1	122.4	464.3
1949	66.7	60.6	54.4	23.0	52.2	43.5	60.6	120.4	450.7
1950	66.6	60.3	51.4	22.6	55.0	45.6	60.5	115.8	414.7
1951	69.0	62.5	50.8	23.6	57.7	49.0	62.7	117.1	413.6
1952	68.4	61.8	51.5	22.5	60.9	47.7	62.7	111.1	399.8
1953	66.6	60.1	49.5	22.1	61.4	46.4	60.5	106.7	383.6
1954	61.9	55.9	46.7	20.5	56.4	43.0	55.9	100.7	354.4
1955	63.2	56.9	43.9	20.7	60.1	44.7	57.7	100.8	350.2
1956	63.3	56.6	43.3	20.2	63.3	44.7	56.7	100.6	335.6
1957	62.2	55.9	43.5	19.9	59.5	44.6	56.6	97.5	333.3
1958	58.1	52.3	44.5	19.6	56.2	42.0	51.7	89.3	292.6
1959	58.1	52.2	43.6	18.9	56.5	42.1	53.2	87.7	284.7
1960	58.0	52.1	44.0	19.1	55.6	42.0	53.6	87.6	281.4
1961	56.1	50.4	42.0	18.1	54.0	41.2	52.1	83.8	267.9
1962	58.1	52.3	42.6	18.0	55.0	42.7	54.6	88.5	277.7
1963	59.5	53.4	42.8	18.2	57.2	44.0	56.3	87.9	277.0
1964	61.4	54.9	43.1	19.1	59.9	47.3	57.6	88.9	263.9
1965	62.3	55.8	43.4	18.7	61.6	47.7	58.8	88.5	268.7
1966	64.8	58.1	44.4	19.9	66.9	49.6	60.7	89.8	267.4
1967	64.0	57.3	42.2	19.4	66.9	49.7	59.2	88.5	257.4
1968	64.3	57.6	40.6	20.5	69.2	50.1	58.5	90.2	244.0
1969	64.6	57.8	40.2	20.0	71.8	51.2	58.4	86.6	232.0
1970	62.5	56.2	38.4	20.1	68.0	49.8	57.6	85.2	219.6
1971	60.7	54.8	37.7	20.1	66.1	48.4	54.7	82.7	213.2
1972	60.7	55.2	35.9	20.6	67.6	47.5	55.2	80.8	214.2
1973	60.1	54.8	35.8	20.6	68.2	48.0	53.3	77.3	206.3

See source and footnotes on page 37.

UNINTENTIONAL-INJURY DEATH RATES[a] BY AGE, UNITED STATES, 1903–1999, Cont.

Year	Index	All Ages	Under 5 Years	5–14 Years	15–24 Years	25–44 Years	45–64 Years	65–74 Years	75 Years & Over[b]
1974	53.5	49.0	32.4	18.2	60.9	42.7	46.7	68.7	186.7
1975	52.0	47.8	30.7	17.8	59.5	42.3	44.9	66.2	175.5
1976	50.1	46.3	30.0	16.7	58.9	40.3	43.2	62.0	168.4
1977	50.6	47.0	28.7	17.0	61.3	40.9	43.4	61.5	164.0
1978	51.2	47.5	30.3	16.9	63.1	42.3	42.4	60.5	159.7
1979	50.4	46.9	27.6	16.1	62.6	42.7	41.3	58.8	154.8
1980	49.7	46.5	27.2	15.0	61.7	42.3	40.8	57.5	158.6
1981	46.8	43.9	24.4	14.2	55.9	41.2	39.0	54.4	147.4
1982	43.2	40.6	23.8	13.2	51.2	37.3	35.8	50.9	140.0
1983	41.8	39.6	22.8	12.7	48.2	36.0	34.7	50.8	142.8
1984	41.5	39.4	20.6	12.4	48.9	35.7	34.3	50.7	142.8
1985	41.3	39.3	21.0	12.6	47.9	35.3	34.2	50.9	143.0
1986	41.7	39.7	21.4	12.6	50.5	36.1	33.0	49.6	141.5
1987	41.1	39.2	21.4	12.4	48.1	35.7	33.0	49.8	141.6
1988	41.5	39.7	20.9	12.3	48.5	36.1	33.4	50.9	145.3
1989	40.1	38.5	20.4	11.8	44.8	35.7	32.8	49.3	141.5
1990	38.5	36.9	18.5	10.4	44.0	34.2	31.6	46.4	136.5
1991	36.8	35.4	18.9	10.2	42.0	32.3	29.3	44.5	136.7
1992	35.1	34.0	16.8	9.3	37.8	31.3	28.7	44.2	134.5
1993	36.2	35.1	17.7	9.4	38.8	33.0	29.1	43.6	139.9
1994	36.1	35.1	17.3	9.4	38.4	32.5	29.9	44.3	139.2
1995	36.4	35.5	15.7	9.3	38.2	33.2	30.6	44.8	140.6
1996	36.5	35.8	15.3	8.9	38.1	32.3	31.1	47.0	145.9
1997[d]	36.2	35.7	14.5	8.7	36.5	32.5	31.6	46.3	146.2
1998[d]	34.8	34.5	12.7	8.2	34.9	30.9	30.9	47.0	140.6
1999[e]	35.6	35.5	13.2	7.8	34.6	31.0	32.9	45.0	151.7
Changes									
1989 to 1999		−8%	−35%	−34%	−23%	−13%	(f)	−9%	+7%
1998 to 1999		+3%	+4%	−5%	−1%	(f)	+6%	−4%	+8%
1999 Population (Millions)									
Total		272.878[g]	18.918	39.511	37.823	82.824	59.224	18.234	16.344
Male		133.352[g]	9.668	20.228	19.356	41.113	28.665	8.205	6.119
Female		139.526[g]	9.250	19.284	18.467	41.712	30.559	10.030	10.226

Source: All figures are National Safety Council estimates. See Technical Appendix for comparability.
[a] *Rates are deaths per 100,000 resident population in each age group. The All Ages crude rates are based on U.S. Census Bureau figures. The index numbers (1912=100.0) are based on rates standardized for age (base 1940) to remove the influence of changes in age distribution between 1903 and 1999.*
[b] *Includes age unknown.*
[c] *In 1948, a revision was made in the International Classification of Diseases. The first figures for 1948 are comparable with those for earlier years, the second with those for later years.*
[d] *Revised.*
[e] *Preliminary.*
[f] *Change less than 0.5%.*
[g] *Sum of parts may not equal total due to rounding.*

UNINTENTIONAL-INJURY DEATHS AND POPULATION BY AGE, UNITED STATES, 1999

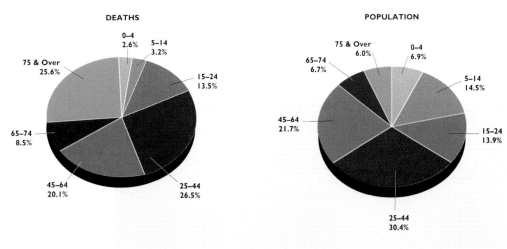

PRINCIPAL TYPES OF
UNINTENTIONAL-INJURY DEATHS

PRINCIPAL TYPES OF UNINTENTIONAL-INJURY DEATHS, UNITED STATES, 1903–1999

Year	Motor-Vehicle	Falls	Drowning[a]	Fires, Burns[b]	Ingest. of Food, Object	Firearms	Poison (Solid, Liquid)	Poison (Gas, Vapor)
1903	(c)	(c)	9,200	(c)	(c)	2,500	(c)	(c)
1904	(c)	(c)	9,300	(c)	(c)	2,800	(c)	(c)
1905	(c)	(c)	9,300	(c)	(c)	2,000	(c)	(c)
1906	400	(c)	9,400	(c)	(c)	2,100	(c)	(c)
1907	700	(c)	9,000	(c)	(c)	1,700	(c)	(c)
1908	800	(c)	9,300	(c)	(c)	1,900	(c)	(c)
1909	1,300	(c)	8,500	(c)	(c)	1,600	(c)	(c)
1910	1,900	(c)	8,700	(c)	(c)	1,900	(c)	(c)
1911	2,300	(c)	9,000	(c)	(c)	2,100	(c)	(c)
1912	3,100	(c)	8,600	(c)	(c)	2,100	(c)	(c)
1913	4,200	15,100	10,300	8,900	(c)	2,400	3,200	(c)
1914	4,700	15,000	8,700	9,100	(c)	2,300	3,300	(c)
1915	6,600	15,000	8,600	8,400	(c)	2,100	2,800	(c)
1916	8,200	15,200	8,900	9,500	(c)	2,200	2,900	(c)
1917	10,200	15,200	7,600	10,800	(c)	2,300	2,800	(c)
1918	10,700	13,200	7,000	10,200	(c)	2,500	2,700	(c)
1919	11,200	11,900	9,100	9,100	(c)	2,800	3,100	(c)
1920	12,500	12,600	6,100	9,300	(c)	2,700	3,300	(c)
1921	13,900	12,300	7,800	7,500	(c)	2,800	2,900	(c)
1922	15,300	13,200	7,000	8,300	(c)	2,900	2,800	(c)
1923	18,400	14,100	6,800	9,100	(c)	2,900	2,800	2,700
1924	19,400	14,700	7,400	7,400	(c)	2,900	2,700	2,900
1925	21,900	15,500	7,300	8,600	(c)	2,800	2,700	2,800
1926	23,400	16,300	7,500	8,800	(c)	2,800	2,600	3,200
1927	25,800	16,500	8,100	8,200	(c)	3,000	2,600	2,700
1928	28,000	17,000	8,600	8,400	(c)	2,900	2,800	2,800
1929	31,200	17,700	7,600	8,200	(c)	3,200	2,600	2,800
1930	32,900	18,100	7,500	8,100	(c)	3,200	2,600	2,500
1931	33,700	18,100	7,600	7,100	(c)	3,100	2,600	2,100
1932	29,500	18,600	7,500	7,100	(c)	3,000	2,200	2,100
1933	31,363	18,962	7,158	6,781	(c)	3,014	2,135	1,633
1934	36,101	20,725	7,077	7,456	(c)	3,033	2,148	1,643
1935	36,369	21,378	6,744	7,253	(c)	2,799	2,163	1,654
1936	38,089	23,562	6,659	7,939	(c)	2,817	2,177	1,665
1937	39,643	22,544	7,085	7,214	(c)	2,576	2,190	1,675
1938	32,582	23,239	6,881	6,491	(c)	2,726	2,077	1,428
1939	32,386	23,427	6,413	6,675	(c)	2,618	1,963	1,440
1940	34,501	23,356	6,202	7,521	(c)	2,375	1,847	1,583
1941	39,969	22,764	6,389	6,922	(c)	2,396	1,731	1,464
1942	28,309	22,632	6,696	7,901	(c)	2,678	1,607	1,741
1943	23,823	24,701	7,115	8,726	921	2,282	1,745	2,014
1944	24,282	22,989	6,511	8,372	896	2,392	1,993	1,860
1945	28,076	23,847	6,624	7,949	897	2,385	1,987	2,120
1946	33,411	23,109	6,442	7,843	1,076	2,801	1,961	1,821
1947	32,697	24,529	6,885	8,033	1,206	2,439	1,865	1,865
1948 (5th Rev.)[d]	32,259	24,836	6,428	7,743	1,315	2,191	1,753	2,045
1948 (6th Rev.)[d]	32,259	22,000	6,500	6,800	1,299	2,330	1,600	2,020
1949	31,701	22,308	6,684	5,982	1,341	2,326	1,634	1,617
1950	34,763	20,783	6,131	6,405	1,350	2,174	1,584	1,769
1951	36,996	21,376	6,489	6,788	1,456	2,247	1,497	1,627
1952	37,794	20,945	6,601	6,922	1,434	2,210	1,440	1,397
1953	37,955	20,631	6,770	6,579	1,603	2,277	1,391	1,223
1954	35,586	19,771	6,334	6,083	1,627	2,271	1,339	1,223
1955	38,426	20,192	6,344	6,352	1,608	2,120	1,431	1,163
1956	39,628	20,282	6,263	6,405	1,760	2,202	1,422	1,213
1957	38,702	20,545	6,613	6,269	2,043	2,369	1,390	1,143
1958	36,981	18,248	6,582 [e]	7,291 [e]	2,191 [e]	2,172	1,429	1,187
1959	37,910	18,774	6,434	6,898	2,189	2,258	1,661	1,141
1960	38,137	19,023	6,529	7,645	2,397	2,334	1,679	1,253
1961	38,091	18,691	6,525	7,102	2,499	2,204	1,804	1,192
1962	40,804	19,589	6,439	7,534	1,813	2,092	1,833	1,376
1963	43,564	19,335	6,347	8,172	1,949	2,263	2,061	1,489
1964	47,700	18,941	6,709	7,379	1,865	2,275	2,100	1,360
1965	49,163	19,984	6,799	7,347	1,836	2,344	2,110	1,526
1966	53,041	20,066	7,084	8,084	1,831	2,558	2,283	1,648
1967	52,924	20,120	7,076	7,423	1,980	2,896	2,506	1,574
1968	54,862	18,651	7,372 [e]	7,335	3,100 [e]	2,394 [e]	2,583	1,526
1969	55,791	17,827	7,699	7,163	3,712	2,309	2,967	1,549
1970	54,633	16,926	7,860	6,718	2,753	2,406	3,679	1,620
1971	54,381	16,755	7,396	6,776	2,877	2,360	3,710	1,646
1972	56,278	16,744	7,586	6,714	2,830	2,442	3,728	1,690
1973	55,511	16,506	8,725	6,503	3,013	2,618	3,683	1,652

See source and footnotes on page 39.

PRINCIPAL TYPES OF UNINTENTIONAL-INJURY DEATHS, UNITED STATES, 1903–1999, Cont.

Year	Motor-Vehicle	Falls	Drowning[a]	Fires, Burns[b]	Ingest. of Food, Object	Firearms	Poison (Solid, Liquid)	Poison (Gas, Vapor)
1974	46,402	16,339	7,876	6,236	2,991	2,513	4,016	1,518
1975	45,853	14,896	8,000	6,071	3,106	2,380	4,694	1,577
1976	47,038	14,136	6,827	6,338	3,033	2,059	4,161	1,569
1977	49,510	13,773	7,126	6,357	3,037	1,982	3,374	1,596
1978	52,411	13,690	7,026	6,163	3,063	1,806	3,035	1,737
1979	53,524	13,216	6,872	5,991	3,243	2,004	3,165	1,472
1980	53,172	13,294	7,257	5,822	3,249	1,955	3,089	1,242
1981	51,385	12,628	6,277	5,697	3,331	1,871	3,243	1,280
1982	45,779	12,077	6,351	5,210	3,254	1,756	3,474	1,259
1983	44,452	12,024	6,353	5,028	3,387	1,695	3,382	1,251
1984	46,263	11,937	5,388	5,010	3,541	1,668	3,808	1,103
1985	45,901	12,001	5,316	4,938	3,551	1,649	4,091	1,079
1986	47,865	11,444	5,700	4,835	3,692	1,452	4,731	1,009
1987	48,290	11,733	5,100	4,710	3,688	1,440	4,415	900
1988	49,078	12,096	4,966	4,965	3,805	1,501	5,353	873
1989	47,575	12,151	4,015	4,716	3,578	1,489	5,603	921
1990	46,814	12,313	4,685	4,175	3,303	1,416	5,055	748
1991	43,536	12,662	4,818	4,120	3,240	1,441	5,698	736
1992	40,982	12,646	3,542	3,958	3,182	1,409	6,449	633
1993	41,893	13,141	3,807	3,900	3,160	1,521	7,877	660
1994	42,524	13,450	3,942	3,986	3,065	1,356	8,309	685
1995	43,363	13,986	4,350	3,761	3,185	1,225	8,461	611
1996	43,649	14,986	3,959	3,741	3,206	1,134	8,872	638
1997[f]	43,458	15,447	4,051	3,490	3,275	981	9,587	576
1998[f]	41,800	16,100	4,200	3,000	3,400	800	9,300	600
1999[g]	41,300	17,100	4,000	3,100	3,200	700	10,500	500
Changes								
1989 to 1999	−13%	+41%	(h)	−34%	−11%	−53%	+87%	−46%
1998 to 1999	−1%	+6%	−5%	+3%	−6%	−13%	+13%	−17%

Source: National Center for Health Statistics and National Safety Council. See Technical Appendix for comparability.
[a] *Includes drowning in water transport accidents.*
[b] *Includes burns by fire, and deaths resulting from conflagration regardless of nature of injury.*
[c] *Comparable data not available.*
[d] *In 1948, a revision was made in the International Classification of Diseases. The first figures for 1948 are comparable with those for earlier years, the second with those for later years.*
[e] *Data are not comparable to previous years shown due to classification changes in 1958 and 1968.*
[f] *Revised.*
[g] *Preliminary.*
[h] *Change less than 0.5%.*

UNINTENTIONAL-INJURY DEATH RATES FOR PRINCIPAL TYPES

UNINTENTIONAL-INJURY DEATH RATES[a] FOR PRINCIPAL TYPES, UNITED STATES, 1903–1999

Year	Motor-Vehicle	Falls	Drowning[b]	Fires, Burns[c]	Ingest. of Food, Object	Firearms	Poison (Solid, Liquid)	Poison (Gas,Vapor)
1903	(d)	(d)	11.4	(d)	(d)	3.1	(d)	(d)
1904	(d)	(d)	11.3	(d)	(d)	3.4	(d)	(d)
1905	(d)	(d)	11.1	(d)	(d)	2.4	(d)	(d)
1906	0.5	(d)	11.0	(d)	(d)	2.4	(d)	(d)
1907	0.8	(d)	10.4	(d)	(d)	2.0	(d)	(d)
1908	0.9	(d)	10.5	(d)	(d)	2.1	(d)	(d)
1909	1.4	(d)	9.4	(d)	(d)	1.8	(d)	(d)
1910	2.0	(d)	9.4	(d)	(d)	2.1	(d)	(d)
1911	2.5	(d)	9.6	(d)	(d)	2.2	(d)	(d)
1912	3.3	(d)	9.0	(d)	(d)	2.2	(d)	(d)
1913	4.4	15.5	10.6	9.1	(d)	2.5	3.3	(d)
1914	4.8	15.1	8.8	9.1	(d)	2.3	3.3	(d)
1915	6.6	14.9	8.6	8.4	(d)	2.1	2.8	(d)
1916	8.1	14.9	8.7	9.3	(d)	2.2	2.8	(d)
1917	10.0	14.7	7.4	10.5	(d)	2.2	2.7	(d)
1918	10.3	12.8	6.8	9.9	(d)	2.4	2.6	(d)
1919	10.7	11.4	6.9	8.7	(d)	2.7	3.0	(d)
1920	11.7	11.8	5.7	8.7	(d)	2.5	3.1	(d)
1921	12.9	11.3	7.2	6.9	(d)	2.6	2.7	(d)
1922	13.9	12.0	6.4	7.5	(d)	2.6	2.5	(d)
1923	16.5	12.6	6.1	8.1	(d)	2.6	2.5	2.4
1924	17.1	12.9	6.5	8.4	(d)	2.5	2.4	2.5
1925	19.1	13.4	6.3	7.4	(d)	2.4	2.3	2.4
1926	20.1	13.9	6.4	7.5	(d)	2.4	2.2	2.7
1927	21.8	13.9	6.8	6.9	(d)	2.5	2.2	2.3
1928	23.4	14.1	7.1	7.0	(d)	2.4	2.3	2.3
1929	25.7	14.5	6.2	6.7	(d)	2.6	2.1	2.3
1930	26.7	14.7	6.1	6.6	(d)	2.6	2.1	2.0
1931	27.2	14.6	6.1	5.7	(d)	2.5	2.1	1.7
1932	23.6	14.9	6.0	5.7	(d)	2.4	1.8	1.7
1933	25.0	15.1	5.7	5.4	(d)	2.4	1.7	1.3
1934	28.6	16.4	5.6	5.9	(d)	2.4	1.7	1.3
1935	28.6	16.8	5.3	5.7	(d)	2.2	1.7	1.3
1936	29.7	18.4	5.2	6.2	(d)	2.2	1.7	1.3
1937	30.8	17.5	5.5	5.6	(d)	2.0	1.7	1.3
1938	25.1	17.9	5.3	5.0	(d)	2.1	1.6	1.1
1939	24.7	17.9	4.9	5.1	(d)	2.0	1.5	1.1
1940	26.1	17.7	4.7	5.7	(d)	1.8	1.4	1.2
1941	30.0	17.1	4.8	5.2	(d)	1.8	1.3	1.1
1942	21.1	16.9	5.0	5.9	(d)	2.0	1.2	1.3
1943	17.8	18.4	5.3	6.5	0.7	1.7	1.3	1.5
1944	18.3	17.3	4.9	6.3	0.7	1.8	1.5	1.4
1945	21.2	18.0	5.0	6.0	0.7	1.8	1.5	1.6
1946	23.9	16.5	4.6	5.6	0.8	2.0	1.4	1.3
1947	22.8	17.1	4.8	5.6	0.8	1.7	1.3	1.3
1948 (5th Rev.)[e]	22.1	17.0	4.4	5.3	0.9	1.5	1.2	1.4
1948 (6th Rev.)[e]	22.1	15.1	4.5	4.7	0.9	1.6	1.1	1.4
1949	21.3	15.0	4.5	4.0	0.9	1.6	1.1	1.1
1950	23.0	13.7	4.1	4.2	0.9	1.4	1.1	1.2
1951	24.1	13.9	4.2	4.4	1.0	1.5	1.0	1.1
1952	24.3	13.5	4.2	4.5	0.9	1.4	0.9	0.9
1953	24.0	13.0	4.3	4.2	1.0	1.4	0.9	0.8
1954	22.1	12.3	3.9	3.8	1.0	1.4	0.8	0.8
1955	23.4	12.3	3.9	3.9	1.0	1.3	0.9	0.7
1956	23.7	12.1	3.7	3.8	1.1	1.3	0.8	0.7
1957	22.7	12.1	3.9	3.7	1.2	1.4	0.8	0.7
1958	21.3	10.5	3.8[f]	4.2[f]	1.3[f]	1.3	0.8	0.7
1959	21.5	10.6	3.7	3.9	1.2	1.3	0.9	0.7
1960	21.2	10.6	3.6	4.3	1.3	1.3	0.9	0.7
1961	20.8	10.2	3.6	3.9	1.4	1.2	1.0	0.7
1962	22.0	10.5	3.5	4.1	1.0	1.1	1.0	0.7
1963	23.1	10.3	3.4	4.3	1.0	1.2	1.1	0.8
1964	25.0	9.9	3.5	3.9	1.0	1.2	1.1	0.7
1965	25.4	10.3	3.5	3.8	1.0	1.2	1.1	0.8
1966	27.1	10.3	3.6	4.8	0.9	1.3	1.2	0.8
1967	26.8	10.2	3.6	3.8	1.0	1.5	1.3	0.8
1968	27.5	9.4	3.7[f]	3.7[f]	1.6[f]	1.2[f]	1.3	0.8
1969	27.7	8.9	3.8	3.6	1.8	1.2	1.5	0.8
1970	26.8	8.3	3.9	3.3	1.4	1.2	1.8	0.8
1971	26.3	8.1	3.6	3.3	1.4	1.1	1.8	0.8
1972	26.9	8.0	3.6	3.2	1.4	1.2	1.8	0.8
1973	26.3	7.8	4.1	3.1	1.4	1.2	1.7	0.8

See source and footnotes on page 41.

UNINTENTIONAL-INJURY DEATH RATES[a] FOR PRINCIPAL TYPES, UNITED STATES, 1903–1999, Cont.

Year	Motor-Vehicle	Falls	Drowning[b]	Fires, Burns[c]	Ingest. of Food, Object	Firearms	Poison (Solid, Liquid)	Poison (Gas, Vapor)
1974	21.8	7.7	3.7	2.9	1.4	1.2	1.8	0.7
1975	21.3	6.9	3.7	2.8	1.4	1.1	2.2	0.7
1976	21.6	6.5	3.1	2.9	1.4	0.9	1.9	0.7
1977	22.5	6.3	3.2	2.9	1.4	0.9	1.5	0.7
1978	23.6	6.2	3.2	2.8	1.4	0.8	1.4	0.8
1979	23.8	5.9	3.1	2.7	1.4	0.9	1.4	0.7
1980	23.4	5.9	3.2	2.6	1.4	0.9	1.4	0.5
1981	22.4	5.5	2.7	2.5	1.5	0.8	1.4	0.6
1982	19.8	5.2	2.7	2.2	1.4	0.8	1.5	0.5
1983	19.0	5.1	2.7	2.2	1.4	0.7	1.4	0.5
1984	19.6	5.1	2.3	2.1	1.5	0.7	1.6	0.5
1985	19.3	5.0	2.2	2.1	1.5	0.7	1.7	0.5
1986	19.9	4.8	2.4	2.0	1.5	0.6	2.0	0.4
1987	19.9	4.8	2.1	1.9	1.5	0.6	1.8	0.4
1988	20.1	4.9	2.0	2.0	1.6	0.6	2.2	0.4
1989	19.3	4.9	1.9	1.9	1.4	0.6	2.3	0.4
1990	18.8	4.9	1.9	1.7	1.3	0.6	2.0	0.3
1991	17.3	5.0	1.8	1.6	1.3	0.6	2.3	0.3
1992	16.1	5.0	1.4	1.6	1.2	0.6	2.5	0.2
1993	16.3	5.1	1.5	1.5	1.2	0.6	3.1	0.2
1994	16.3	5.2	1.5	1.5	1.2	0.5	3.2	0.3
1995	16.5	5.3	1.7	1.4	1.2	0.5	3.2	0.2
1996	16.5	5.6	1.5	1.4	1.2	0.4	3.3	0.2
1997[g]	16.2	5.8	1.5	1.3	1.2	0.4	3.6	0.2
1998[g]	15.5	6.0	1.6	1.1	1.3	0.3	3.4	0.2
1999[h]	15.1	6.3	1.5	1.1	1.2	0.3	3.8	0.2
Changes								
1989 to 1999	−22%	+29%	−21%	−42%	−14%	−50%	+65%	−50%
1998 to 1999	−3%	+5%	−6%	0%	−8%	0%	+12%	0%

Source: National Safety Council estimates. See Technical Appendix for comparability.
[a] Deaths per 100,000 population.
[b] Includes drowning in water transport accidents.
[c] Includes burns by fire, and deaths resulting from conflagration regardless of nature of injury.
[d] Comparable data not available.
[e] In 1948, a revision was made in the International Classification of Diseases. The first figures for 1948 are comparable with those for earlier years, the second with those for later years.
[f] Data are not comparable to previous years shown due to classification changes in 1958 and 1968.
[g] Revised.
[h] Preliminary.

UNINTENTIONAL-INJURY DEATH RATES FOR PRINCIPAL TYPES, UNITED STATES, 1989, 1998, 1999

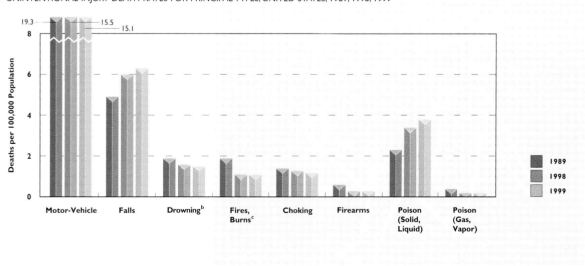

WORK

WORK, 1999

Between 1912 and 1999, unintentional work deaths per 100,000 population were reduced 90%, from 21 to 2. In 1912, an estimated 18,000 to 21,000 workers' lives were lost. In 1999, in a workforce nearly quadrupled in size and producing nine times the goods and services, there were only 5,100 work deaths.

The National Safety Council adopted the Bureau of Labor Statistics' Census of Fatal Occupational Injuries (CFOI) figure, beginning with the 1992 data year, as

the authoritative count of work-related deaths. The Technical Appendix discusses the change in the Council's estimating procedures.

The CFOI system counts intentional as well as unintentional work injuries. Each year approximately 900 to 1,300 homicides and suicides are identified and counted. These fatal injuries are not included in the unintentional-injury estimates below.

Unintentional-Injury Deaths 5,100
Unintentional-Injury Deaths per 100,000 workers 3.8
Disabling Injuries 3,800,000
Workers 134,688,000
Costs . . . . $122.6 billion

UNINTENTIONAL INJURIES AT WORK BY INDUSTRY, UNITED STATES, 1999

Industry Division	Workers[a] (000)	Deaths[a]		Deaths per 100,000 Workers[a]		Disabling Injuries
		1999	Change from 1998	1999	Change from 1998	
All industries	**134,688**	**5,100**	+([b])%	**3.8**	0%	**3,800,000**
Agriculture[c]	3,348	770	−4%	22.5	+([b])%	150,000
Mining, quarrying[c]	562	130	−8%	23.1	+([b])%	20,000
Construction	8,479	1,190	+5%	14.0	−1%	400,000
Manufacturing	19,993	600	−4%	3.0	0%	670,000
Transportation and public utilities	7,948	850	+3%	10.7	0%	370,000
Trade[c]	27,473	450	+2%	1.6	0%	710,000
Services[c]	46,766	640	+2%	1.4	0%	900,000
Government	20,118	470	+1%	2.3	−4%	580,000

Source: National Safety Council estimates based on data from the Bureau of Labor Statistics, National Center for Health Statistics, state vital statistics departments, and state industrial commissions.
[a] Deaths include persons of all ages. Workers and death rates include persons 16 years and older.
[b] Less than 0.5%.
[c] Agriculture includes forestry, fishing, and agricultural services. Mining includes oil and gas extraction. Trade includes wholesale and retail trade. Services includes finance, insurance, and real estate.

WORKERS, UNINTENTIONAL-INJURY DEATHS, AND DEATH RATES, UNITED STATES, 1992–1999

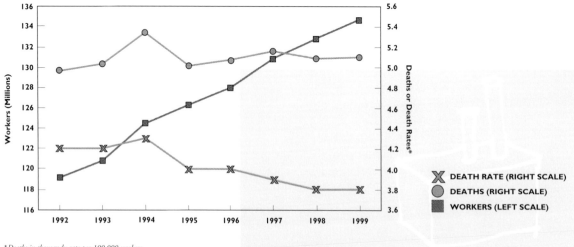

DEATH RATE (RIGHT SCALE)
DEATHS (RIGHT SCALE)
WORKERS (LEFT SCALE)

Deaths in thousands; rate per 100,000 workers.

UNINTENTIONAL WORK-INJURY DEATHS AND DEATH RATES, UNITED STATES, 1933–1999

Year	Deaths	Workers[a]	Death Rate[b]	Year	Deaths	Workers[a]	Death Rate[b]
1933	14,500	39,000	37	1967	14,200	74,700	19
1934	16,000	41,500	39	1968	14,300	76,900	19
1935	16,500	42,500	39	1969	14,300	79,000	18
1936	18,500	44,000	42	1970	13,800	77,700	18
1937	19,000	44,100	43	1971	13,700	78,500	17
1938	16,000	42,100	38	1972	14,000	81,300	17
1939	15,500	43,600	36	1973	14,300	84,300	17
1940	17,000	45,200	38	1974	13,500	86,200	16
1941	18,000	48,100	37	1975	13,000	85,200	15
1942	18,000	51,500	35	1976	12,500	88,100	14
1943	17,500	52,200	34	1977	12,900	91,500	14
1944	16,000	51,800	31	1978	13,100	95,500	14
1945	16,500	50,200	33	1979	13,000	98,300	13
1946	16,500	52,400	31	1980	13,200	98,800	13
1947	17,000	54,900	31	1981	12,500	99,800	13
1948	16,000	56,000	29	1982	11,900	98,800	12
1949	15,000	55,200	27	1983	11,700	100,100	12
1950	15,500	56,400	27	1984	11,500	104,300	11
1951	16,000	57,450	28	1985	11,500	106,400	11
1952	15,000	57,800	26	1986	11,100	108,900	10
1953	15,000	58,050	26	1987	11,300	111,700	10
1954	14,000	57,500	24	1988	11,000	114,300	10
1955	14,200	59,400	24	1989	10,700	116,700	9
1956	14,300	61,100	23	1990	10,100	116,700	9
1957	14,200	61,300	23	1991	9,800	116,400	8
1958	13,300	59,900	22	1992	4,968[c]	119,168[c]	4.2[c]
1959	13,800	61,300	23	1993	5,035	120,778	4.2
1960	13,800	64,400	21	1994	5,338	124,470	4.3
1961	13,500	64,500	21	1995	5,018	126,248	4.0
1962	13,700	65,200	21	1996	5,069	127,997	4.0
1963	14,200	66,200	21	1997[d]	5,160	130,810	3.9
1964	14,200	67,600	21	1998[d]	5,090	132,772	3.8
1965	14,100	69,700	20	1999[e]	5,100	134,688	3.8
1966	14,500	72,600	20				

Source: Deaths for 1992–1998 are from Bureau of Labor Statistics, Census of Fatal Occupational Injuries. Employment for 1992–1998 are from Bureau of Labor Statistics. All other figures are National Safety Council estimates.
[a] *In thousands. Workers are persons ages 16 and older gainfully employed, including owners, managers, other paid employees, the self-employed, unpaid family workers, and active duty resident military personnel. Due to changes in estimating procedures, the numbers of workers for 1970–1991 and 1992–1999 are not comparable to other years.*
[b] *Deaths per 100,000 workers.*
[c] *Deaths include persons of all ages. Workers and death rates include persons 16 years and older. Because of adoption of the Census of Fatal Occupational Injuries, deaths and rates from 1992 to the present are not comparable to prior years. See Technical Appendix for change in estimating procedure.*
[d] *Revised.*
[e] *Preliminary.*

OCCUPATIONAL-INJURY DEATHS AND DEATH RATES, UNITED STATES, 1992–1999

Year	Total	Homicide & Suicide	Unintentional								
			All Industries[a]	Agri-culture[b]	Mining, Quarrying[c]	Construc-tion	Manufac-turing	Transpor-tation & Public Utilities	Trade[d]	Services[e]	Govern-ment
Deaths											
1992	6,217	1,249	4,968	779	175	889	707	769	415	601	585
1993	6,331	1,296	5,035	842	169	895	698	754	450	633	524
1994	6,632	1,294	5,338	814	177	1,000	734	820	492	676	531
1995	6,275	1,257	5,018	770	155	1,021	640	785	462	608	527
1996	6,202	1,133	5,069	768	152	1,073	663	923	454	671	321
1997[f]	6,238	1,078	5,160	799	156	1,075	678	882	451	593	504
1998[f]	6,026	936	5,090	799	142	1,133	628	828	442	629	464
1999[g]	—	—	5,100	770	130	1,190	600	850	450	640	470
Deaths per 100,000 Workers											
1992	5.2	1.0	4.2	23.2	26.4	13.7	3.6	11.5	1.7	1.6	3.0
1993	5.2	1.0	4.2	26.0	25.3	13.3	3.6	11.0	1.8	1.6	2.6
1994	5.3	1.0	4.3	22.8	26.5	14.4	3.7	11.6	1.9	1.7	2.7
1995	4.9	0.9	4.0	21.5	24.8	14.3	3.1	11.0	1.8	1.5	2.7
1996	4.8	0.9	4.0	21.3	26.8	14.4	3.2	12.7	1.7	1.6	1.6
1997[f]	4.8	0.8	3.9	22.5	24.7	13.7	3.3	11.6	1.7	1.3	2.6
1998[f]	4.5	0.7	3.8	22.4	23.0	14.1	3.0	10.7	1.6	1.4	2.4
1999[g]	—	—	3.8	22.5	23.1	14.0	3.0	10.7	1.6	1.4	2.3

Source: Deaths are from Bureau of Labor Statistics, Census of Fatal Occupational Injuries, except 1999 which are National Safety Council estimates. Rates are National Safety Council estimates based on Bureau of Labor Statistics employment data. Deaths include persons of all ages. Death rates include persons 16 years and older. Dashes indicate data not available.
[a] Includes deaths with industry unknown.
[b] Agriculture includes forestry, fishing, and agricultural services.
[c] Mining includes oil and gas extraction.
[d] Trade includes wholesale and retail trade.
[e] Services includes finance, insurance, and real estate.
[f] Revised.
[g] Preliminary.

OCCUPATIONAL UNINTENTIONAL-INJURY DEATH RATES, UNITED STATES, 1999

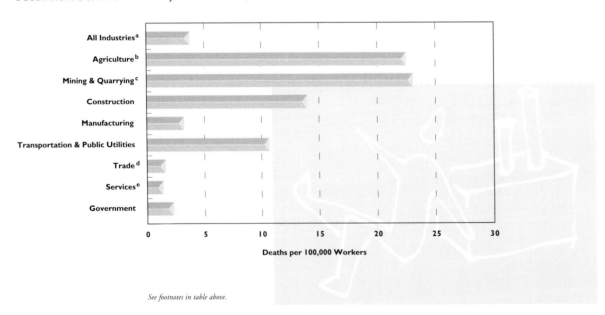

See footnotes in table above.

WORK INJURY COSTS

The true cost to the nation, to employers, and to individuals of work-related deaths and injuries is much greater than the cost of workers' compensation insurance alone. The figures presented below show the National Safety Council's estimates of the total costs of occupational deaths and injuries. Cost estimating procedures were revised for the 1993 edition of *Accident Facts®*. In general, cost estimates are not comparable from year to year. As additional or more precise data become available, they are used from that year forward. Previously estimated figures are not revised.

Total Cost in 1998 . . . . **$122.6 billion**
Includes wage and productivity losses of $63.9 billion, medical costs of $19.9 billion, and administrative expenses of $23.5 billion. Includes employer costs of $11.0 billion such as the money value of time lost by workers other than those with disabling injuries, who

are directly or indirectly involved in injuries, and the cost of time required to investigate injuries, write up injury reports, etc. Also includes damage to motor vehicles in work injuries of $2.0 billion and fire losses of $2.3 billion.

Cost per Worker **$910**
This figure indicates the value of goods or services each worker must produce to offset the cost of work injuries. It is *not* the average cost of a work injury.

Cost per Death **$940,000**

Cost per Disabling Injury **$28,000**
These figures include estimates of wage losses, medical expenses, administrative expenses, and employer costs, and exclude property damage costs except to motor vehicles.

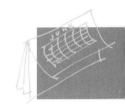

TIME LOST BECAUSE OF WORK INJURIES

DAYS LOST
TOTAL TIME LOST IN 1999 . . . . **125,000,000**
Due to injuries in 1999 . . . . **80,000,000**
Includes primarily the actual time lost during the year from disabling injuries, except that it does not include time lost on the day of the injury or time required for further medical treatment or check-up following the injured person's return to work.

Fatalities are included at an average loss of 150 days per case, and permanent impairments are included at actual days lost plus an allowance for lost efficiency resulting from the impairment.

Not included is time lost by persons with nondisabling injuries or other persons directly or indirectly involved in the incidents.

DAYS LOST
Due to injuries in prior years **45,000,000**
This is an indicator of the productive time lost in 1999 due to permanently disabling injuries that occurred in prior years.

DAYS LOST
**TIME LOSS IN FUTURE YEARS FROM
1999 INJURIES** **60,000,000**
Includes time lost in future years due to on-the-job deaths and permanently disabling injuries that occurred in 1999.

FATAL OCCUPATIONAL INJURIES

Highway traffic incidents were the leading cause of all work-related fatal injuries in 1998 and the leading cause within the Transportation and Public Utilities, Services, and Government industries. Assaults and violent acts by persons (homicide) was the second leading cause overall and the leading cause in the Wholesale and Retail Trade industry. Falls to a lower level was the third leading cause for all industries and the leading cause in the Construction industry.

FATAL OCCUPATIONAL INJURIES BY TYPE OF EVENT AND INDUSTRY, UNITED STATES, 1998

Type of Event or Exposure	All Industries	Agriculture[a]	Mining[a]	Construction	Manufac-turing	Trans. & Pub. Util.	Wholesale & Retail Trade	Services[a]	Government
Total	**6,026**	**831**	**146**	**1,171**	**694**	**908**	**797**	**849**	**598**
Highway accident	1,431	107	17	147	110	443	216	203	181
Assaults and violent acts by persons	709	19	—	20	37	69	307	159	93
Fall to lower level	623	51	15	372	46	25	33	59	18
Struck by object	517	97	18	93	151	48	36	53	19
Pedestrian, nonpassenger struck by vehicle, mobile equipment	413	48	—	103	31	81	32	52	65
Nonhighway accident, except rail, air, water	384	212	15	42	32	24	13	29	16
Contact with electric current	334	40	5	171	42	27	11	28	10
Caught in or compressed by equipment or object	266	66	10	45	77	17	27	15	8
Aircraft accident	223	12	—	—	12	57	12	54	70
Self-inflicted injury	223	13	—	18	29	12	47	60	39
Caught in or crushed in collapsing materials	140	18	19	68	12	9	5	—	—
Fire—unintended or uncontrolled	116	7	12	10	28	5	16	15	22
Water vehicle accident	112	68	5	—	5	23	—	6	—
Exposure to caustic, noxious, or allergenic substances	104	12	—	15	18	11	9	29	—
Explosion	89	—	10	17	24	13	5	12	5
Oxygen deficiency, n.e.c.	87	20	—	14	—	11	—	17	17
Railway accident	60	—	—	6	11	17	6	8	8
All other events or exposures	195	37	—	28	25	16	21	46	17

Source: National Safety Council tabulation of Bureau of Labor Statistics, Census of Fatal Occupational Injuries data. "All Industries" includes 32 cases for which industry or ownership was unclassifiable.
[a]Agriculture includes forestry and fishing; mining includes quarrying and oil and gas extraction; services includes finance, insurance and real estate.
Dash indicates less than five cases.
n.e.c. = not elsewhere classified.

FATAL OCCUPATIONAL INJURIES, 1998

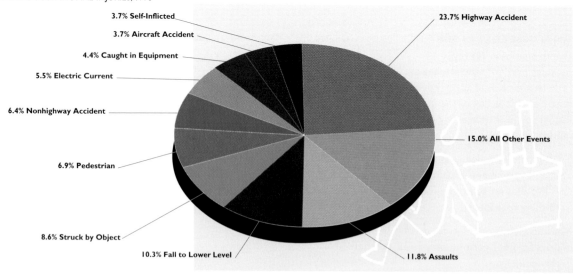

- 3.7% Self-Inflicted
- 3.7% Aircraft Accident
- 4.4% Caught in Equipment
- 5.5% Electric Current
- 6.4% Nonhighway Accident
- 6.9% Pedestrian
- 8.6% Struck by Object
- 10.3% Fall to Lower Level
- 11.8% Assaults
- 23.7% Highway Accident
- 15.0% All Other Events

NONFATAL OCCUPATIONAL INJURIES INVOLVING DAYS AWAY FROM WORK

More than half of the 1,730,500 nonfatal occupational injuries and illnesses in private industry involving days away from work result from contacts with objects or equipment or from overexertions, according to data from the Bureau of Labor Statistics 1998 Survey of Occupational Injuries and Illnesses. The injury and

illness total from the annual survey is lower than the Council's estimate in part because it excludes the self-employed, private household workers, and government employees. The table below shows the percent distributions by type of event or exposure for major industry divisions.

NONFATAL OCCUPATIONAL INJURIES AND ILLNESSES INVOLVING DAYS AWAY FROM
WORK BY EVENT OR EXPOSURE AND INDUSTRY DIVISION, UNITED STATES, 1998

Event or Exposure	Private Industry[a]	Agriculture[a,b]	Mining[b]	Construction	Manufacturing	Trans. and Pub. Util.	Trade[b]	Services[b]
Total	**100.0%**	**100.0%**	**100.0%**	**100.0%**	**100.0%**	**100.0%**	**100.0%**	**100.0%**
Contact with objects, equipment	27.6	35.8	41.8	35.3	34.5	22.5	27.9	18.4
Struck by object	*13.3*	*14.5*	*21.8*	*19.3*	*14.6*	*10.9*	*14.9*	*8.9*
Struck against object	*7.3*	*11.0*	*9.9*	*8.6*	*8.1*	*5.9*	*7.5*	*5.5*
Caught in object, equipment	*4.5*	*4.4*	*9.0*	*3.8*	*8.5*	*2.9*	*3.6*	*2.3*
Overexertion	27.6	16.2	26.0	20.3	25.6	30.7	27.9	32.0
Overexertion in lifting	*16.2*	*10.5*	*8.5*	*11.7*	*13.5*	*17.8*	*18.8*	*18.2*
Fall on same level	10.7	8.6	8.8	6.9	7.4	8.5	13.5	13.9
Fall to lower level	5.5	7.5	8.7	11.8	3.4	7.3	4.6	4.8
Exposure to harmful substances	4.7	5.3	3.8	4.0	5.3	3.0	4.9	4.7
Transportation accidents	4.0	4.2	1.9	3.9	2.0	8.8	3.9	4.1
Repetitive motion	3.8	0.9	0.6	1.4	7.6	2.0	2.3	3.8
Slips, trips	3.2	3.5	0.8	2.9	2.8	3.4	3.5	3.3
Assaults and violent act by person	1.0	0.1	(c)	0.1	0.1	0.4	0.6	3.1
Fires, explosions	0.2	0.2	0.5	0.6	0.2	0.1	0.2	0.2
All other	11.7	17.7	7.1	12.8	11.1	13.3	10.7	11.7

Source: Bureau of Labor Statistics. (2000, April 20). Lost-worktime injuries and illnesses: Characteristics and resulting time away from work, 1998. (News Release USDL-00-115). Washington, DC: U.S. Department of Labor.
[a] *Excludes farms with less than 11 employees.*
[b] *Agriculture includes forestry and fishing; mining includes quarrying and oil and gas extraction; trade includes wholesale and retail; services includes finance, insurance, and real estate.*
[c] *No data or data do not meet publication guidelines.*

NONFATAL OCCUPATIONAL INJURIES AND ILLNESSES INVOLVING DAYS AWAY FROM WORK, 1998

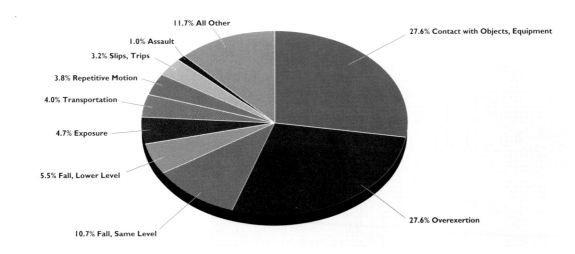

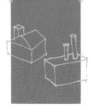

WORKER DEATHS AND INJURIES
ON AND OFF THE JOB

Nearly 9 out of 10 deaths and about three fifths of the disabling injuries suffered by workers in 1999 occurred off the job. The ratios of off-the-job deaths and injuries to on-the-job were 8.0 to 1 and 1.7 to 1, respectively. Production time lost due to off-the-job injuries totaled about 160,000,000 days in 1999, compared with 80,000,000 days lost by workers injured on the job. Production time lost in future years due to off-the-job injuries in 1999 will total an estimated 380,000,000 days, more than six times the 60,000,000 days lost in

future years from 1999's on-the-job injuries. Off-the-job injuries to workers cost the nation at least $159.0 billion in 1999.

The basis of the rates shown in the table below was changed from 1,000,000 hours to 200,000 hours beginning with the 1998 edition. This change was made so that the rates would be on the same basis as the occupational injury and illness incidence rates shown elsewhere in *Injury Facts*™.

ON- AND OFF-THE-JOB INJURIES, UNITED STATES, 1999

| Place | Deaths | | Disabling Injuries | |
	Number	Rate[a]	Number	Rate[a]
On- and off-the-job	**45,700**	**0.012**	**10,400,000**	**2.6**
On-the-job	5,100	0.004	3,800,000	2.6
Off-the-job	40,600	0.016	6,600,000	2.6
Motor-vehicle	21,000	0.078	1,100,000	4.1
Public nonmotor-vehicle	9,100	0.022	3,000,000	7.2
Home	10,500	0.006	2,500,000	1.3

Source: National Safety Council estimates. Procedures for allocating time spent on and off the job were revised for the 1990 edition. Rate basis changed to 200,000 hours for the 1998 edition. Death and injury rates are not comparable to rate estimates prior to the 1998 edition.
[a] *Per 200,000 hours exposure by place.*

WORKERS' ON- AND OFF-THE-JOB INJURIES, 1999

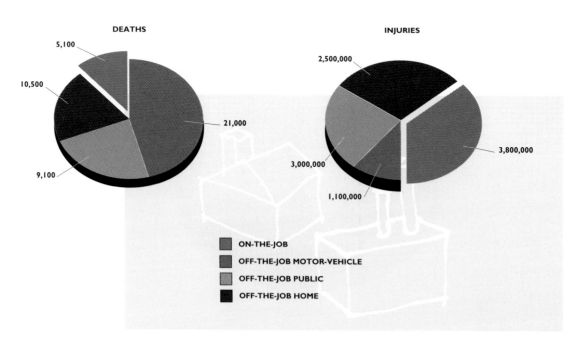

WORKERS' COMPENSATION CASES

According to the National Academy of Social Insurance, an estimated $40.6 billion, including benefits under deductible provisions, was paid out under workers' compensation in 1997 (the latest year for which data were available), a decrease of about 4.4% from 1996. Of this total, $25.1 billion was for income benefits and $15.5 billion was for medical and hospitalization costs. Private carriers paid about $20.6 billion of the total workers' compensation benefits in 1997. In 1998,

approximately 120.9 million workers were covered by workers' compensation—an increase of 2.7% over the 117.7 million in 1997.

The table below shows the trend in the number of compensated or reported cases in each reporting state. Due to the differences in population, industries, and coverage of compensation laws, comparison among states should not be made.

WORKERS' COMPENSATION CASES, UNITED STATES, 1997—1999

State	Deaths[a]			Cases[a]			1998 Compensation Paid ($000)
	1999	1998	1997	1999	1998	1997	
Alabama	101	98	49	27,170	27,820	22,336	615,316
Alaska[b]	31	33	38	27,037	28,565	29,165	110,866
Arizona	75	89	69	145,709	151,581	150,462	417,673
Arkansas	88	96	96	13,351	13,979	14,140	161,146
Colorado[c]	—	104	108	—	33,441	34,036	656,894
Connecticut	60	43	54	75,175	61,659	70,884	711,130
Delaware[d]	14	11	17	20,550	18,410	20,617	118,511
District of Columbia	9	5	16	12,072	11,957	12,261	70,608
Georgia[b]	—	97	132	—	33,336	33,762	807,562
Hawaii	—	17	30	—	30,727	33,255	194,680
Idaho	36	51	46	44,763	46,278	45,224	165,764
Iowa	54	69	70	30,027	34,219	37,077	292,002
Kansas	68	—	—	96,234	—	—	318,352
Kentucky	86	74	77	49,214	49,460	44,717	510,938
Louisiana	—	107	112	—	18,975	23,843	364,656
Maine	47	37	41	16,599	12,690	12,642	288,146
Maryland	66	49	37	28,704	29,556	30,228	510,527
Massachusetts	508	718	534	41,404	41,238	41,335	641,409
Michigan[d]	134	155	128	64,952	64,903	71,873	1,366,963
Minnesota[b,e]	—	64	54	—	33,100	33,700	732,300
Mississippi[f]	—	100	87	—	16,335	16,814	234,700
Missouri	145	139	160	173,079	170,727	187,424	527,587
Montana	24	24	17	31,268	31,876	33,774	155,019
Nebraska	53	53	45	67,339	68,206	69,036	164,382
New Hampshire[g]	29	45	28	57,668	57,785	58,201	163,885
New Mexico[h]	—	37	32	—	46,651	48,700	116,799
North Carolina[d]	161	143	130	68,469	74,939	74,303	765,817
North Dakota	—	16	19	—	—	20,901	81,403
Ohio	194	123	115	288,242	296,158	287,701	2,335,022
Oregon[i]	46	52	43	25,700[i]	27,049	27,922	492,854
Pennsylvania	121	96	137	82,676	85,783	88,451	2,447,909
Rhode Island	7	7	5	33,254	34,495	32,159	104,199
South Carolina	116	113	106	30,159	32,143	37,272	483,606
South Dakota[b]	25	19	18	29,646	28,656	29,474	72,722
Vermont	18	16	12	25,817	25,016	25,012	87,925
Virginia	143	138	155	49,003	50,220	51,661	591,868
Washington	64	71	65	257,587	254,160	259,678	1,481,587
West Virginia	—	391	470	—	61,090	62,820	468,555
Wisconsin[b,e]	67[i]	63	90	58,620[i]	48,047	52,839	621,973
Wyoming	—	22	24	—	17,293	17,837	74,469

Source: Deaths and Cases—State workers' compensation authorities for calendar or fiscal year. Compensation Paid—National Academy of Social Insurance. (2000). Workers' compensation: benefits, coverage, and costs, 1997–1998 new estimates. Washington, DC: Author. States not listed did not respond to the survey. Dash (—) indicates data not available.

Definitions:
Reported case—a reported case may or may not be work-related and may not receive compensation.
Compensated case—a case determined to be work-related and for which compensation was paid.

[a] *Reported cases involving medical and indemnity benefits, unless otherwise noted.*
[b] *Closed or compensated cases.*
[c] *Lost-time claims.*
[d] *Reported cases only, not specified whether they are medical benefits only or medical and indemnity benefits.*
[e] *Indemnity benefits only.*

[f] *Reported and compensated cases.*
[g] *Medical benefit cases only.*
[h] *Compensated and compensable claims and indemnity cases only.*
[i] *Cases included are both those reported and closed or compensated.*
[j] *Preliminary.*

WORKERS' COMPENSATION
CLAIMS COSTS, 1997–1998

The data in the graphs below and on page 53 are from the National Council on Compensation Insurance (NCCI) Detailed Claim Information (DCI) file, a stratified random sample of lost-time claims in 41 states. Total incurred costs consist of medical and indemnity payments plus case reserves on open claims, and are calculated as of the second report (18 months after the initial report of injury). Injuries that result in medical payments only, without lost time, are not included. For open claims, costs include all payments as of the second report plus case reserves for future payments.

Cause of Injury. The most costly lost-time workers' compensation claims, according to the NCCI data, are for those resulting from motor-vehicle crashes. These injuries averaged in excess of $21,600 per workers' compensation claim filed in 1997 and 1998. The other types with above average costs were those involving a burn ($13,361), fall or slip ($11,670), miscellaneous causes ($10,500), and cumulative trauma ($10,310). The average cost for all claims combined was $10,130.

Nature of Injury. The most costly lost-time workers' compensation claims by the nature of the injury are for those resulting from amputation. These injuries averaged $16,468 per workers' compensation claim filed in 1997 and 1998. The next highest costs were for injuries resulting in fracture ($13,554), "other trauma" ($12,692), carpal tunnel syndrome ($11,944), and burns ($10,575). The average cost for all natures of injury combined was $10,130.

Part of Body. When viewed by part of body, the most costly lost-time workers' compensation claims are for those involving the head or central nervous system. These injuries averaged $25,650 per workers' compensation claim filed in 1997 and 1998. The next highest costs were for injuries involving multiple body parts ($17,398), neck ($15,448), leg ($13,688), knee ($11,007), arm or shoulder ($10,855), and lower back ($10,450). The average cost for all parts of body combined was $10,130.

AVERAGE TOTAL INCURRED COSTS PER CLAIM BY CAUSE OF INJURY, 1997–1998

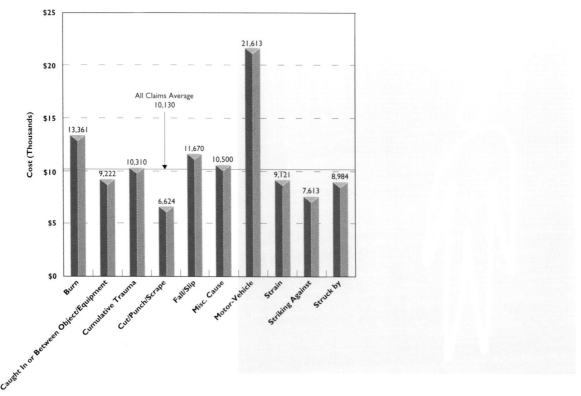

AVERAGE TOTAL INCURRED COSTS PER CLAIM BY NATURE OF INJURY, 1997–1998

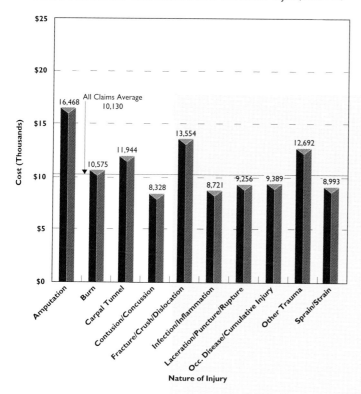

AVERAGE TOTAL INCURRED COSTS PER CLAIM BY PART OF BODY, 1997–1998

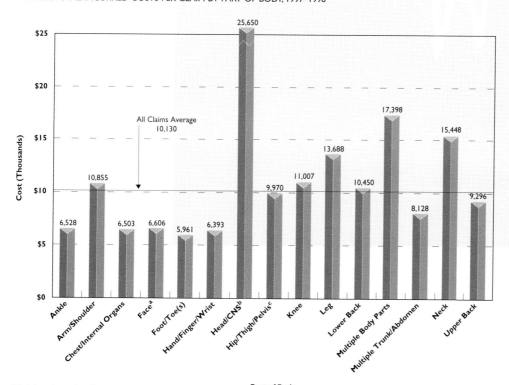

a Includes teeth, mouth, and eyes.
b Central nervous system.
c Includes sacrum and coccyx.

**Work-related homicides decreased
34% from 1994 to 1998.**

WORK-RELATED HOMICIDES

According to the BLS Census of Fatal Occupational Injuries (CFOI), homicide accounted for 709 (12%) of the 6,026 fatal occupational injuries in 1998, an 18% decrease from 860 in 1997. In 1998, robbers were the perpetrators of most (67%) work-related homicides, followed by coworkers (15%), customers (8%), acquaintances of the victim (7%), and relatives of the victim (4%).

In 1998, the rate of work-related homicides for all occupations was 0.5 homicides per 100,000 workers. The occupation with the highest rate of work-related homicide was taxi drivers and chauffeurs (17.9), followed by public police and detectives (4.4), private guards and police (4.1), supervisors and sales proprietors (2.5), managerial executives (0.5), cashiers (1.5), and truck drivers (0.7).

Women accounted for 7% of all work-related fatalities from 1992 to 1998. In 1998, women were victim to about 23% of all work-related homicides, the leading cause of fatal injuries for women in the workplace.

In 1998, there were about as many work-related homicides from 8 a.m. to noon as there were from 8 p.m. to midnight. The 4-hour periods with the fewest homicides were from midnight to 4 a.m. and from 4 a.m. to 8 a.m. Except for the preceding time frames, the frequency of work-related homicides stays fairly consistent throughout the day. Work-related homicides were more frequent during late hours for nighttime industries like taxis, bars, and restaurants.

Source: Synatur, E. F., & Toscano, G. A. (2000). Work-related Homicides: The Facts. Compensation and Working Conditions, Vol. 4 (1), 3-8.

WORK-RELATED HOMICIDES BY OCCUPATION, 1998

Occupation[a]	Annual Average Employment (000)[b]	Homicide	
		Number	Rate
All Occupations	131,463	709	0.5
Taxi drivers and chauffeurs	273	49	17.9
Police and detectives, public	1,180	52	4.4
Guards and police, except public	946	39	4.1
Supervisors and proprietors, sales	4,719	117	2.5
Executive, administrative, managerial	19,054	102	0.5
Managers, Food and Lodging	1,453	36	2.5
Cashiers	3,025	45	1.5
Truck drivers	3,012	22	0.7

Source: U.S. Department of Labor, Bureau of Labor Statistics, Census of Fatal Occupational Injuries.
[a] Occupations with more than 20 homicides and employment exceeding 100,000 workers.
[b] Annual average employment estimates of employed civilians 16 years of age and older are based on the 1998 Current Population Survey.

WORK-RELATED HOMICIDES BY YEAR, UNITED STATES, 1992-1998

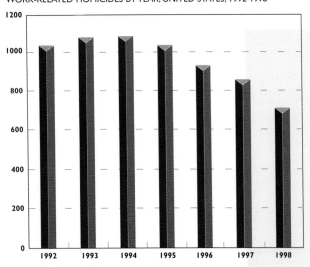

Fatal work injuries involving forklifts averaged 101 per year for the 5-year period 1992-1996, according to information from the Bureau of Labor Statistics' (BLS) Census of Fatal Occupational Injuries. Work fatalities involving forklifts in 1996 and 1997 totaled 115 and 110, respectively. About 69% of the fatalities were associated with forklifts as a primary source of the injury and 34% had forklifts listed as a secondary source of the injury[a].

In 1997, manufacturing had a higher tally of fatalities than any other industry with 33 of the 110 total deaths. Transportation and trade were next with 20 deaths

each. Workers aged 25 to 34 and 35 to 44 each accounted for 24% of the 1997 total.

By activity, 45% of the fatalities occurred while the worker was operating the vehicle. About 14% occurred during materials handling operations; 13% occurred while using or operating tools or machinery; an additional 13% occurred while constructing, repairing, or cleaning; and 11% occurred while doing physical activities.

[a] *The primary source of injury or illness identifies the object, substance, bodily motion, or exposure that directly produced or inflicted the injury or illness. The secondary source of injury or illness identifies the object, substance, or person that generated the primary source of injury or illness or that contributed to the event or exposure.*

CHARACTERISTICS OF FORKLIFT-RELATED FATALITIES, UNITED STATES, 1992-1997

Characteristic	Fatalities		
	1992–1996 Average[a]	1996	1997
Total	101	115	110
Industry			
Agriculture, Forestry, and Fishing	6	6	7
Mining	—	—	4
Construction	13	13	18
Manufacturing	36	42	33
Transportation and Public Utilities	12	11	20
Wholesale and Retail Trade	25	33	20
Services	6	7	5
Age			
19 & Under	4	3	3
20–24	12	11	12
25–34	22	25	26
35–44	25	32	26
45–54	18	24	23
55–64	14	14	13
65 & Over	5	6	7
Worker Activity			
Vehicular & Transportation Operations	43	53	50
Driving, Operating Industrial/Construction Vehicle	*33*	*41*	*34*
Operating Tools, Machinery	13	13	14
Constructing, Repairing, Cleaning	15	13	14
Materials Handling	14	18	15
Physical Activities	9	11	12
Other/Not Reported	5	5	3
Event or Exposure			
Contact with Objects, Equipment	33	34	34
Struck by	*23*	*25*	*19*
Caught in	*9*	*9*	*15*
Falls	11	13	18
Exposure to Harmful Substances or Environments	—	—	7
Transportation Incidents	54	64	51
Nonhighway Incident, Except Rail, Air, Water	*38*	*45*	*32*
Worker Struck by Vehicle, Mobile Equipment	*14*	*18*	*17*
Other/Not Reported	—	—	—

Source: U.S. Department of Labor, Bureau of Labor Statistics, Census of Fatal Occupational Injuries, 1992–97.
Note: Dashes indicate no data or less than 3 work fatalities. Totals for major categories may include subcategories not shown separately. Averages may not add to totals because of rounding.
[a] *Number of fatalities involving forklifts by year: 1992 = 86; 1993 = 89; 1994 = 120; 1995 = 95.*

TRENDS IN OCCUPATIONAL INCIDENCE RATES

All four occupational injury and illness incidence rates published by the Bureau of Labor Statistics for 1998 decreased from 1997. The incidence rate for total nonfatal cases was 6.7 per 100 full-time workers in 1998, down 6% from the 1997 rate of 7.1. The 1998 incidence rate for total lost workday cases was 3.1, down 6% from 3.3 in 1997. The incidence rate for lost workday cases with days away from work was 2.0 in 1998, down 5% from 2.1 in 1997. The incidence rate in 1998 for nonfatal cases without lost workdays was 3.5, a decrease of 8% from the 1997 rate of 3.8.

Beginning with 1992 data, the Bureau of Labor Statistics revised its annual survey to include only nonfatal cases and stopped publishing the incidence rate of lost workdays.

OCCUPATIONAL INJURY AND ILLNESS INCIDENCE RATES, BUREAU OF LABOR STATISTICS, UNITED STATES, 1973–1998

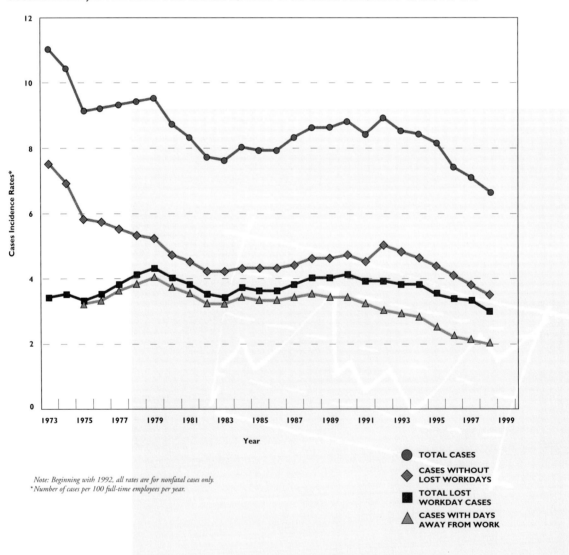

Note: Beginning with 1992, all rates are for nonfatal cases only.
*Number of cases per 100 full-time employees per year.

● TOTAL CASES

◆ CASES WITHOUT LOST WORKDAYS

■ TOTAL LOST WORKDAY CASES

▲ CASES WITH DAYS AWAY FROM WORK

OCCUPATIONAL INJURIES AND ILLNESSES

The tables below and on pages 58–60 present the results of the 1998 Survey of Occupational Injuries and Illnesses conducted by the Bureau of Labor Statistics (BLS), U.S. Department of Labor. The survey collects data on injuries and illnesses (from the OSHA 200 Log) and employee-hours worked from a nationwide sample of about 169,000 establishments representing the private sector of the economy. The survey excludes public employees, private households, the self-employed, and farms with fewer than 11 employees. The incidence rates give the number of cases per 100 full-time workers per year using 200,000 employee-hours as the equivalent. Definitions of the terms are given in the Glossary on page 159.

Beginning with 1992 data, the BLS revised its annual survey to include only nonfatal cases and stopped publishing incidence rates of lost workdays.

BLS ESTIMATES OF NONFATAL OCCUPATIONAL INJURY AND ILLNESS INCIDENCE RATES BY INDUSTRY DIVISION, 1997-1998

Industry Division	Incidence Rates[a]							
	Total Cases		Lost Workday Cases				Cases Without Lost Workdays	
			Total		With Days Away from Work			
	1998	1997	1998	1997	1998	1997	1998	1997
Private Sector[b]	**6.7**	**7.1**	**3.1**	**3.3**	**2.0**	**2.1**	**3.5**	**3.8**
Agriculture, forestry, and fishing[b]	7.9	8.4	3.9	4.1	3.0	3.0	4.0	4.2
Mining	4.9	5.9	2.9	3.7	2.2	2.9	2.0	2.1
Construction	8.8	9.5	4.0	4.4	3.3	3.6	4.8	5.0
Manufacturing	9.7	10.3	4.7	4.8	2.3	2.4	5.0	5.4
Transportation and public utilities	7.3	8.2	4.3	4.8	3.2	3.7	3.0	3.4
Wholesale and retail trade	6.5	6.7	2.8	3.0	1.8	2.0	3.6	3.7
Finance, insurance, and real estate	1.9	2.2	0.7	0.9	0.5	0.7	1.2	1.4
Services	5.2	5.6	2.4	2.5	1.5	1.7	2.9	3.1

Source: Bureau of Labor Statistics.

[a] Incidence Rate = $\dfrac{\text{Number of injuries \& illnesses} \times 200{,}000}{\text{Total hours worked by all employees during period covered}}$

where 200,000 is the base for 100 full-time workers (working 40 hours per week, 50 weeks per year). The "Total Cases" rate is based on the number of cases with check marks in columns 2, 6, 9, and 13 of the OSHA 200 Log. The "Total Lost Workday Cases" rate is based on columns 2 and 9. The "Lost Workday Cases With Days Away From Work" rate is based on columns 3 and 10. The "Cases Without Lost Workdays" rate is based on columns 6 and 13.

[b] Excludes farms with less than 11 employees.

[c] Industry Division and 2 and 3 digit SIC code totals on pages 58–60 include data for industries not shown separately.

[d] Standard Industrial Classification Manual, 1987 Edition, for industries shown on pages 58–60.

BLS ESTIMATES OF NONFATAL OCCUPATIONAL INJURY AND ILLNESS INCIDENCE RATES FOR SELECTED INDUSTRIES, 1998

Industry[c]	SIC Code[d]	Incidence Rates[a]			
		Total Cases	Lost Workday Cases		Cases Without Lost Workdays
			Total	With Days Away from Work	
PRIVATE SECTOR[b]	**—**	**6.7**	**3.1**	**2.0**	**3.5**
Agriculture, Forestry, and Fishing[b]	**—**	**7.9**	**3.9**	**3.0**	**4.0**
Agricultural production	01-02	8.4	4.1	2.8	4.3
Agricultural services	07	7.6	3.9	3.1	3.8
Forestry	08	7.3	2.6	2.3	4.7
Mining	**—**	**4.9**	**2.9**	**2.2**	**2.0**
Metal mining	10	5.2	2.9	1.8	2.3
Coal mining	12	8.2	6.0	5.6	2.2
Oil and gas extraction	13	4.1	2.0	1.4	2.1
Crude petroleum and natural gas	131	1.6	0.8	0.6	0.8
Oil and gas field services	138	5.7	2.8	1.9	2.9
Nonmetallic minerals, except fuels	14	4.6	3.0	2.2	1.6
Construction	**—**	**8.8**	**4.0**	**3.3**	**4.8**
General building contractors	15	8.4	3.9	3.1	4.6
Residential building construction	152	7.6	3.5	3.1	4.1
Nonresidential building construction	154	9.5	4.3	3.2	5.2
Heavy construction, except building	16	8.2	4.1	3.2	4.1
Highway and street construction	161	9.3	4.3	3.2	5.0
Heavy construction, except highway	162	7.8	4.0	3.3	3.8
Special trade contractors	17	9.1	4.1	3.3	5.0
Plumbing, heating, air-conditioning	171	10.1	3.9	3.1	6.2
Painting and paper hanging	172	6.1	3.4	2.9	2.7
Electrical work	173	8.1	3.3	2.5	4.8
Masonry, stonework and plastering	174	10.0	4.8	4.2	5.2
Carpentry and floor work	175	10.9	4.9	4.3	6.0
Roofing, siding, and sheet metal work	176	9.1	5.1	4.4	3.9
Miscellaneous special trade contractors	179	8.2	3.8	3.1	4.4
Manufacturing	**—**	**9.7**	**4.7**	**2.3**	**5.0**
Durable goods	—	*10.7*	*5.0*	*2.5*	*5.7*
Lumber and wood products	24	13.2	6.8	3.8	6.4
Logging	241	8.4	5.5	5.2	2.9
Sawmills and planing mills	242	13.8	6.9	4.3	6.9
Millwork, plywood and structural members	243	12.6	6.1	3.2	6.5
Wood containers	244	14.7	8.4	5.2	6.3
Wood buildings and mobile homes	245	19.8	10.0	3.8	9.8
Furniture and fixtures	25	11.4	5.7	2.7	5.7
Household furniture	251	9.7	5.1	2.4	4.7
Office furniture	252	11.5	5.2	1.9	6.3
Public building and related furniture	253	15.6	8.3	3.1	7.4
Stone, clay, and glass products	32	11.8	6.0	3.3	5.8
Flat glass	321	17.5	5.9	3.3	11.6
Glass and glassware, pressed or blown	322	9.8	5.1	2.2	4.7
Products of purchased glass	323	12.4	5.5	2.1	6.9
Structural clay products	325	10.9	6.7	2.5	4.1
Concrete, gypsum, and plaster products	327	13.4	7.1	4.4	6.2
Miscellaneous nonmetallic mineral products	329	8.4	3.6	2.2	4.7
Primary metal industries	33	14.0	7.0	3.5	7.0
Blast furnace and basic steel products	331	11.4	5.4	2.8	5.9
Iron and steel foundries	332	22.1	10.6	5.5	11.5
Primary nonferrous metals	333	13.3	6.9	3.4	6.4
Nonferrous rolling and drawing	335	10.0	5.2	2.3	4.8
Nonferrous foundries (castings)	336	17.6	9.7	5.2	8.0
Fabricated metal products	34	13.9	6.5	3.4	7.4
Metal cans and shipping containers	341	11.1	4.4	2.0	6.7
Cutlery, hand tools, and hardware	342	13.8	6.8	2.7	7.1
Plumbing and heating, except electric	343	10.7	4.7	1.7	6.0
Fabricated structural metal products	344	14.5	6.6	4.1	7.9
Screw machine products, bolts, etc.	345	12.5	5.8	3.1	6.7
Metal forgings and stampings	346	17.9	8.1	3.6	9.9
Metal services, n.e.c.	347	12.5	6.1	3.2	6.3
Ordnance and accessories, n.e.c.	348	5.7	3.2	1.8	2.5
Miscellaneous fabricated metal products	349	12.7	6.1	3.2	6.6
Industrial machinery and equipment	35	9.5	4.0	2.2	5.5
Engines and turbines	351	9.1	3.6	2.0	5.5
Farm and garden machinery	352	12.2	5.0	2.7	7.2
Construction and related machinery	353	14.1	6.1	3.7	8.0
Metalworking machinery	354	9.3	3.5	2.0	5.8
Special industry machinery	355	8.9	3.3	1.7	5.5
General industrial machinery	356	10.7	4.4	2.6	6.3
Computer and office equipment	357	3.2	1.5	0.5	1.6
Refrigeration and service machinery	358	13.0	5.6	2.3	7.4

See source and footnotes on page 57.
n.e.c. = not elsewhere classified.

Industry[c]	SIC Code[d]	Incidence Rates[a]			
			Lost Workday Cases		Cases Without Lost Workdays
		Total Cases	Total	With Days Away from Work	
Industrial machinery, n.e.c.	359	9.9	4.4	2.7	5.5
Electronic and other electric equipment	36	5.9	2.8	1.3	3.1
Electric distribution equipment	361	9.9	5.0	2.8	5.0
Electrical industrial apparatus	362	7.2	3.3	1.4	3.9
Household appliances	363	10.9	4.8	1.9	6.1
Electric lighting and wiring equipment	364	7.3	3.5	1.7	3.8
Household audio and video equipment	365	6.4	3.5	1.7	2.9
Communications equipment	366	3.3	1.7	0.8	1.6
Electronic components and accessories	367	4.6	2.2	1.1	2.4
Misc. electrical equipment and supplies	369	7.4	3.3	1.4	4.1
Transportation equipment	37	14.6	6.6	2.7	8.0
Motor vehicles and equipment	371	17.9	7.8	3.0	10.1
Aircraft and parts	372	8.7	4.2	1.8	4.5
Ship and boat building and repairing	373	20.5	10.2	4.7	10.3
Railroad equipment	374	11.6	5.1	2.9	6.5
Guided missiles, space vehicles, parts	376	3.3	1.5	0.7	1.8
Instruments and related products	38	4.0	1.9	0.8	2.1
Search and navigation equipment	381	1.9	0.9	0.5	1.0
Measuring and controlling devices	382	4.0	1.9	0.8	2.2
Medical instruments and supplies	384	4.7	2.3	0.9	2.4
Ophthalmic goods	385	6.8	3.8	1.6	3.0
Miscellaneous manufacturing industries	39	8.1	3.9	2.2	4.2
Musical instruments	393	10.0	5.3	3.2	4.8
Toys and sporting goods	394	9.9	4.6	2.4	5.3
Pens, pencils, office, and art supplies	395	6.7	3.8	2.0	2.9
Costume jewelry and notions	396	5.7	2.2	1.5	3.5
Nondurable goods	—	8.2	4.3	2.0	3.9
Food and kindred products	20	13.6	7.5	2.9	6.0
Meat products	201	20.1	11.4	2.3	8.7
Dairy products	202	11.3	6.3	4.2	4.9
Preserved fruits and vegetables	203	10.2	4.9	2.5	5.3
Grain mill products	204	8.6	4.3	2.9	4.3
Bakery products	205	10.3	6.6	2.7	3.7
Sugar and confectionery products	206	10.4	5.2	2.9	5.2
Fats and oils	207	12.1	5.2	3.1	6.9
Beverages	208	12.3	7.0	3.9	5.2
Miscellaneous foods and kindred products	209	11.5	6.2	3.7	5.3
Tobacco products	21	6.4	3.1	2.1	3.3
Textile mill products	22	6.7	3.4	1.3	3.3
Broadwoven fabric mills, cotton	221	5.2	2.6	0.4	2.6
Broadwoven fabric mills, manmade	222	9.2	4.7	2.0	4.5
Broadwoven fabric mills, wool	223	4.3	2.5	0.7	1.8
Knitting mills	225	6.3	3.6	1.2	2.7
Textile finishing, except wool	226	7.4	3.4	1.8	4.0
Carpets and rugs	227	5.9	2.8	1.1	3.1
Yarn and thread mills	228	5.6	2.5	0.7	3.1
Miscellaneous textile goods	229	9.3	4.4	2.6	4.8
Apparel and other textile products	23	6.2	2.6	1.2	3.6
Men's and boys' suits and coats	231	5.7	3.1	2.1	2.7
Men's and boys' furnishings	232	8.5	3.7	1.7	4.8
Women's and misses' outerwear	233	3.2	1.1	0.6	2.1
Women's and children's undergarments	234	5.3	2.3	0.9	3.0
Girls' and children's outerwear	236	5.2	1.9	1.1	3.3
Miscellaneous apparel and accessories	238	4.5	2.0	1.5	2.5
Miscellaneous fabricated textile products	239	7.8	3.4	1.4	4.4
Paper and allied products	26	7.1	3.7	2.0	3.3
Paper mills	262	6.5	2.9	1.6	3.5
Paperboard mills	263	4.2	2.1	1.2	2.2
Paperboard containers and boxes	265	8.2	4.5	2.5	3.8
Printing and publishing	27	5.4	2.8	1.7	2.6
Newspapers	271	5.4	2.7	2.0	2.7
Books	273	6.0	3.0	1.8	3.0
Commercial printing	275	6.3	3.4	1.9	3.0
Manifold business forms	276	7.0	3.7	2.2	3.2
Blankbooks and bookbinding	278	6.3	3.8	2.3	2.5
Chemicals and allied products	28	4.2	2.1	1.0	2.1
Industrial inorganic chemicals	281	3.7	1.8	0.9	1.9
Plastics materials and synthetics	282	3.1	1.6	0.7	1.5
Drugs	283	4.2	1.8	0.9	2.4
Soap, cleaners, and toilet goods	284	4.8	2.5	1.3	2.3
Paints and allied products	285	6.7	3.8	2.2	2.9
Industrial organic chemicals	286	2.7	1.3	0.6	1.3
Agricultural chemicals	287	5.3	2.8	1.5	2.5
Miscellaneous chemical products	289	6.1	3.3	1.8	2.8

See source and footnotes on page 57.
n.e.c. = not elsewhere classified.

BLS ESTIMATES OF NONFATAL OCCUPATIONAL INJURY AND ILLNESS INCIDENCE RATES FOR SELECTED INDUSTRIES, 1998, Cont.

Industry[c]	SIC Code[d]	Incidence Rates[a]			
		Total Cases	Lost Workday Cases		Cases Without Lost Workdays
			Total	With Days Away from Work	
Petroleum and coal products	29	3.9	1.8	1.1	2.2
Petroleum refining	291	1.9	1.0	0.6	0.9
Asphalt paving and roofing materials	295	10.3	4.0	2.7	6.3
Rubber and miscellaneous plastics products	30	11.2	5.8	2.7	5.4
Tires and inner tubes	301	10.5	6.2	2.5	4.3
Rubber and plastics footwear	302	5.9	3.0	1.0	2.9
Hose and belting and gaskets and packing	305	10.3	5.4	2.2	4.8
Fabricated rubber products, n.e.c.	306	11.5	6.3	3.4	5.2
Miscellaneous plastic products, n.e.c.	308	11.4	5.7	2.7	5.7
Leather and leather products	31	9.8	4.5	2.2	5.2
Leather tanning and finishing	311	12.7	7.7	2.5	5.0
Footwear, except rubber	314	11.3	4.4	2.5	6.9
Transportation and Public Utilities	—	**7.3**	**4.3**	**3.2**	**3.0**
Railroad transportation	40	3.4	2.5	2.1	0.9
Local and interurban passenger transit	41	8.8	4.4	3.5	4.4
Local and suburban transportation	411	10.8	5.7	4.5	5.1
School buses	415	7.3	3.0	2.3	4.3
Trucking and warehousing	42	8.4	4.6	3.8	3.7
Trucking & courier services, except air	421	8.4	4.7	3.9	3.7
Public warehousing and storage	422	8.6	4.6	2.7	4.0
Water transportation	44	7.5	3.9	3.4	3.6
Transportation by air	45	14.5	10.0	7.4	4.5
Air transportation, scheduled	451	15.9	11.2	8.4	4.7
Transportation services	47	3.4	1.8	1.1	1.6
Communications	48	3.0	1.6	1.2	1.4
Telephone communications	481	2.6	1.5	1.1	1.1
Cable and other pay television services	484	6.6	3.4	2.1	3.2
Electric, gas, and sanitary services	49	6.3	3.3	1.8	3.0
Electric services	491	5.1	2.4	1.2	2.7
Gas production and distribution	492	4.9	2.9	1.7	2.0
Combination utility services	493	4.9	2.4	1.2	2.4
Sanitary services	495	11.0	6.0	3.5	5.1
Wholesale and Retail Trade	—	**6.5**	**2.8**	**1.8**	**3.6**
Wholesale trade	—	*6.5*	*3.3*	*2.1*	*3.2*
Wholesale trade—durable goods	50	5.9	2.8	1.7	3.1
Lumber and construction materials	503	9.3	4.4	2.8	4.8
Electrical goods	506	3.3	1.6	1.0	1.7
Machinery, equipment, and supplies	508	5.8	2.5	1.6	3.3
Wholesale trade—nondurable goods	51	7.4	4.1	2.6	3.3
Groceries and related products	514	10.8	6.4	3.9	4.4
Petroleum and petroleum products	517	4.7	2.5	1.8	2.2
Retail trade	—	*6.5*	*2.7*	*1.8*	*3.8*
Building materials and garden supplies	52	8.9	4.4	2.7	4.6
General merchandise stores	53	9.0	4.7	2.6	4.4
Food stores	54	8.4	3.6	2.4	4.8
Automotive dealers and service stations	55	5.8	2.2	1.7	3.6
Apparel and accessory stores	56	3.2	1.3	0.8	1.9
Home furniture, furnishings, and equipment	57	4.7	2.2	1.4	2.5
Eating and drinking places	58	6.3	2.1	1.5	4.3
Miscellaneous retail	59	3.9	1.7	1.1	2.2
Finance, Insurance, and Real Estate	—	**1.9**	**0.7**	**0.5**	**1.2**
Depository institutions	60	1.5	0.4	0.3	1.1
Insurance agents, brokers, and service	64	1.1	0.4	0.4	0.6
Real estate	65	4.0	1.8	1.4	2.2
Services	—	**5.2**	**2.4**	**1.5**	**2.9**
Hotels and other lodging places	70	7.3	3.6	2.0	3.7
Personal services	72	3.1	1.6	1.1	1.5
Business services	73	3.6	1.6	1.1	1.9
Services to buildings	734	6.5	3.1	2.2	3.4
Auto repair, services, and parking	75	5.2	2.2	1.7	3.0
Miscellaneous repair services	76	6.4	3.3	2.5	3.2
Amusement and recreation services	79	8.2	3.5	1.8	4.7
Health services	80	7.7	3.6	2.2	4.2
Nursing and personal care facilities	805	14.2	8.1	4.5	6.1
Hospitals	806	9.2	3.8	2.6	5.4
Legal services	81	0.8	0.4	0.3	0.4
Educational services	82	3.1	1.2	0.9	1.9
Social services	83	6.4	2.9	2.0	3.5
Residential care	836	9.8	4.6	3.0	5.2
Engineering and management services	87	2.1	0.8	0.5	1.3

See source and footnotes on page 57.
n.e.c. = not elsewhere classified.

BLS ESTIMATES OF NONFATAL OCCUPATIONAL INJURY AND ILLNESS INCIDENCE RATES FOR SELECTED INDUSTRIES, 1998

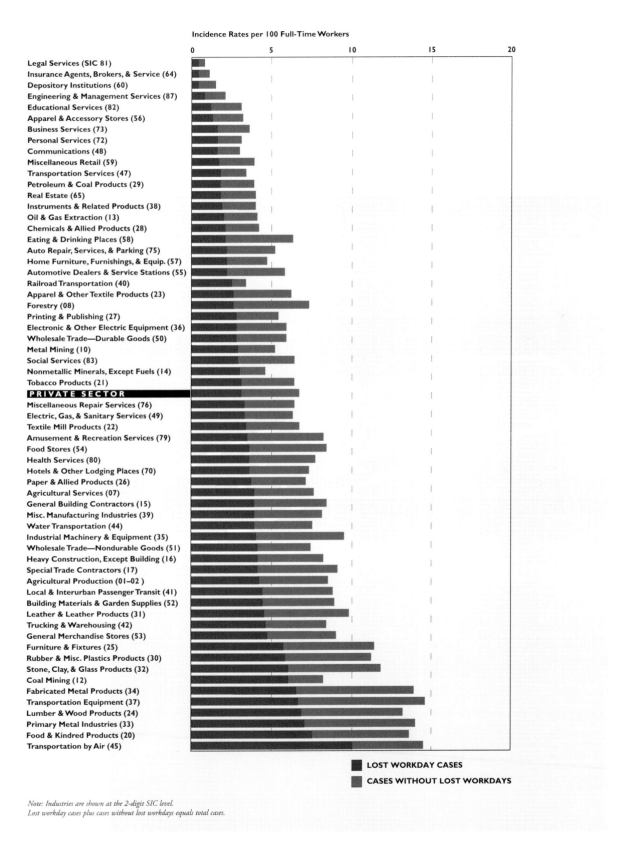

Incidence Rates per 100 Full-Time Workers

Legal Services (SIC 81)
Insurance Agents, Brokers, & Service (64)
Depository Institutions (60)
Engineering & Management Services (87)
Educational Services (82)
Apparel & Accessory Stores (56)
Business Services (73)
Personal Services (72)
Communications (48)
Miscellaneous Retail (59)
Transportation Services (47)
Petroleum & Coal Products (29)
Real Estate (65)
Instruments & Related Products (38)
Oil & Gas Extraction (13)
Chemicals & Allied Products (28)
Eating & Drinking Places (58)
Auto Repair, Services, & Parking (75)
Home Furniture, Furnishings, & Equip. (57)
Automotive Dealers & Service Stations (55)
Railroad Transportation (40)
Apparel & Other Textile Products (23)
Forestry (08)
Printing & Publishing (27)
Electronic & Other Electric Equipment (36)
Wholesale Trade—Durable Goods (50)
Metal Mining (10)
Social Services (83)
Nonmetallic Minerals, Except Fuels (14)
Tobacco Products (21)
PRIVATE SECTOR
Miscellaneous Repair Services (76)
Electric, Gas, & Sanitary Services (49)
Textile Mill Products (22)
Amusement & Recreation Services (79)
Food Stores (54)
Health Services (80)
Hotels & Other Lodging Places (70)
Paper & Allied Products (26)
Agricultural Services (07)
General Building Contractors (15)
Misc. Manufacturing Industries (39)
Water Transportation (44)
Industrial Machinery & Equipment (35)
Wholesale Trade—Nondurable Goods (51)
Heavy Construction, Except Building (16)
Special Trade Contractors (17)
Agricultural Production (01–02)
Local & Interurban Passenger Transit (41)
Building Materials & Garden Supplies (52)
Leather & Leather Products (31)
Trucking & Warehousing (42)
General Merchandise Stores (53)
Furniture & Fixtures (25)
Rubber & Misc. Plastics Products (30)
Stone, Clay, & Glass Products (32)
Coal Mining (12)
Fabricated Metal Products (34)
Transportation Equipment (37)
Lumber & Wood Products (24)
Primary Metal Industries (33)
Food & Kindred Products (20)
Transportation by Air (45)

■ LOST WORKDAY CASES
■ CASES WITHOUT LOST WORKDAYS

Note: Industries are shown at the 2-digit SIC level.
Lost workday cases plus cases without lost workdays equals total cases.

OCCUPATIONAL INJURY AND ILLNESS INCIDENCE RATES BY INDUSTRY, 1999, REPORTERS TO THE NATIONAL SAFETY COUNCIL

Industry	SIC Code[b]	Incidence Rates per 100 Full-Time Employees[a]					
		Total Cases	Lost Workday Cases	Cases Involving Days Away from Work & Deaths	Nonfatal Cases Without Lost Workdays	Lost Workdays[c]	Days Away from Work
All Industries[d]		**7.99**	**3.37**	**1.11**	**4.62**	**84**	**25**
Agriculture, forestry, and fishing		**3.75**	**1.20**	**0.85**	**2.55**	**27**	**22**
Mining		**4.01**	**1.43**	**0.46**	**2.58**	**40**	**18**
Metal mining	10	4.90	2.70	1.02	2.19	96	58
Coal mining	12	3.13	0.73	0.31	2.39	30	12
Oil and gas extraction	13	1.13	0.43	0.09	0.69	10	3
Crude petroleum and natural gas	131	0.83	0.24	0.00	0.60	5	0
Nonmetallic minerals, except fuels	14	4.88	1.75	0.49	3.14	38	15
Crushed and broken stone	142	3.33	1.37	0.51	1.96	22	11
Sand and gravel	144	9.36	3.18	0.71	6.18	67	18
Construction		**3.00**	**1.24**	**0.51**	**1.76**	**32**	**14**
General building contractors	15	6.87	3.49	0.82	3.37	67	21
Nonresidential building construction	154	6.99	3.36	0.83	3.62	71	23
Heavy construction, except building	16	2.55	0.98	0.50	1.57	28	14
Highway and street construction	161	7.82	2.70	2.12	5.11	68	29
Heavy construction, except highway	162	1.87	0.76	0.29	1.11	23	12
Special trade contractors	17	2.78	1.10	0.41	1.68	31	13
Misc. special trade contractors	179	2.50	1.24	0.32	1.26	35	13
Manufacturing		**10.06**	**4.07**	**1.19**	**5.99**	**102**	**27**
Durable goods		*14.69*	*5.70*	*1.68*	*8.99*	*146*	*38*
Lumber and wood products	24	4.62	2.48	0.64	2.14	66	19
Sawmills and planing mills	242	5.64	3.14	0.69	2.50	86	18
Millwork, plywood and structural members	243	3.77	2.32	1.16	1.45	79	36
Miscellaneous wood products	249	4.16	1.96	0.36	2.20	44	16
Furniture and fixtures	25	8.73	4.12	1.55	4.60	86	26
Stone, clay, and glass products	32	10.62	3.98	1.53	6.64	121	44
Cement, hydraulic	324	7.45	2.86	1.55	4.59	93	69
Concrete, gypsum, and plaster products	327	5.80	1.64	0.88	4.15	47	35
Miscellaneous nonmetallic general products	329	5.47	3.18	1.61	2.28	102	48
Primary metal industries	33	10.93	4.32	1.27	6.61	88	25
Blast furnace and basic steel products	331	5.12	1.80	0.97	3.32	54	26
Iron and steel foundries	332	16.32	5.97	1.59	10.35	107	31
Primary nonferrous metals	333	13.63	7.88	2.92	5.74	167	40
Nonferrous rolling and drawing	335	5.16	1.94	0.46	3.22	39	8
Fabricated metal products	34	24.71	9.40	2.35	15.31	211	47
Fabricated structural metal products	344	8.92	3.96	2.16	4.97	84	43
Metal forgings and stampings	346	44.11	16.08	3.77	28.03	366	76
Metal services, n.e.c.	347	3.80	1.72	0.30	2.08	34	14
Ordnance and accessories, n.e.c.	348	5.16	3.37	0.98	1.79	70	19
Miscellaneous fabricated metal products	349	4.78	2.14	0.47	2.63	42	7
Industrial machinery and equipment	35	7.65	2.79	1.09	4.86	74	20
Construction and related machinery	353	10.00	3.29	1.98	6.71	113	54
Metalworking machinery	354	7.72	3.69	0.70	4.03	86	19
Special industry machinery	355	11.29	6.15	1.47	5.14	88	15
General industrial machinery	356	10.10	3.20	1.34	6.90	78	24
Computer and office equipment	357	1.49	0.92	0.42	0.57	16	3
Refrigeration and service machinery	358	9.94	3.74	0.98	6.21	75	15
Industrial machinery, n.e.c.	359	23.17	8.15	3.67	15.02	284	44
Electronic and other electric equipment	36	2.33	1.26	0.43	1.07	28	8
Electrical industrial apparatus	362	4.64	2.66	0.97	1.98	54	12
Electric lighting and wiring equipment	364	10.20	5.87	0.55	4.33	112	9
Communications equipment	366	1.51	0.84	0.27	0.67	19	4
Electronic components and accessories	367	1.50	0.67	0.50	0.83	20	11
Miscellaneous electrical equipment & supplies	369	7.41	4.58	0.54	2.83	76	11
Transportation equipment	37	18.15	6.97	2.02	11.18	183	48

See source and footnotes on page 64.
n.e.c. = not elsewhere classified.

Industry	SIC Code[b]	Incidence Rates per 100 Full-Time Employees[a]					
		Total Cases	Lost Workday Cases	Cases Involving Days Away from Work & Deaths	Nonfatal Cases Without Lost Workdays	Lost Workdays[c]	Days Away from Work
Motor vehicles and equipment	371	19.80	7.61	2.17	12.19	200	52
Aircraft and parts	372	5.44	2.63	0.79	2.80	83	28
Ship and boat building and repairing	373	11.11	2.88	2.15	8.23	48	24
Guided missiles, space vehicles, parts	376	2.50	1.00	0.32	1.50	28	12
Instruments and related products	38	4.66	2.18	0.90	2.48	57	20
Measuring and controlling devices	382	6.18	1.60	1.01	4.58	73	26
Miscellaneous manufacturing industries	39	10.12	5.22	0.75	4.90	151	16
Miscellaneous manufactures	399	10.07	4.86	0.73	5.21	166	17
Nondurable goods		*3.94*	*1.91*	*0.54*	*2.04*	*45*	*13*
Food and kindred products	20	7.01	3.62	1.38	3.38	89	33
Meat products	201	7.59	3.23	1.40	4.36	67	11
Dairy products	202	5.27	3.17	1.30	2.10	64	19
Preserved fruits and vegetables	203	10.81	4.77	2.16	6.04	100	45
Grain mill products	204	5.41	1.99	0.88	3.43	37	13
Bakery products	205	7.41	5.03	1.29	2.38	124	22
Sugar and confectionery products	206	6.85	3.85	1.12	3.00	100	27
Beverages	208	10.74	4.81	2.41	5.93	175	104
Textile products	22	2.78	1.49	0.22	1.29	28	7
Broadwoven fabric mills, cotton	221	2.95	1.81	0.06	1.14	36	1
Broadwoven fabric mills, manmade	222	3.11	1.46	0.11	1.65	32	4
Knitting mills	225	5.17	3.12	0.49	2.05	48	2
Textile finishing, except wool	226	3.45	2.04	0.12	1.40	28	6
Carpets and rugs	227	5.69	3.51	0.42	2.18	57	10
Yarn and thread mills	228	2.46	1.14	0.17	1.32	30	12
Miscellaneous textile goods	229	4.33	2.80	1.15	1.53	70	29
Apparel and other textile products	23	19.39	7.90	0.73	11.50	199	17
Miscellaneous fabricated textile products	239	28.77	10.64	1.04	18.13	305	22
Paper and allied products	26	4.81	2.19	0.81	2.62	63	26
Paper mills	262	4.96	2.14	0.88	2.83	75	28
Paperboard mills	263	3.45	1.11	0.48	2.34	32	22
Paperboard containers and boxes	265	5.34	2.75	0.79	2.60	69	31
Miscellaneous converted paper products	267	5.38	2.81	1.08	2.57	60	22
Printing and publishing	27	5.17	2.33	1.32	2.84	39	16
Commercial printing	275	6.38	2.87	1.22	3.51	48	14
Chemicals and allied products	28	1.75	0.87	0.26	0.88	16	5
Industrial inorganic chemicals	281	1.52	0.65	0.24	0.86	20	7
Plastics materials and synthetics	282	2.03	1.06	0.30	0.97	27	7
Drugs	283	1.99	0.92	0.48	1.07	12	4
Soap, cleaners, and toilet goods	284	2.40	1.21	0.35	1.20	24	4
Paints and allied products	285	1.95	1.25	0.46	0.70	34	13
Industrial organic chemicals	286	2.14	1.09	0.37	1.04	38	14
Agricultural chemicals	287	2.13	0.87	0.39	1.26	16	5
Miscellaneous chemical products	289	2.27	1.32	0.34	0.95	34	9
Petroleum and coal products	29	2.28	1.23	0.50	1.06	48	13
Petroleum refining	291	2.27	1.23	0.50	1.04	49	13
Asphalt paving and roofing materials	295	2.78	1.39	0.17	1.39	16	5
Rubber and miscellaneous plastics products	30	10.41	5.19	1.37	5.22	125	30
Tires and inner tubes	301	9.17	6.78	2.25	2.39	167	58
Hose, belting, gaskets, and packing	305	4.56	1.19	0.76	3.36	50	17
Fabricated rubber products, n.e.c.	306	3.95	2.60	0.42	1.35	61	23
Miscellaneous plastics products, n.e.c.	308	12.17	5.60	1.36	6.57	133	26
Transportation and public utilities		**4.16**	**2.20**	**1.11**	**1.96**	**51**	**22**
Local and interurban passenger transit	41	5.29	3.01	3.01	2.29	109	96
Local and suburban transportation	411	4.00	2.61	2.61	1.38	107	92
Trucking and warehousing	42	10.58	6.43	4.06	4.15	121	67
Trucking and courier services, except air	421	10.10	5.87	4.79	4.23	115	78
Water transportation	44	2.08	1.29	0.86	0.80	51	42
Water transportation of freight, n.e.c.	444	2.59	1.63	0.27	0.95	38	22

See source and footnotes on page 64.
n.e.c. = not elsewhere classified.

OCCUPATIONAL INJURY AND ILLNESS INCIDENCE RATES BY INDUSTRY, 1999, REPORTERS TO THE NATIONAL SAFETY COUNCIL, Cont.

Industry	SIC Code[b]	Incidence Rates per 100 Full-Time Employees[a]					
		Total Cases	Lost Workday Cases	Cases Involving Days Away from Work & Deaths	Nonfatal Cases Without Lost Workdays	Lost Workdays[c]	Days Away from Work
Water transportation services	449	3.15	1.83	1.69	1.32	65	62
Pipelines, except natural gas	46	1.15	0.29	0.21	0.86	8	3
Communication	48	3.38	1.72	1.38	1.66	39	25
Telephone communication	481	3.32	1.70	1.36	1.62	37	25
Electric, gas, and sanitary services	49	3.95	2.05	0.86	1.90	49	18
Electric services	491	3.46	1.73	0.60	1.73	38	11
Gas production and distribution	492	5.22	3.14	1.51	2.08	72	32
Combination utility services	493	3.77	1.87	0.88	1.90	60	20
Water supply	494	8.08	3.51	2.94	4.57	70	56
Sanitary services	495	7.18	3.71	1.73	3.46	98	58
Wholesale and retail trade		**8.14**	**4.49**	**1.79**	**3.65**	**100**	**45**
Wholesale trade		*10.83*	*6.67*	*2.95*	*4.16*	*159*	*76*
Wholesale trade—durable goods	50	12.87	7.57	3.52	5.30	197	98
Machinery, equipment and supplies	508	2.90	1.58	1.15	1.31	53	35
Wholesale trade—nondurable products	51	6.26	4.67	1.67	1.59	74	26
Petroleum and petroleum products	517	2.91	1.31	1.17	1.60	51	41
Retail trade		*5.17*	*2.07*	*0.51*	*3.10*	*35*	*11*
Finance, Insurance & Real Estate		**0.48**	**0.00**	**0.00**	**0.48**	**0**	**0**
Services		**2.23**	**1.11**	**0.59**	**1.12**	**28**	**10**
Business services	73	1.62	0.90	0.42	0.72	21	9
Services to buildings	734	4.09	2.55	1.01	1.54	45	14
Health services	80	4.78	2.73	2.17	2.05	89	29
Engineering and management services	87	1.79	0.71	0.22	1.08	16	1
Engineering and architectural services	871	1.87	0.58	0.08	1.29	12	0
Research, development and testing services	873	0.82	0.38	0.15	0.44	10	1
Management and public relations	874	2.72	1.14	0.39	1.58	26	2
Public administration		**5.36**	**2.44**	**1.49**	**2.92**	**52**	**29**
Executive, legislative, and general	91	5.72	2.48	1.39	3.23	57	28
Public works departments	9191	9.05	3.34	1.81	5.71	47	17
Justice, public order and safety	92	6.78	1.33	1.18	5.46	14	10
Administration of economic programs	96	3.22	1.70	0.71	1.52	26	7
Offices	0001	0.95	0.35	0.15	0.61	7	2
Research and development or laboratory	0002	3.14	1.49	0.51	1.66	37	11
Warehouse or storage yard	0003	2.38	0.60	0.40	1.79	5	0

Source: Reports of National Safety Council members participating in the Occupational Safety/Health Award Program.

Note: These rates should not be interpreted as representative of the industries listed or of Council member companies. Rates for each industry may not be comparable to previous years due to changes in numbers of reporters and adoption of the 1987 SIC manual in 1990.

[a] Based on OSHA definitions. 200,000 employee-hours used as the equivalent of 100 full-time employees. See page 61 for the incidence rate formula.

[b] Standard Industrial Classification (SIC) Manual, 1987 Edition.

[c] Lost workdays include both days away from work and days of restricted work activity.

[d] Division and 2- and 3-digit SIC codes include data for 4-digit codes not shown separately.

n.e.c. = not elsewhere classified.

COMPARISON OF OCCUPATIONAL INJURY AND ILLNESS INCIDENCE RATES FOR SELECTED INDUSTRIES, 1999

	Cases Involving Days Away from Work and Deaths[a]		Days Away from Work[a]
Offices	0.15 (0.95)[b]	2	Offices
Pipeline Transportation	0.21 (1.15)	3	Pipeline Transportation
Textile	0.22 (2.78)	5	Agricultural Chemicals
Chemical	0.26 (1.75)	5	Chemical
Agricultural Chemicals	0.39 (2.13)	7	Textile
Electronic Equipment	0.43 (2.33)	8	Electronic Equipment
Mining	0.46 (4.01)	8	Nonferrous Rolling, Drawing
Nonferrous Rolling, Drawing	0.46 (5.16)	10	Services
Petroleum and Coal Products	0.49 (2.28)	11	Electric Services
Research and Development Labs	0.51 (3.14)	11	Research and Development Labs
Construction	0.51 (3.00)	13	Petroleum and Coal Products
Services	0.59 (2.23)	14	Construction
Electric Services	0.60 (3.46)	16	Printing and Publishing
Lumber and Wood Products	0.64 (4.62)	17	Apparel
Apparel	0.73 (19.39)	17	Public Works Departments
Aircraft	0.79 (5.44)	18	Mining
Paper	0.81 (4.81)	19	Lumber and Wood Products
Agriculture, Forestry	0.85 (3.75)	20	Industrial Machinery & Equip.
Water Transportation	0.86 (2.08)	22	Agriculture, Forestry
Steel	0.97 (5.12)	24	Ship and Boat Building
Industrial Machinery & Equip.	1.09 (7.65)	25	ALL INDUSTRIES
ALL INDUSTRIES	1.11 (7.99)	25	Communication
Printing and Publishing	1.32 (5.17)	26	Furniture and Fixtures
Rubber and Plastics	1.37 (10.41)	26	Paper
Communication	1.38 (3.38)	26	Steel
Food	1.38 (7.01)	28	Aircraft
Government	1.49 (5.36)	29	Government
Gas Production and Dist.	1.51 (5.22)	30	Rubber and Plastics
Stone, Clay and Glass	1.53 (10.62)	31	Iron and Steel Foundries
Furniture and Fixtures	1.55 (8.73)	32	Gas Production and Dist.
Iron and Steel Foundries	1.59 (16.32)	33	Food
Sanitary Services	1.73 (7.18)	42	Water Transportation
Wholesale and Retail Trade	1.79 (8.14)	44	Stone, Clay and Glass
Public Works Departments	1.81 (9.05)	45	Wholesale and Retail Trade
Ship and Boat Building	2.15 (11.11)	47	Fabricated Metal Products
Motor Vehicles	2.17 (19.80)	52	Motor Vehicles
Fabricated Metal Products	2.35 (24.71)	56	Water Supply
Water Supply	2.94 (8.08)	58	Sanitary Services
Transit	3.01 (5.29)	67	Trucking
Trucking	4.06 (10.58)	96	Transit

Source: Based on reports of National Safety Council members participating in the Occupational Safety/Health Award Program. These rates should not be interpreted as representative of the industries listed or of Council member organizations. Data compiled in accordance with OSHA recordkeeping definitions.
[a] *Incidence rates per 100 full-time employees using 200,000 employee hours as the equivalent.*
[b] *Rates in parentheses are for Total Cases.*

OCCUPATIONAL HEALTH

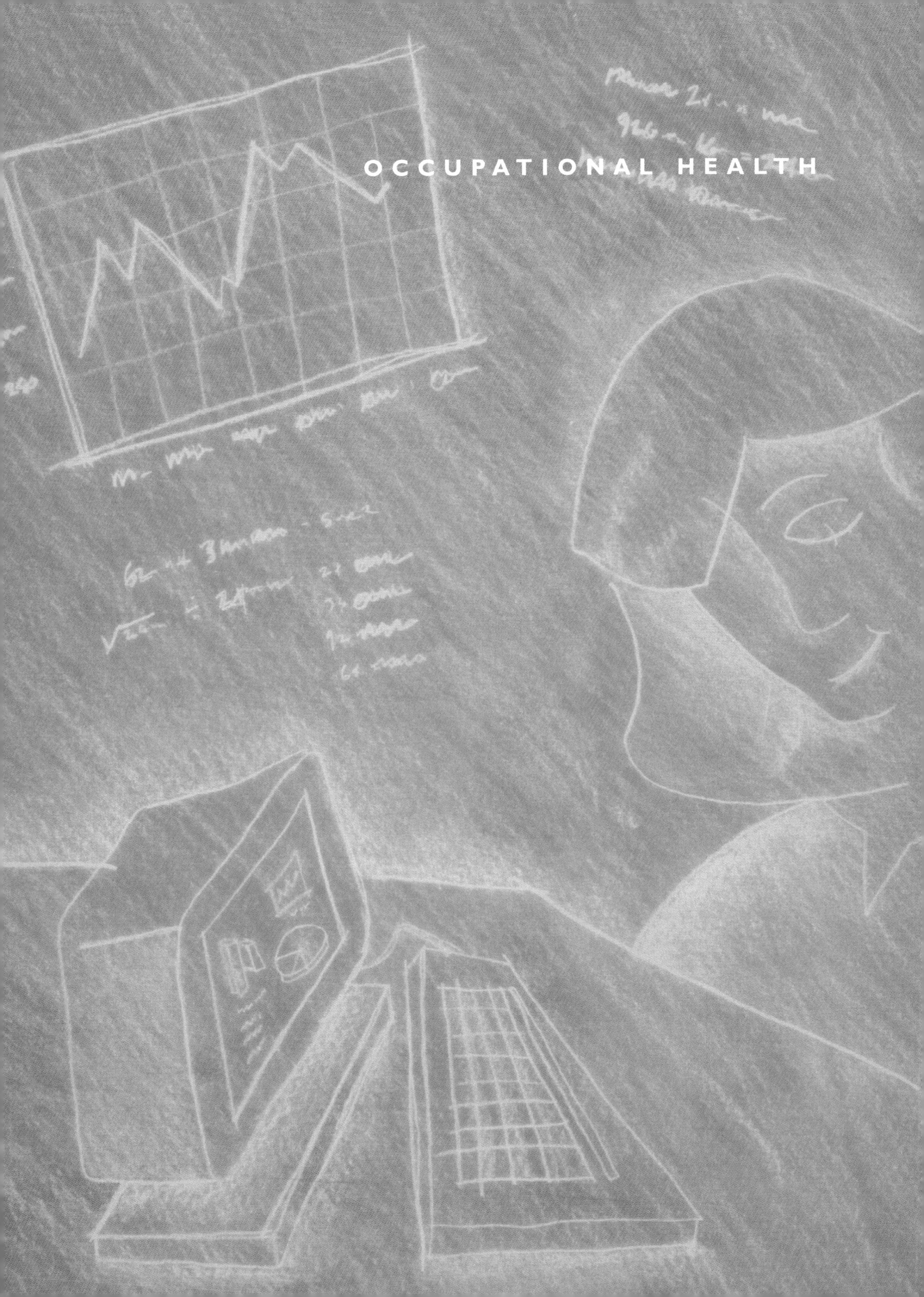

Disorders associated with repeated trauma were the most common illness with over 253,000 new cases in 1998.

OCCUPATIONAL HEALTH

Approximately 391,900 occupational illnesses were recognized or diagnosed in 1998 according to the Bureau of Labor Statistics (BLS). Disorders associated with repeated trauma were the most common illness with 253,300 new cases, followed by skin diseases and disorders (over 53,000), and respiratory conditions due to toxic agents (17,500).

The overall incidence rate of occupational illness for all workers was 44.2 per 10,000 full-time workers. Of the major industry divisions, manufacturing had the highest rate in 1998, 125.5 per 10,000 full-time workers. Workers in manufacturing also had the highest rates for disorders associated with repeated trauma, respiratory conditions due to toxic agents, disorders due to physical agents, and poisoning. Agriculture

had the second highest incidence rate, 30.9, although agricultural workers had the highest rate of all the industry divisions for skin diseases and disorders. Mining had the highest incidence rate for dust diseases of the lungs.

The table below shows the number of occupational illnesses and the incidence rate per 10,000 full-time workers as measured by the 1998 BLS survey. To convert these to incidence rates per 100 full-time workers, which are comparable to other published BLS rates, divide the rates in the table by 100. The BLS survey records illnesses only for the year in which they are recognized or diagnosed as work-related. Since only recognized cases are included, the figures underestimate the incidence of occupational illness.

NUMBER OF OCCUPATIONAL ILLNESSES AND INCIDENCE RATES BY INDUSTRY AND TYPE OF ILLNESS, UNITED STATES, 1998

Occupational Illness	Private Sector[a]	Agriculture[a, b]	Mining[b]	Construction	Manufacturing	Trans. & Pub. Util.	Trade[b]	Finance[b]	Services
Number of Illnesses (in thousands)									
All Illnesses	391.9	4.3	1.3	7.7	236.3	16.6	38.8	15.2	71.7
Disorders associated with repeated trauma	253.3	0.6	0.8	2.0	180.9	9.2	20.9	12.0	27.0
Skin diseases, disorders	53.1	2.4	0.1	1.8	24.4	1.7	4.3	0.8	17.7
Respiratory conditions due to toxic agents	17.5	0.5	(c)	0.8	6.6	1.2	2.6	0.6	5.1
Disorders due to physical agents	16.6	0.1	(c)	1.2	9.0	1.2	2.2	0.1	2.7
Poisoning	4.0	0.1	(c)	0.3	2.2	0.3	0.3	(c)	0.8
Dust diseases of the lungs	2.1	(c)	0.3	0.2	0.8	0.3	0.2	(c)	0.4
All other occupational diseases	45.4	0.5	0.1	1.5	12.5	2.7	8.4	2.2	18.0
Incidence Rate per 10,000 Full-Time Workers									
All Illnesses	44.2	30.9	20.8	14.2	125.5	26.7	16.7	23.1	27.2
Disorders associated with repeated trauma	28.5	4.4	12.2	3.6	96.0	14.8	9.0	18.3	10.2
Skin diseases, disorders	6.0	17.2	0.9	3.3	12.9	2.8	1.9	1.1	6.7
Respiratory conditions due to toxic agents	2.0	3.7	0.8	1.4	3.5	2.0	1.1	1.0	1.9
Disorders due to physical agents	1.9	1.0	0.7	2.2	4.8	2.0	0.9	0.2	1.0
Poisoning	0.5	0.5	0.1	0.5	1.2	0.4	0.1	0.1	0.3
Dust diseases of the lungs	0.2	0.2	4.3	0.3	0.4	0.4	0.1	0.1	0.2
All other occupational diseases	5.1	3.8	1.9	2.8	6.6	4.3	3.6	2.4	6.8

Source: Bureau of Labor Statistics, U.S. Department of Labor. Components may not add to totals due to rounding.
[a] *Private sector includes all industries except government, but excludes farms with less than 11 employees.*
[b] *Agriculture includes forestry and fishing; mining includes quarrying and oil and gas extraction; trade includes wholesale and retail; finance includes insurance and real estate.*
[c] *Fewer than 50 cases.*

NONFATAL OCCUPATIONAL ILLNESS INCIDENCE RATES, U.S. PRIVATE INDUSTRY, 1992–1998

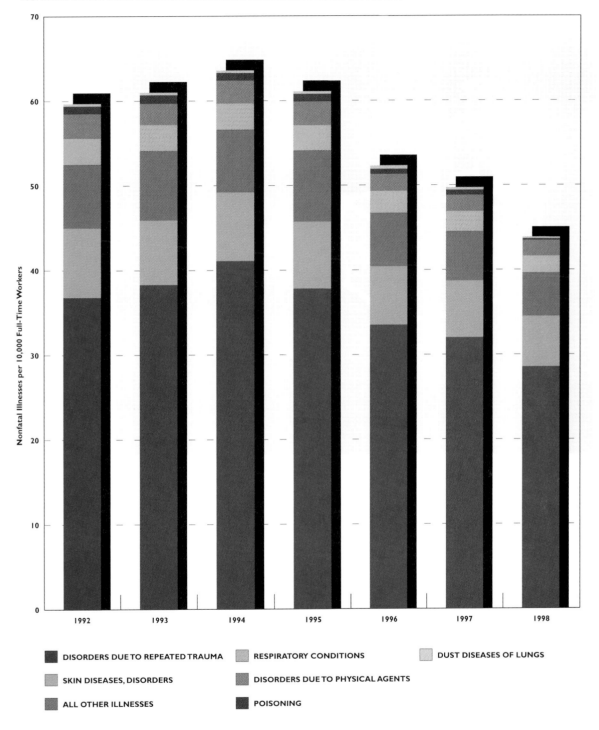

BACK INJURIES

A recent study[a] of nonfatal occupational injuries in the United States found that in 1995, about 27% of all injuries in private industry involved the back as the injured body part. The service sector had the highest proportion of injuries involving the back with 31%, followed by transportation and public utilities with 28% and wholesale and retail trade with 26%. The services and manufacturing industries had the highest proportion of injuries to the entire back, including those to the spine and spinal column, with 27% and 23%, respectively. The services and manufacturing industries also had the highest proportion of injuries to the lumbar region (27% and 24%, respectively), and multiple back regions (38% and 26%, respectively). For all industries, injuries to the lumbar region of the back were the most numerous.

Overexertion in lifting was the leading exposure resulting in back injury, accounting for about 75% of the injuries to the entire back (including the spine and spinal column) in 1995. Falls to the same level (10%) and slips or trips without fall (7%) were the next highest injury-producing exposures. These three exposures were also involved in 94% of the injuries to the lumbar region and 90% of those to multiple back regions, with overexertion in lifting the leading exposure in injuries to both regions at 79% and 71%, respectively.

Sprains and strains accounted for the most injuries to the entire back (84%) and the lumbar region (86%). In addition, sprains and strains were involved in nearly 75% of injuries to multiple back regions. Although a significant portion of the injuries that occurred to the lumbar region resulted in low back pain, injuries such as fractures, cuts and punctures, bruises, and so forth, did not significantly affect any of the back regions.

The major sources of injury causing the greatest number and incidence of back injuries included containers, worker motion or position while at work, walkways or ground surfaces, parts and materials, and healthcare patients. Containers were associated with over 25% of the injuries to the entire back, nearly 25% of the injuries to the lumbar region, and about 18% of the injuries to multiple back regions. Worker motion or position while at work accounted for 10–18% of the injuries to different regions of the back, except for the coccygeal region.

About 25% of the injuries to the entire back resulted in 21 or more lost workdays. An identical portion of the injuries to the lumbar region resulted in 21 or more lost workdays, while another 25% of the injuries to this region resulted in 3–5 lost workdays. Nearly 25% of injuries to the multiple back regions resulted in 21 or more lost workdays. Once again, the lumbar region of the back was the most commonly affected region across the different number of workday losses.

The use of back belts has been suggested to lessen the risk of back injury among uninjured workers. A recent report[b] by the National Institute for Occupational Safety and Health (NIOSH) concluded that the effectiveness of back belts in reducing back injury remains unproven and the use of back belts to prevent injuries among uninjured workers is not recommended. The report emphasized that back belts do not mitigate the hazards to workers posed by repeated lifting, pushing, pulling, twisting, or bending.

The report recommended that the most effective means to minimize the likelihood of back injury is to develop and implement a comprehensive ergonomics program that includes ergonomic assessment of jobs and workstations; ongoing, comprehensive training for all workers regarding lifting mechanics and techniques; a surveillance program to identify work-related musculoskeletal problems; and a medical management program.

[a] Mital, A., Pennathur, A., & Kansal, A. (1999). Nonfatal occupational injuries in the United States, Part II - back injuries. *International Journal of Industrial Ergonomics, 25* (2), *131-150*.
[b] National Institute for Occupational Safety and Health. (July, 1994). Workplace use of back belts. Cincinnati, OH: Author.

WORKPLACE HEALTH PROMOTION

Physical Activity/Diet

A study by Emmins, Linnan, and Shadel (1999) in the *Journal of Occupational and Environmental Medicine* showed that worksite intervention programs can significantly raise the physical fitness level of the employee population. Before intervention, about 39% of the control group and 39% of the intervention group claimed to exercise on a regular basis. After the intervention period, only 41% of the control group exercised regularly, compared to 51% for the intervention group. While subjects in the intervention program showed only a small increase in fruit and vegetable consumption, the group showed a statistically significant increase in fiber consumption, increasing from 8.3 to 9.2 daily grams of fiber. Reduction of the percentage of calories from fat was not related to the intervention program.

Smoking

In 1993 the Centers for Disease Control and Prevention estimated that over 400,000 deaths each year are linked to smoking, totaling over 5 million years of potential life lost. According to Jason, Salina, and McMahon (1997), participants in worksite interventions were 58% more likely to quit smoking than those in corresponding control conditions. The study found that 25.6% of subjects given access to group help, incentives, and self-help manuals at the worksite were able to successfully quit smoking for two years following the study. About 17.5% of those given only

self-help manuals were able to quit two years following the study. The results immediately following the three-week intervention were more compelling with 47.7% of the subjects receiving treatment successfully quitting, compared to 5.2% of the subjects only receiving self-help manuals.

Influenza Vaccinations

According to Dille's (1999) writing in the *AAOHN Journal*, as much as 20% of the population may have an influenza-like illness in any given year. During epidemic years, estimated annual costs associated with influenza can exceed $12 billion. The influenza vaccine is about 70% effective in protecting against the symptoms of influenza. Studies of the effectiveness of the vaccination are compelling. Episodes of influenza were reported at a higher rate in unvaccinated employees (78 per 100) compared to vaccinated employees (59 per 100). The rate of lost workday cases resulting from influenza-like illness was higher in unvaccinated employees (63 per 100) than in vaccinated employees (35 per 100). Results from the immunization program study show that the vaccine saved about $45.72 per person in avoided direct health care costs and about $38.12 per employee in indirect costs. The combined savings were approximately $83.84 per vaccinated employee.

Source: Dille, J.H. (1999). A Worksite Influenza Immunization Program. AAOHN Journal, 47(7), 301–309. Emmons, K.M., Linnan, L.A., & Shadel, W.G. (1999). The Working Healthy Project. Journal of Occupational and Environmental Medicine, 41(7), 545–555. Jason, L.A., Salina, P., & McMahon, S.D. (1997). A Worksite Smoking Intervention. Health Education Research, Vol. 12(1), 129–138.

ECONOMIC BENEFITS ASSOCIATED WITH INFLUENZA VACCINATION

Outcome Variable	Estimated Cost (Savings) per 100 Subjects in 1994 Dollars
Direct Costs	**($4,572)**
Vaccination	$1,000
Potential Physician Visit Avoided	($530)
Potential Hospitalization Avoided	($4,600)
Potential Antibiotic Therapy Avoided	($442)
Indirect Costs	**($3,812)**
Estimated Work Time Lost for Vaccination	$1,095
Potential Lost Work Days Avoided	($4,907)
Net Savings	**($8,384)**

Source: Dille (1999).

MOTOR VEHICLE, 1999

Between 1912 and 1999, motor-vehicle deaths per 10,000 registered vehicles were reduced 94%, from 33 to about 2. In 1912, there were 3,100 fatalities when the number of registered vehicles totaled only 950,000. In 1999, there were 41,300 fatalities, but registrations soared to more than 218 million.

While mileage data were not available in 1912, the 1999 mileage death rate of 1.54 per 100,000,000 vehicle miles was the lowest rate on record. Disabling injuries in motor-vehicle accidents totaled 2,200,000 in 1999, and total motor-vehicle costs were estimated at $181.5 billion. Costs include wage and productivity losses, medical expenses, administrative expenses, motor-vehicle property damage, and employer costs.

Motor-vehicle deaths decreased 1% from 1998 to 1999, the third consecutive decrease following four years of increases. Miles traveled and the number of registered vehicles increased 2% each, while the population increased 1%. As a result, the mileage, registration, and death rates decreased 3% from 1998 to 1999.

Compared with 1989, 1999 motor-vehicle deaths decreased by about 13%. However, mileage, registration, and population death rates were all sharply lower in 1999 compared to 1989 (see chart on opposite page).

Deaths 41,300
Disabling injuries 2,200,000
Cost . . . . $181.5 billion
Motor-vehicle mileage . . . . 2,679 billion
Registered vehicles in the United States 218,300,000
Licensed drivers in the United States 188,200,000
Death rate per 100,000,000 vehicle miles 1.54
Death rate per 10,000 registered vehicles 1.89
Death rate per 100,000 population 15.1

ACCIDENT AND VEHICLE TOTALS, 1999

Severity of Accident	Number of Accidents	Drivers (Vehicles) Involved
Fatal	34,700	42,200
Disabling injury	1,400,000	2,300,000
Property damage and nondisabling injury[a]	10,000,000	15,700,000
Total (rounded)	11,400,000	18,000,000

[a] Estimating procedures for these figures were revised beginning with the 1990 edition.

TRAVEL DEATHS AND DEATH RATES, UNITED STATES, 1925–1999

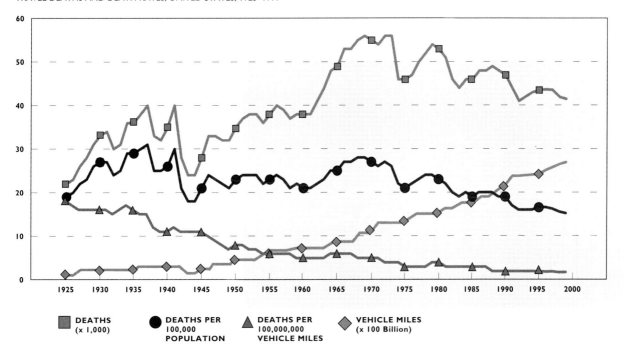

DEATHS DUE TO MOTOR-VEHICLE ACCIDENTS, 1999

TYPE OF ACCIDENT AND AGE OF VICTIM

All Motor-Vehicle Accidents

Includes deaths involving mechanically or electrically powered highway-transport vehicles in motion (except those on rails), both on and off the highway or street.

	Total	Change from 1998	Death Rate[a]
Deaths	41,300	−1%	15.1
Nonfatal Injuries	2,200,000		

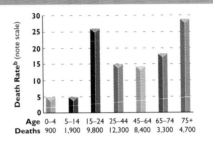

Age	0–4	5–14	15–24	25–44	45–64	65–74	75+
Deaths	900	1,900	9,800	12,300	8,400	3,300	4,700

Collision Between Motor Vehicles

Includes deaths from collisions of two or more motor vehicles. Motorized bicycles and scooters, trolley buses, and farm tractors or road machinery traveling on highways are motor vehicles.

	Total	Change from 1998	Death Rate[a]
Deaths	18,800	+2%	6.9
Nonfatal Injuries	1,580,000		

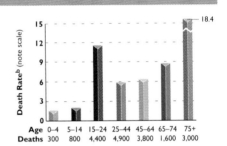

Age	0–4	5–14	15–24	25–44	45–64	65–74	75+
Deaths	300	800	4,400	4,900	3,800	1,600	3,000

Collision with Fixed Object

Includes deaths from collisions in which the first harmful event is the striking of a fixed object such as a guardrail, abutment, impact attenuator, etc.

	Total	Change from 1998	Death Rate[a]
Deaths	11,100	−8%	4.1
Nonfatal Injuries	330,000		

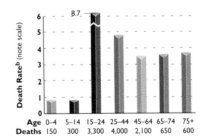

Age	0–4	5–14	15–24	25–44	45–64	65–74	75+
Deaths	150	300	3,300	4,000	2,100	650	600

Pedestrian Accidents

Includes all deaths of persons struck by motor vehicles, either on or off a street or highway, regardless of the circumstances of the accident.

	Total	Change from 1998	Death Rate[a]
Deaths	5,800	−2%	2.1
Nonfatal Injuries	95,000		

See footnotes on page 77.

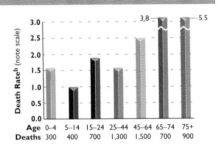

Age	0–4	5–14	15–24	25–44	45–64	65–74	75+
Deaths	300	400	700	1,300	1,500	700	900

Noncollision Accidents

Includes deaths from accidents in which the first injury or damage-producing event was an overturn, jackknife, or other type of noncollision.

	Total	Change from 1998	Death Rate[a]
Deaths	4,300	+2%	1.6
Nonfatal Injuries	110,000		

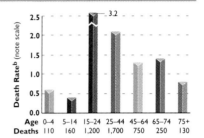

Age	0–4	5–14	15–24	25–44	45–64	65–74	75+
Deaths	110	160	1,200	1,700	750	250	130

Collision with Pedalcycle

Includes deaths of pedalcyclists and motor-vehicle occupants from collisions between pedalcycles and motor vehicles on streets, highways, private driveways, parking lots, etc.

	Total	Change from 1998	Death Rate[a]
Deaths	900	+29%	0.3
Nonfatal Injuries	70,000		

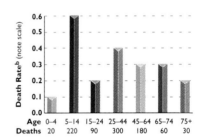

Age	0–4	5–14	15–24	25–44	45–64	65–74	75+
Deaths	20	220	90	300	180	60	30

Collision with Railroad Train

Includes deaths from collisions of motor vehicles (moving or stalled) and railroad vehicles at public or private grade crossings. In other types of accidents, classification requires motor vehicle to be in motion.

	Total	Change from 1998	Death Rate[a]
Deaths	300	−25%	0.1
Nonfatal Injuries	2,000		

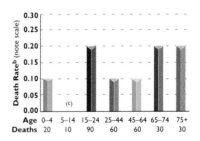

Age	0–4	5–14	15–24	25–44	45–64	65–74	75+
Deaths	20	10	90	60	60	30	30

Other Collision

Includes deaths from motor-vehicle collisions not specified in other categories above. Most of the deaths arose out of accidents involving animals or animal-drawn vehicles.

	Total	Change from 1996	Death Rate[a]
Deaths	100	0%	(c)
Nonfatal Injuries	13,000		

Note: Procedures and benchmarks for estimating deaths by type of accident and age were changed in 1990. Estimates for 1987 and later years are not comparable to earlier years. The noncollision and fixed object categories were most affected by the changes.
[a] Deaths per 100,000 population.
[b] Deaths per 100,000 population in each age group.
[c] Death rate was less than 0.05.

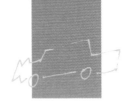

TYPE OF MOTOR-VEHICLE ACCIDENT

Although motor-vehicle deaths occur more often in collisions between motor vehicles than any other type of accident, this type represents only about 46% of the total. Collisions between a motor vehicle and a fixed object were the next most common type, with about 27% of the deaths, followed by pedestrian accidents and noncollisions (rollovers, etc.).

While collisions between motor vehicles accounted for less than half of motor-vehicle fatalities, this accident type represented 72% of injuries, 72% of injury accidents, and 75% of all accidents. Single-vehicle accidents involving collisions with fixed objects, pedestrians, and noncollisions, on the other hand,

accounted for a greater proportion of fatalities and fatal accidents compared to less serious accidents. These three accident types made up 51% of fatalities and 54% of fatal accidents, but less than 25% of injuries, injury accidents, or all accidents.

Of collisions between motor vehicles, angle collisions cause the greatest number of deaths, about 9,200 in 1999 and the greatest number of nonfatal injuries as well as fatal, injury, and all accidents. The table below shows the estimated number of motor-vehicle deaths, injuries, fatal accidents, injury accidents, and all accidents, for various types of accidents.

MOTOR-VEHICLE DEATHS AND INJURIES AND NUMBER OF ACCIDENTS BY TYPE OF ACCIDENT, 1999

Type of Accident	Deaths	Nonfatal Injuries	Fatal Accidents	Injury Accidents	All Accidents
Total	**41,300**	**2,200,000**	**34,700**	**1,400,000**	**11,400,000**
Collision with—					
Pedestrian	5,800	95,000	4,000	75,000	120,000
Other motor vehicle	18,800	1,580,000	15,000	1,010,000	8,590,000
Angle collision	*9,200*	*866,000*	*7,700*	*535,000*	*4,310,000*
Head-on collision	*7,300*	*75,000*	*5,400*	*37,000*	*180,000*
Rear-end collision	*1,700*	*599,000*	*1,400*	*411,000*	*3,550,000*
Sideswipe and other two-vehicle collisions	*600*	*40,000*	*500*	*27,000*	*550,000*
Railroad train	300	2,000	200	1,000	5,000
Pedalcycle	900	70,000	500	40,000	85,000
Animal, animal-drawn vehicle	100	13,000	100	5,000	430,000
Fixed object	11,100	330,000	10,900	189,000	1,850,000
Noncollision	**4,300**	**110,000**	**4,000**	**80,000**	**320,000**

Source: National Safety Council estimates, based on reports from state traffic authorities. Procedures for estimating the number of accidents by type were changed for the 1998 edition and are not comparable to estimates in previous editions (see Technical Appendix).

ESTIMATING MOTOR-VEHICLE ACCIDENT COSTS

There are two methods currently used to measure the costs of motor-vehicle accidents. One is the *economic cost* framework and the other is the *comprehensive cost* framework.

Economic costs may be used by a community or state to estimate the economic impact of motor-vehicle accidents that occurred within its jurisdiction in a given time period. It is a measure of the productivity lost and expenses incurred because of the accidents. Economic costs, however, should not be used for cost-benefit analysis because they do not reflect what society is willing to pay to prevent a statistical fatality or injury.

There are five economic cost components: (a) wage and productivity losses, which include wages, fringe benefits, household production, and travel delay; (b) medical expenses including emergency service costs; (c) administrative expenses, which include the administrative cost of private and public insurance plus police and legal costs; (d) motor-vehicle damage including the value of damage to property; and (e) employer costs for accidents to workers.

The information below shows the average economic costs in 1999 per death (*not* per fatal accident), per injury (*not* per injury accident), and per property damage accident.

ECONOMIC COSTS, 1999

Death	**$970,000**
Nonfatal disabling injury	**$35,300**
Incapacitating injury[a]	*$45,800*
Nonincapacitating evident injury[a]	*$15,300*
Possible injury[a]	*$8,700*
Property damage accident (including minor injuries)	**$6,400**

Comprehensive costs include not only the economic cost components, but also a measure of the value of lost quality of life associated with the deaths and injuries, that is, what society is willing to pay to prevent them. The values of lost quality of life were obtained through empirical studies of what people actually pay to reduce their safety and health risks, such as through the purchase of air bags or smoke detectors. Comprehensive costs should be used for cost-benefit analysis, but because the lost quality of life represents only a dollar equivalence of intangible qualities, they do not represent real economic losses and should not be used to determine the economic impact of past accidents.

The information below shows the average comprehensive costs in 1999 on a per person basis.

COMPREHENSIVE COSTS, 1999

Death	**$3,100,150**
Incapacitating injury[a]	*$153,453*
Nonincapacitating evident injury[a]	*$39,481*
Possible injury[a]	*$18,782*
No injury	**$1,787**

Source: National Safety Council estimates (see the Technical Appendix) and Children's Safety Network Economics and Insurance Resource Center, National Public Services Research Institute.
[a]*Committee on Motor Vehicle Traffic Accident Classification. (1997). Manual on Classification of Motor Vehicle Traffic Accidents, ANSI D16.1-1996 (6th ed.). Itasca, IL: National Safety Council.*
Note: The National Safety Council's cost estimating procedures were extensively revised for the 1993 edition. New components were added, new benchmarks adopted, and a new discount rate assumed. The costs are not comparable with those of prior years.

STATE LEGISLATION

Currently all states and the District of Columbia have 21-year-old drinking age and child safety seat laws. Breath alcohol ignition interlock device laws are currently in effect in 38 states. Mandatory belt use laws are in effect in 49 states plus the District of Columbia.

As of January 2000, graduated licensing laws will be in effect in 40 states, 30 of which prohibit young drivers from driving during high-risk nighttime and early morning hours.

STATE LEGISLATION

State	Alcohol Legislation				Mandatory Belt Use Law		Graduated Licensing Law			
	Admin-istrative License Revocation Since[a]	BAC Limit[b]	Zero Tolerance Limit[c] for Minors	Alcohol Ignition Interlock Device[d]	Enforce-ment	Seating Positions Covered by Law	Gradu-ated Licensing Law	Minimum Instruc-tional Permit Period	Night-time Driving Restric-tions	Unrestricted License Minimum Age
Alabama	1996	0.08	0.02	no	standard	front	yes	6 mo.	yes	17 yrs.
Alaska	1983	0.10	0.00	yes	secondary	all	no	none	no	16 yrs.
Arizona	1992	0.10	0.00	yes	secondary	front	yes	5 mo.	no	18 yrs.
Arkansas	1995	0.10	0.02	yes	secondary	front	no	none	no	16 yrs.
California	1989	0.08	0.01	yes[e]	standard	all	yes	6 mo.	yes	17 yrs.
Colorado	1983	0.10	0.02	yes[e]	secondary	front	yes	6 mo.	yes	17 yrs.
Connecticut	1990	0.10	0.02	no	standard	front[f]	yes	6 mo.	no	16 yrs. & 6 mo.
Delaware	yes	0.10	0.02	yes[e]	secondary	front	yes	6 mo.	yes	16 yrs. & 10 mo.
District of Columbia	yes	0.08	0.00	no	standard	all	yes	6 mo.	yes	18 yrs.
Florida	1990	0.08	0.02	yes	secondary	front	yes	6 mo.	yes	18 yrs.
Georgia	1995	0.10	0.02	yes[e]	standard	front[f]	yes	12 mo.	yes	18 yrs.
Hawaii	1990	0.08	0.02	no	standard	front	no	none	no	15 yrs. & 3 mo.
Idaho	1994	0.08	0.02	yes	secondary	front	no	none	no	16 yrs.
Illinois	1986	0.08	0.00	yes	secondary	front	yes	6 mo.	yes	17 yrs.
Indiana	yes	0.10	0.02	yes	standard	front	yes	3 mo.	yes	18 yrs.
Iowa	1982	0.10	0.02	yes	standard	front	yes	6 mo.	yes	17 yrs.
Kansas	1988	0.08	0.02	yes	secondary	front	yes	6 mo.	no	16 yrs.
Kentucky	no	0.10	0.02	no	secondary	all	yes	6 mo.	yes	18 yrs.
Louisiana	1984	0.10	0.02	yes	standard	front[f]	yes	3 mo.	yes	17 yrs.
Maine	1984	0.08	0.00	yes[e]	secondary	all	no	none	no	16 yrs.
Maryland	1989	0.10[g]	0.02	yes	standard	front[f,h]	yes	4 mo.	yes	18 yrs.
Massachusetts	1994	0.08	0.02	no	secondary	all	yes[i]	6 mo.	yes	18 yrs.
Michigan	no	0.10	0.02	yes	standard	front[f]	yes	6 mo.	yes	17 yrs.
Minnesota	1976	0.10	0.01	no	secondary	front[f]	no	none	no	16 yrs.
Mississippi	1983	0.10	0.02	no[j]	secondary	front	no[k]	none	no	16 yrs.
Missouri	1987	0.10	0.02	yes[e]	secondary	front[f]	yes[k]	6 mo.	yes	18 yrs.
Montana	no	0.10	0.02	yes	secondary	all	no	none	no	15 yrs.
Nebraska	1993	0.10	0.02	yes	secondary	front[f,j,l]	yes	none	yes	18 yrs.
Nevada	1983	0.10	0.02	yes[e]	secondary	all	yes	6 mo.	no	16 yrs.
New Hampshire	1994	0.08	0.02	no	no	—	yes	3 mo.	yes	18 yrs.
New Jersey	no	0.10	0.01	yes	standard[m]	front	yes[k]	6 mo.	—	18 yrs.
New Mexico	1984	0.08	0.02	yes	standard	front	yes	6 mo.	yes	16 yrs. & 6 mo.
New York	1994[n]	0.10[g]	0.02	yes[e]	standard	front[f]	yes	—	yes	17 yrs.
North Carolina	1983	0.08	0.00	yes[e]	standard	front[f]	yes	12 mo.	yes	16 yrs. & 6 mo.
North Dakota	1983	0.10	0.02	yes[e]	secondary	front	yes	6 mo.	no	18 yrs.
Ohio	1993	0.10	0.02	yes	secondary	front	yes	6 mo.	yes	17 yrs.
Oklahoma	1983	0.10	0.00	yes	standard	front	yes	none	no	16 yrs.
Oregon	1983	0.08	0.00	yes	secondary	all	yes	6 mo.	yes	18 yrs.
Pennsylvania	no	0.10	0.02	no	secondary	front	yes	6 mo.	yes	18 yrs.
Rhode Island	no	0.10	0.02	yes[e]	secondary	all	yes	6 mo.	yes	17 yrs. & 6 mo.
South Carolina	1998	0.10	0.02	no	secondary	front[f,o]	yes	3 mo.	yes	16 yrs. & 3 mo.
South Dakota[i]	no	0.10	0.02	no	secondary	front	yes	—	—	—
Tennessee	no	0.10	0.02	yes	secondary	front[f]	yes	3 mo.	no	16 yrs.
Texas	1995	0.08	0.00	yes[e]	standard	front[f]	no	none	no	16 yrs.
Utah	1983	0.08	0.00	yes[e]	secondary[p]	all	no	none	no	16 yrs.
Vermont	1969[n]	0.08	0.02 (<18)	no	secondary	all	yes	none	no	18 yrs.
Virginia	1995	0.08	0.02	yes	secondary	front	yes	6 mo.	no	17 yrs.
Washington	1998	0.08	0.02	yes[e]	secondary	all	yes	6 mo.	yes	18 yrs.
West Virginia	1981	0.10	0.02	yes	secondary	front[f]	yes[k]	6 mo.	yes	17 yrs.
Wisconsin	1988	0.10[q]	0.00 (<19)	yes[e]	secondary	front[o]	yes	6 mo.	yes	19 yrs.
Wyoming	1973	0.10	0.02	no	secondary	front	no	none	no	16 yrs.

Source: Offices of State Governor's Highway Safety Representatives (review of state legislation as of May 1999).

Dash (—) indicates data not available.

[a] Year original law became effective, not when grandfather clauses expired.

[b] Blood alcohol concentration that constitutes the threshold of legal intoxication.

[c] Blood alcohol concentration that constitutes "zero tolerance" threshold for minors (<21 years of age unless otherwise noted).

[d] Legislation for instruments designed to prevent drivers from starting their cars when breath alcohol content is at or above a set point.

[e] Primarily for repeat offenders (GA, ME, NY, NC, ND, RI, TX, WI), but may also be applied to first-time offenders under certain circumstances.

[f] Required for certain ages at all seating positions.

[g] BAC of 0.07 is prima facie evidence of DUI (MD); BAC of 0.05–0.10 constitutes driving while ability impaired (NY).

[h] Excluding front center seat.

[i] Most recent data from 1999.

[j] Legislation pending.

[k] Legislation becomes effective 1/1/01.

[l] Legislation becomes effective 7/1/00.

[m] Legislation becomes effective 5/1/00.

[n] Revocation by judicial action (NY) or Department of Motor Vehicles (VT).

[o] Belt use required in rear seat if lap/shoulder belt is available.

[p] Secondary for 19 and older, standard for under 19.

[q] 0.08 after second DUI conviction.

TRENDS IN MOTOR-VEHICLE DEATH RATES

The use of motor vehicles was just beginning to grow in 1906. There were 108,100 vehicles registered—about 1 for every 790 people—and 400 people died in motor-vehicle crashes for a death rate of 0.5 per 100,000 population. In 1999, on the other hand, there were about 218,300,000 registered vehicles—about 4 vehicles for every 5 people. An estimated 41,300 people died in crashes for a rate of 15.1 per 100,000 population. The 1999 death rate was less than half of the maximum rate (30.8) that was reached in 1937.

Death rates for all age groups generally increased prior to World War II, showed a sharp dip and recovery during and immediately after the war, and then generally decreased. A sharp drop associated with the Arabian oil embargo is also noticeable in the early 1970s.

Through the early 1950s the 65 and older age group had the highest death rates. Since then the 15–24 year age group has had the highest death rates. The 0–4 and 5–14 year age groups have had the lowest death rates since the early 1920s.

See also the graph on page 75 which shows the trends in numbers of deaths, miles traveled, and mileage death rates.

MOTOR-VEHICLE DEATH RATES BY AGE GROUP, UNITED STATES, 1906–1999

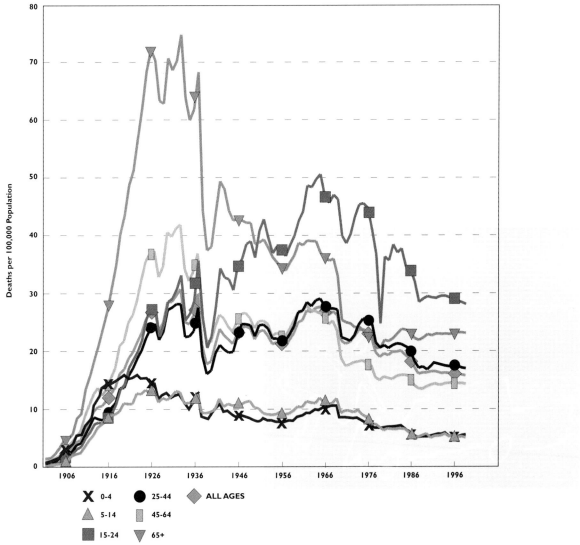

ALCOHOL

According to studies conducted by the National Highway Traffic Safety Administration, about 38% of all traffic fatalities in 1998 involved an intoxicated or alcohol-impaired driver or nonmotorist. In 1998, 30% of all traffic fatalities occurred in crashes where at least one driver or nonoccupant was intoxicated (blood alcohol concentration [BAC] of 0.10 or greater). Of the 12,456 people killed in such crashes, 70% were themselves intoxicated. The other 30% were passengers, nonintoxicated drivers, or nonintoxicated nonoccupants. The following data summarizes the extent of alcohol involvement in motor-vehicle accidents:

• Traffic fatalities in alcohol-related crashes fell by 1% from 1997 to 1998 and declined by 33% from 1988 to 1998. (See corresponding chart.) In 1988, alcohol-related fatalities accounted for 50% of all traffic deaths.

• According to NHTSA, alcohol was involved in 39% of fatal crashes and 7% of all traffic accidents, both fatal and nonfatal, in 1998.

• Approximately 1.5 million drivers were arrested in 1997 for driving under the influence of alcohol or narcotics.

• About 3 in every 10 Americans will be involved in an alcohol-related traffic accident at some time in their lives.

• There were 15,935 alcohol-related traffic fatalities in 1998, an average of one alcohol-related fatality every 33 minutes. An average of one person every 2 minutes is injured in a traffic accident where alcohol is present.

• In 1998, alcohol was present in 29% of all fatal traffic accidents on weekdays, compared to 52% on weekends. The rate of alcohol involvement in fatal crashes during the day is 17%, compared to 60% at night.

PERCENT OF TOTAL TRAFFIC FATALITIES WITH ALCOHOL PRESENT, BY STATE, 1998

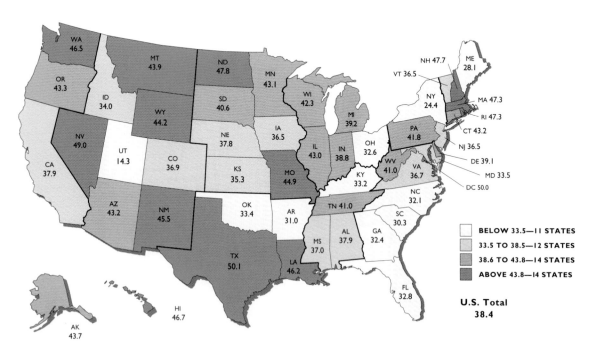

- From 1988 to 1998, intoxication rates decreased for drivers of all age groups. The greatest decrease was for 16-to-20-year-old drivers (33%). NHTSA estimates that 18,220 lives have been saved by 21-year-old minimum drinking age laws since 1975. All states and the District of Columbia now have such laws.

- Safety belts were used by about 19% of fatally injured intoxicated drivers, compared to 32% of fatally injured alcohol-impaired drivers and 49% of fatally injured sober drivers.

- The driver, pedestrian, or both were intoxicated in 37% of all fatal pedestrian traffic accidents in 1998. In these crashes, the intoxication rate for pedestrians was more than double the rate for drivers.

- The cost of alcohol-related motor-vehicle accidents is estimated by the National Safety Council at $25.8 billion in 1999.

Source: National Center for Statistics and Analysis. (1999). Traffic Safety Facts 1998—Alcohol. Washington, DC: National Highway Traffic Safety Administration.

PERCENT OF ALL TRAFFIC FATALITIES THAT OCCURRED IN ALCOHOL-RELATED CRASHES, 1988–1998

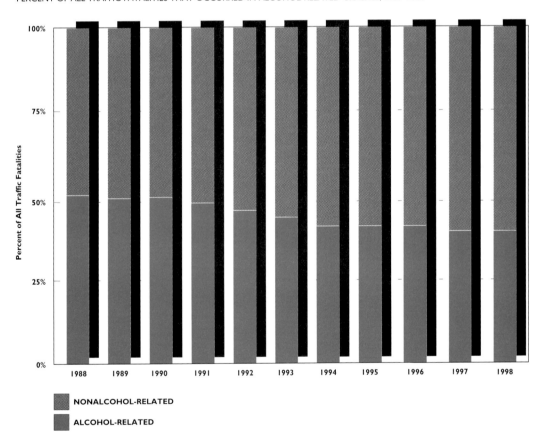

NONALCOHOL-RELATED

ALCOHOL-RELATED

OCCUPANT PROTECTION

Safety Belts

- When used, lap/shoulder safety belts reduce the risk of fatal injury to front seat passenger car occupants by 45% and reduce the risk of moderate-to-critical injury by 50%.

- For light truck occupants, safety belts reduce the risk of fatal injury by 60% and moderate-to-critical injury by 65%.

- Forty-nine states and the District of Columbia have mandatory belt use laws in effect, the only exception being New Hampshire. Thirty-three of the states with belt use laws in effect in 1998 specified secondary enforcement (i.e., police officers are permitted to write a citation only after a vehicle is stopped for some other traffic infraction). Sixteen states and the District of Columbia had laws that allowed primary enforcement, enabling officers to stop vehicles and write citations whenever they observe violations of the belt law.

- Safety belts saved an estimated 11,088 lives in 1998 among passenger vehicle occupants over 4 years old. An *additional* 9,267 lives could have been saved in 1998 if all passenger vehicle occupants over age 4 wore safety belts. From 1975 through 1998, an estimated 112,086 lives were saved by safety belts.

- Safety belts provide the greatest protection against occupant ejection. Among crashes in which a fatality occurred in 1998, only 1% of restrained passenger car occupants were ejected, compared to 21% of unrestrained occupants.

- The belt use rate reported by states with secondary enforcement laws was 62%, compared to 79% in states with primary enforcement laws. New Hampshire, which has no adult belt use law, reported a 56% use rate.

Air Bags

- Air bags, combined with lap/shoulder belts, offer the most available protection for passenger vehicle occupants. The overall fatality-reducing effectiveness for air bags is estimated at 11% over and above the benefits from using safety belts.

- Lap/shoulder belts should always be used, even in a vehicle with an air bag. Air bags are a supplemental form of protection and are not designed to deploy in crashes that are not severe.

- Children in rear-facing child seats should not be placed in the front seat of vehicles equipped with passenger-side air bags. The impact of the deploying air bag could result in injury to the child.

- An estimated 1,043 lives were saved by air bags in 1998 and a total of 3,706 lives were saved from 1987 through 1998.

- Beginning September 1997, all new passenger cars were required to have driver and passenger side air bags. In 1998, the same requirement went into effect for light trucks.

ESTIMATED LIVES SAVED BY SAFETY BELTS, 1975–1998

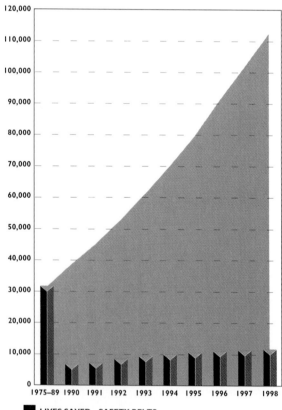

- LIVES SAVED—SAFETY BELTS
- CUMULATIVE LIVES SAVED—SAFETY BELTS

Child Restraints

• Child restraints saved an estimated 299 lives in 1998 among children under the age of 5. Of the 299 lives, 244 were attributed to the use of child safety seats while 55 lives were spared with the use of adult belts.

• At 100% child safety seat use for children under the age of 5, an estimated additional 173 lives could have been saved in 1998.

• All states and the District of Columbia have had child restraint use laws in effect since 1985.

• Research has shown that child safety seats reduce fatal injury in passenger cars by 71% for infants (less than 1 year old), and by 54% for toddlers (1–4 years old). For infants and toddlers in light trucks, the corresponding reductions are 58% and 59% respectively.

• In 1998, there were 575 occupant fatalities among children less than 5 years of age. Of these, an estimated 51% were totally unrestrained.

• An estimated 4,193 lives have been saved by child restraints from 1975 through 1998.

Motorcycle Helmets

• Motorcycle helmets are estimated to be 29% effective in preventing fatal injuries to motorcyclists.

• Helmets saved the lives of 500 motorcyclists in 1998. An additional 307 lives could have been saved if all motorcyclists had worn helmets.

• According to the latest observational survey by the National Highway Traffic Safety Administration (NHTSA), helmet use was at 67% in 1998. Previous NHTSA surveys have reported helmet use to be essentially 100% in areas with helmet use laws governing all riders, compared to 34% to 54% at sites with no helmet use laws or laws limited to minors. Reported helmet use rates for fatally injured motorcyclists in 1998 were 54% for operators and 45% for passengers, compared with 57% and 49%, respectively, in 1997.

• In 1998, 22 states, the District of Columbia, and Puerto Rico required helmet use by all motorcycle operators and passengers. In another 25 states, only persons under 18 were required to wear helmets. Three states had no laws requiring helmet use.

Source: National Center for Statistics and Analysis. (1999). Traffic Safety Facts 1998— Occupant Protection; Traffic Safety Facts 1998—Motorcycles. Washington, DC: National Highway Traffic Safety Administration.

ESTIMATED LIVES SAVED BY CHILD RESTRAINTS AND AIR BAGS, 1975–1998

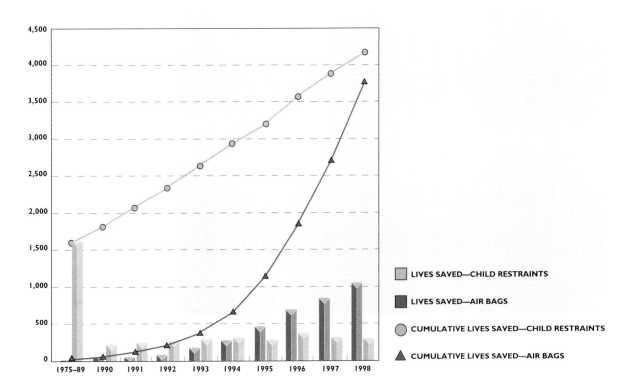

DEATHS AND DEATH RATES BY DAY AND NIGHT

About three-fifths of all motor-vehicle deaths in 1999 occurred during the day, while the remainder occurred at night. Death rates based on mileage, however, were nearly two times higher at night than during the day with vehicle miles traveled by night representing only 25% of the total.

Source: State traffic authorities and the Federal Highway Administration.

DEATH RATES BY DAY AND NIGHT, 1999

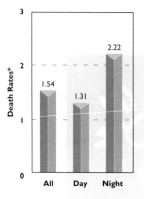

*Per 100,000,000 vehicle miles

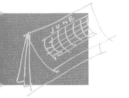

DEATHS AND MILEAGE DEATH RATES BY MONTH

Motor-vehicle deaths in 1999 were at their lowest level in February and increased to their highest level in July. In 1999, the highest monthly mileage death rate of 1.67 deaths per 100,000,000 vehicle miles occurred in September. The overall rate for the year was 1.54.

Source: Deaths—National Safety Council estimates. Mileage—Federal Highway Administration, Traffic Volume Trends.

MOTOR-VEHICLE DEATHS AND MILEAGE DEATH RATES BY MONTH, 1999

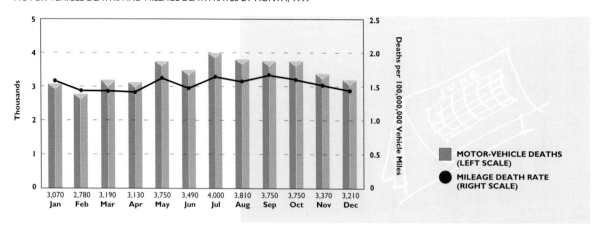

MOTOR-VEHICLE ACCIDENTS
BY TIME OF DAY AND DAY OF WEEK

More fatal accidents occurred on Saturday than any other day of the week in 1999, according to reports from state traffic authorities. Approximately 18% of fatal accidents occurred on Saturday, compared to about 12% on Mondays. For all accidents, Friday had the highest percentage with more than 17%.

Patterns by hour of day for fatal accidents show peaks during afternoon rush hour for weekdays and, especially, late night for weekends. For all accidents, peaks occur during both morning and afternoon rush hour.

PERCENT OF WEEKLY ACCIDENTS BY HOUR OF DAY AND DAY OF WEEK, UNITED STATES, 1999

Time of Day	Fatal Accidents								All Accidents							
	Total	Mon.	Tues.	Wed.	Thurs.	Fri.	Sat.	Sun.	Total	Mon.	Tues.	Wed.	Thurs.	Fri.	Sat.	Sun.
All Hours	100.0%	12.1%	12.5%	12.4%	13.4%	16.5%	18.1%	15.0%	100.0%	14.3%	14.5%	14.6%	14.8%	17.7%	13.4%	10.5%
Midnight–3:59 A.M.	14.7%	0.8%	0.9%	1.5%	1.6%	2.2%	4.1%	3.7%	6.0%	0.5%	0.5%	0.5%	0.6%	0.8%	1.5%	1.5%
4:00–7:59 A.M.	11.6%	1.5%	1.9%	1.6%	1.7%	1.7%	1.7%	1.6%	10.4%	1.8%	1.8%	1.8%	1.7%	1.7%	0.9%	0.7%
8:00–11:59 A.M.	14.2%	1.9%	2.0%	2.0%	2.1%	2.4%	2.1%	1.6%	17.3%	2.7%	2.7%	2.6%	2.6%	2.9%	2.4%	1.5%
Noon–3:59 P.M.	21.1%	3.2%	2.5%	2.7%	2.9%	3.3%	3.4%	3.0%	26.1%	3.9%	3.8%	3.8%	3.9%	4.7%	3.4%	2.6%
4:00–7:59 P.M.	22.2%	2.8%	3.2%	2.6%	3.2%	3.8%	3.3%	3.2%	27.4%	4.0%	4.2%	4.2%	4.3%	5.1%	3.0%	2.6%
8:00–11:59 P.M.	16.1%	1.8%	2.0%	1.9%	2.0%	3.1%	3.5%	1.9%	12.8%	1.4%	1.6%	1.6%	1.8%	2.6%	2.3%	1.6%

Source: Based on reports from 10 state traffic authorities.
Note: Column and row totals may not equal sums of parts due to rounding.

PERCENT OF ACCIDENTS BY TIME OF DAY AND DAY OF WEEK, 1999

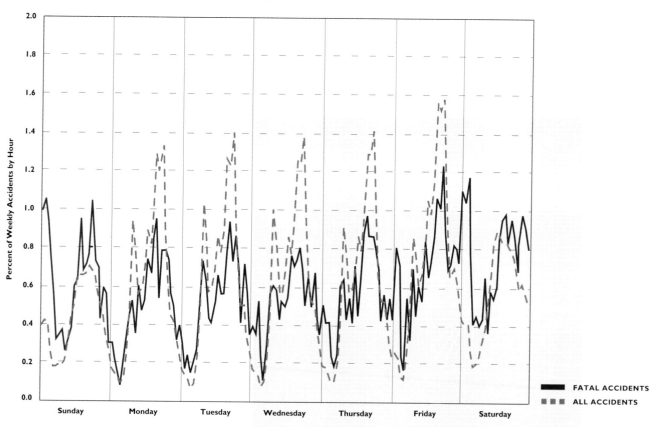

TYPE OF MOTOR VEHICLE

The types of vehicles listed in the table below are classified by body style, not by vehicle use. The light truck category includes both commercial and noncommercial trucks under 10,000 pounds gross vehicle weight. It also includes minivans and sport-utility vehicles. The medium/heavy truck category includes truck tractors with or without semi-trailers.

Passenger Cars

In 1999, passenger cars comprised about 61% of the registered vehicles and were involved in more than their share of the fatal accidents (64.5%). Approximately three fifths of all motor-vehicle occupant fatalities are passenger car occupants. (See corresponding chart.)

Trucks

Light trucks represent about 33% of all motor-vehicle registrations and about 35% of vehicles involved in fatal accidents. Medium and heavy trucks account for about 4% of registered vehicles and about 9% of vehicles involved in fatal accidents. Medium and heavy truck occupants as well as light truck occupants are slightly under-represented in motor-vehicle occupant fatalities compared to their proportion of registrations. Medium and heavy truck occupants account for only about 2%

of all motor-vehicle occupant fatalities and light truck occupants account for 31%.

There were 773,000 light truck occupants and 29,000 large truck occupants injured in 1998, according to the National Highway Traffic Safety Administration.

Motorcycles

The number of registered motorcycles in the United States totaled about 3,900,000 in 1999, compared to approximately 4,700,000 a decade earlier. Although motorcycles accounted for less than 2% of the total 218,300,000 vehicle registrations in 1999, they were over-represented in the distribution of fatalities by type of vehicle. Of the 34,500 occupant deaths in motor-vehicle accidents in 1999, about 2,500 (7%) were motorcycle riders. Approximately 51,000 riders and passengers were injured in 1998 according to the National Highway Traffic Safety Administration.

Motorcycles traveled an estimated 10.4 billion miles in 1999. The 1999 mileage death rate for motorcycle riders is estimated to be about 18 occupant deaths per 100,000,000 miles of motorcycle travel, more than 14 times the mileage death rate for occupants of other types of vehicles (passenger autos, trucks, buses, etc.).

TYPES OF MOTOR VEHICLES INVOLVED IN ACCIDENTS, 1999

Type of Vehicle	In Fatal Accidents		In All Accidents		Percent of Total Vehicle Registrations[a]	No. of Occupant Fatalities
	Number	Percent	Number	Percent		
All Types	**42,200**	**100.0%**	**18,000,000**	**100.0%**	**100.0%**	**34,500[b]**
Passenger cars	20,900	49.5	11,610,000	64.5	60.9	19,900
Trucks	18,500	43.9	6,200,000	34.4	36.4	11,410
Light trucks	_14,800_	_35.1_	_5,560,000_	_30.9_	_32.6_	_10,700_
Medium/heavy trucks	_3,700_	_8.8_	_640,000_	_3.6_	_3.8_	_710_
Farm tractor, equipment	100	0.2	6,000	(c)	(d)	80
Buses, commercial	100	0.2	51,000	0.3	0.2	20
Buses, school	100	0.2	39,000	0.2	0.7	10
Motorcycles	1,900	4.5	70,000	0.4	} 1.8	2,400
Motor scooters, motor bikes	(c)	(c)	6,000	(c)		0
Other	600	1.4	18,000	0.1	(d)	680

Source: Based on reports from 9 state traffic authorities. Vehicle registrations based on data from Federal Highway Administration. Estimating procedures were changed for the 1998 edition and are not comparable to estimates in previous editions.
[a] Percentage figures are based on numbers of vehicles and do not reflect miles traveled or place of travel, both of which affect accident experience. Percents may not add due to rounding.
[b] In addition to these occupant fatalities, there were 5,800 pedestrian, 900 pedalcyclist, and 100 other deaths.
[c] Less than 0.05% or less than 50.
[d] Data not available.

REGISTRATIONS, INVOLVEMENTS, AND OCCUPANT FATALITIES BY TYPE OF VEHICLE, 1999

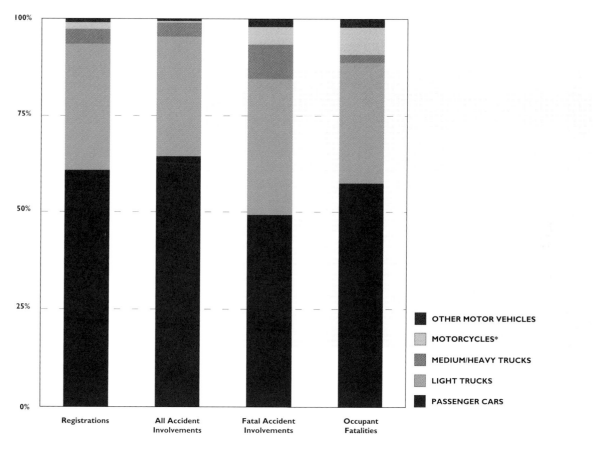

*Includes motor scooters and motorbikes.

SCHOOL BUS TRANSPORTATION, 1998

School bus-related crashes killed 126 persons and injured an estimated 17,000 persons nationwide in 1998, according to data from the National Highway Traffic Safety Administration's Fatality Analysis Reporting System (FARS) and General Estimates System (GES).

A school bus-related crash is defined by NHTSA to be any crash in which a vehicle, regardless of body design, used as a school bus is directly or indirectly involved, such as a crash involving school children alighting from a vehicle.

Over the past six years, about 67% of the deaths in fatal school bus-related crashes were occupants of vehicles other than the school bus and 23% were pedestrians. About 6% were school bus passengers and 2% were school bus drivers.

Of the pedestrians killed in school bus-related crashes over this period, approximately 78% were struck by the school bus.

Out of the people injured in school bus-related crashes from 1993 through 1998, about 42% were school bus passengers, 9% were school bus drivers, and another 44% were occupants of other vehicles. The remaining 5% were pedestrians, pedalcyclists, and other or unknown type persons.

Characteristics of school bus transportation
School Bus Fleet (http://www.schoolbusfleet/resource/98stats.htm) found that in the 1997–1998 school year, 44 states reported about 21.3 million public school pupils were transported at public expense and 29 states reported another 0.9 million private school pupils were transported at public expense. This compares to estimates from the U.S. Department of Education of enrollments in grades K–12 of about 46.8 million public school pupils and 5.9 million private school pupils nationwide. About 442,000 school buses were reported in use in 49 states and the District of Columbia and the buses in 40 states traveled about 3.2 billion route miles.

FATALITIES IN SCHOOL BUS-RELATED CRASHES, U.S., 1987–1998

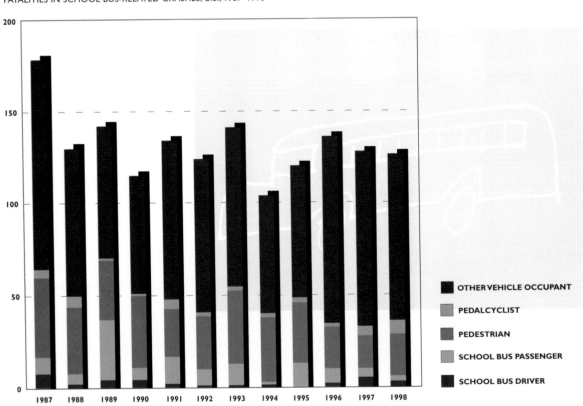

DEATHS AND INJURIES IN SCHOOL BUS-RELATED CRASHES, U.S., 1993–1998

	1993	1994	1995	1996	1997	1998
Deaths						
Total	141	104	121	136	128	126
School bus driver	1	1	0	2	5	3
School bus passenger	12	2	13	8	5	3
Pedestrian	40	35	33	23	18	23
Pedalcyclist	2	2	3	2	5	7
Occupant of other vehicle	86	64	71	101	95	90
Other or unknown	0	0	1	0	0	0
Injuries						
Total	20,000	18,000	18,000	15,000	19,000	17,000
School bus driver	2,000	1,000	2,000	1,000	2,000	2,000
School bus passenger	7,000	8,000	7,000	7,000	10,000	6,000
Pedestrian	1,000	1,000	(a)	(a)	(a)	(a)
Pedalcyclist	(a)	(a)	(a)	(a)	(a)	(a)
Occupant of other vehicle	10,000	7,000	8,000	6,000	7,000	9,000
Other or unknown	(a)	(a)	(a)	(a)	(a)	(a)

Source: National Highway Traffic Safety Administration. Traffic Safety Facts, *1993–1998 editions. Washington, DC: Author.*
[a] *Less than 500.*

PEDESTRIAN DEATHS IN SCHOOL BUS-RELATED CRASHES, U.S., 1993–1998

		Age Group			
Year	All Ages	Under 5	5–9	10–15	16 and older
1993	40	0	18	7	15
Struck by bus	*32*	*0*	*15*	*4*	*13*
1994	35	2	15	8	10
Struck by bus	*27*	*2*	*9*	*7*	*9*
1995	33	3	12	7	11
Struck by bus	*23*	*3*	*7*	*2*	*11*
1996	23	1	11	3	8
Struck by bus	*16*	*0*	*7*	*1*	*8*
1997	18	0	8	3	7
Struck by bus	*16*	*0*	*6*	*3*	*7*
1998	23	3	9	1	10
Struck by bus	*20*	*3*	*6*	*1*	*10*

Source: National Highway Traffic Safety Administration. Traffic Safety Facts, *1993–1998 editions. Washington, DC: Author.*

AGE OF DRIVER

The table below shows the total number of licensed drivers and drivers involved in accidents by selected ages and age groups. The figures in the last two columns indicate the frequency of accident involvement on the basis of the number of drivers in each age group. The fatal accident involvement rates per 100,000 drivers in each age group ranged from a low of 16 for drivers 65 to 74 years of age to a high of 57 for drivers 19 and under. The all accident involvement rates per 100 drivers in each age group ranged from 5 for drivers 65 to 74 to 29 for drivers 19 and under.

On the basis of miles driven by each age group, however, involvement rates (not shown in the table) are highest for young and old drivers. For drivers aged 16 to 19, the fatal involvement rate per 100 million vehicle miles traveled was 9.2 in 1990, about three times the overall rate for all drivers in passenger vehicles, 3.0. The rate for drivers aged 75 and over was 11.5, the highest of all age groups. The same basic U-shaped curve is found for injury accident involvement rates.[*]

[*] *Massie, D., Campbell, K., & Williams, A. (1995). Traffic accident involvement rates by driver age and gender. Accident Analysis and Prevention, 27 (1), 73-87.*

AGE OF DRIVER—TOTAL NUMBER AND NUMBER IN ACCIDENTS, 1999

| Age Group | Licensed Drivers | | Drivers in Accidents | | | | | |
| | Number | Percent | Fatal | | All | | Per No. of Drivers | |
			Number	Percent	Number	Percent	Fatal[a]	All[b]
Total	**188,167,000**	**100.0%**	**42,200**	**100.0%**	**18,000,000**	**100.0%**	**22**	**10**
Under 16	31,000	(c)	300	0.7	130,000	0.7	(d)	(d)
16	1,707,000	0.9	1,100	2.6	660,000	3.7	64	39
17	2,403,000	1.3	1,200	2.8	730,000	4.1	50	30
18	2,805,000	1.5	1,500	3.6	730,000	4.1	53	26
19	3,040,000	1.6	1,600	3.8	660,000	3.7	53	22
19 and under	9,986,000	5.4	5,700	13.5	2,910,000	16.2	57	29
20	3,106,000	1.7	1,100	2.6	560,000	3.1	35	18
21	3,030,000	1.6	1,100	2.6	530,000	2.9	36	17
22	3,027,000	1.6	1,000	2.4	490,000	2.7	33	16
23	3,141,000	1.7	900	2.1	450,000	2.5	29	14
24	3,300,000	1.8	900	2.1	430,000	2.4	27	13
20-24	15,604,000	8.4	5,000	11.8	2,460,000	13.7	32	16
25-34	53,385,000	20.1	8,100	19.2	3,780,000	21.0	21	10
35-44	42,307,000	22.5	8,100	19.4	3,580,000	19.9	19	8
45-54	34,050,000	18.1	6,100	14.5	2,490,000	13.8	18	7
55-64	21,651,000	11.5	3,800	9.0	1,340,000	7.4	18	6
65-74	16,069,000	8.5	2,500	5.9	840,000	4.7	16	5
75 and over	10,719,000	5.7	2,900	6.9	600,000	3.3	27	6

Source: National Safety Council estimates. Drivers in accidents based on reports from 11 state traffic authorities. Total licensed drivers from the Federal Highway Administration; age distribution by National Safety Council.
Note: Percents may not add to total due to rounding.
[a] *Drivers in fatal accidents per 100,000 licensed drivers in each age group.*
[b] *Drivers in all accidents per 100 licensed drivers in each age group.*
[c] *Less than 0.05.*
[d] *Rates for drivers under age 16 are substantially overstated due to the high proportion of unlicensed drivers involved.*

Of the estimated 188,167,000 licensed drivers in 1999, about 94,062,000 (50.0%) were males and 94,105,000 (50.0%) were females. Males account for about 63% of the miles driven each year, according to the latest estimates, and females for 37%. At least part of the difference in involvement rates, cited below, may be due to differences in the time, place, and circumstances of driving.

For fatal accidents, males have higher involvement rates than females. About 30,400 male drivers and 11,800

female drivers were involved in fatal accidents in 1999. The involvement rate per one billion miles driven was 18 for males and 12 for females. For all accidents, females have higher involvement rates than males. About 10,600,000 male drivers and 7,400,000 female drivers were involved in all accidents in 1999. Their involvement rates per 10 million miles driven were 63 and 74, respectively.

IMPROPER DRIVING

In most motor-vehicle accidents, factors are present relating to the driver, the vehicle and the road, and it is the interaction of these factors that often sets up the series of events that results in an accident. The table below relates only to the driver, and shows the principal kinds of improper driving in accidents in 1999 as reported by police.

Exceeding the posted speed limit or driving at an unsafe speed was the most common error in fatal accidents. Right-of-way violations predominated in the injury and all accidents categories.

While some drivers were under the influence of alcohol or other drugs, this represents the driver's physical condition—not a driving error. See page 82 for a discussion of alcohol involvement in traffic accidents.

Correcting the improper practices listed below could reduce the number of accidents. This does not mean, however, that road and vehicle conditions can be disregarded.

IMPROPER DRIVING REPORTED IN ACCIDENTS, 1999

Kind of Improper Driving	Fatal Accidents	Injury Accidents	All Accidents
Total	**100.0%**	**100.0%**	**100.0%**
Improper driving	**72.6**	**67.2**	**62.2**
Speed too fast or unsafe	23.0	13.0	10.6
Right of way	20.1	25.8	22.9
Failed to yield	*10.8*	*19.2*	*13.8*
Disregarded signal	*4.7*	*4.9*	*5.9*
Passed stop sign	*4.6*	*1.7*	*3.2*
Drove left of center	9.6	1.7	1.3
Made improper turn	1.2	2.4	3.0
Improper overtaking	1.1	0.9	1.2
Followed too closely	0.5	3.4	6.3
Other improper driving	17.1	20.3	16.9
No improper driving stated	**27.4**	**32.8**	**37.8**

Source: Based on reports from 7 state traffic authorities.

MOTOR-VEHICLE DEATHS BY STATE, UNITED STATES, 1996–1999

State	Motor-Vehicle *Traffic* Deaths (Place of Accident)				Total Motor-Vehicle Deaths[a] (Place of Residence)			
	Number		Mileage Rate[b]		Number		Population Rate[b]	
	1999	1998	1999	1998	1997[c]	1996	1997	1996
Total U.S.[a]	41,300	41,800	1.5	1.6	43,458	43,649	16.2	16.5
Alabama	1,107	1,069	2.0	2.0	1,211	1,176	28.0	27.4
Alaska	76	72	1.7	1.6	85	98	14.0	15.9
Arizona	1,024	980	2.2	2.2	971	996	21.3	22.5
Arkansas	602	625	2.1	2.2	692	636	27.4	25.4
California	3,204	3,161	1.1	1.1	3,749	4,224	11.6	13.3
Colorado	—	524	—	1.4	648	669	16.7	17.5
Connecticut	301	329	1.0	1.1	337	326	10.3	10.0
Delaware	103	115	1.2	1.4	142	105	19.3	14.4
Dist. of Columbia	46	58	1.4	1.7	87	59	16.5	10.9
Florida	2,920	2,804	2.1	2.0	2,840	2,809	19.3	19.5
Georgia	1,514	1,580	1.5	1.7	1,618	1,588	21.6	21.7
Hawaii	98	120	1.2	1.5	138	139	11.6	11.7
Idaho	278	265	2.0	2.0	283	282	23.4	23.8
Illinois	1,456	1,392	1.4	1.4	1,261	1,600	10.5	13.4
Indiana	1,019	978	1.5	1.4	960	969	16.3	16.6
Iowa	489	444	1.7	1.6	484	490	17.0	17.2
Kansas	532	493	1.9	1.8	487	521	18.6	20.2
Kentucky	819	868	1.7	1.9	845	808	21.6	20.8
Louisiana	923	812	2.2	2.0	963	911	22.1	21.0
Maine	179	184	1.3	1.4	201	177	16.1	14.3
Maryland	598	606	1.2	1.3	627	652	12.3	12.9
Massachusetts	414	406	0.8	0.8	486	458	7.9	7.5
Michigan	1,386	1,367	1.4	1.5	1,472	1,579	15.0	16.2
Minnesota	626	650	1.2	1.3	565	634	12.1	13.6
Mississippi	926	948	2.7	2.9	892	867	32.7	32.0
Missouri	1,094	1,169	1.7	1.8	1,276	1,127	23.6	21.0
Montana	220	237	2.2	2.5	270	191	30.7	21.8
Nebraska	295	315	1.6	1.8	305	301	18.4	18.3
Nevada	350	360	2.0	2.2	400	328	23.9	20.5
New Hampshire	141	129	1.2	1.1	143	134	12.2	11.6
New Jersey	665	755	1.0	1.2	814	834	10.1	10.4
New Mexico	461	424	2.0	1.9	503	443	29.2	25.9
New York	1,473	1,405	1.2	1.1	1,719	1,761	9.5	9.7
North Carolina	1,506	1,574	1.7	1.9	1,588	1,511	21.4	20.7
North Dakota	119	92	1.6	1.3	126	108	19.7	16.8
Ohio	1,430	1,421	1.3	1.3	1,407	1,429	12.5	12.8
Oklahoma	740	769	1.7	1.8	852	809	25.7	24.5
Oregon	413	538	1.2	1.6	566	533	17.5	16.7
Pennsylvania	1,549	1,485	1.5	1.5	1,648	1,594	13.7	13.2
Rhode Island	88	74	1.1	1.0	91	78	9.2	7.9
South Carolina	1,064	1,001	2.4	2.4	917	901	24.2	24.1
South Dakota	150	165	1.8	2.0	155	172	21.2	23.3
Tennessee	1,282	1,208	2.0	2.0	1,445	1,308	26.9	24.6
Texas	3,517	3,516	1.7	1.7	3,736	3,956	19.3	20.8
Utah	360	346	1.7	1.7	403	342	19.5	16.9
Vermont	92	104	1.4	1.6	86	84	14.6	14.3
Virginia	877	934	1.2	1.3	962	886	14.3	13.3
Washington	637	665	1.2	1.3	704	793	12.6	14.4
West Virginia	395	351	2.1	1.9	406	337	22.4	18.5
Wisconsin	745	709	1.3	1.3	759	798	14.6	15.4
Wyoming	189	154	2.3	2.0	133	118	27.7	24.6

Source: Motor-Vehicle Traffic Deaths are provisional counts from state traffic authorities; Total Motor-Vehicle Deaths are from the National Center for Health Statistics (see also page 144).
[a] *Includes both traffic and nontraffic motor-vehicle deaths. See definitions of motor-vehicle traffic and nontraffic accidents on page 159.*
[b] *The mileage death rate is deaths per 100,000,000 vehicle miles; the population death rate is deaths per 100,000 population. Death rates are National Safety Council estimates.*
[c] *Latest year available. See Technical Appendix for comparability.*
Note: Dash (—) indicates data not reported.

MILEAGE DEATH RATES, 1999
MOTOR-VEHICLE TRAFFIC DEATHS PER 100,000,000 VEHICLE MILES

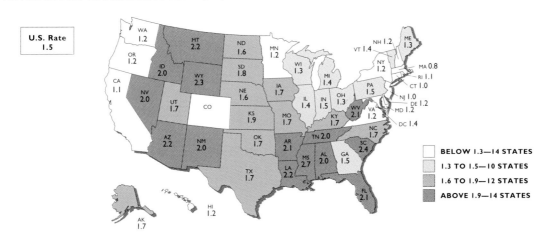

U.S. Rate
1.5

BELOW 1.3—14 STATES
1.3 TO 1.5—10 STATES
1.6 TO 1.9—12 STATES
ABOVE 1.9—14 STATES

REGISTRATION DEATH RATES, 1999
MOTOR-VEHICLE TRAFFIC DEATHS PER 10,000 MOTOR VEHICLES

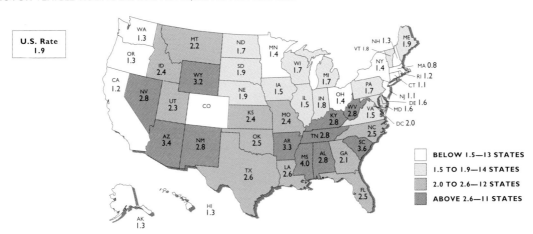

U.S. Rate
1.9

BELOW 1.5—13 STATES
1.5 TO 1.9—14 STATES
2.0 TO 2.6—12 STATES
ABOVE 2.6—11 STATES

POPULATION DEATH RATES, 1999
MOTOR-VEHICLE TRAFFIC DEATHS PER 100,000 POPULATION

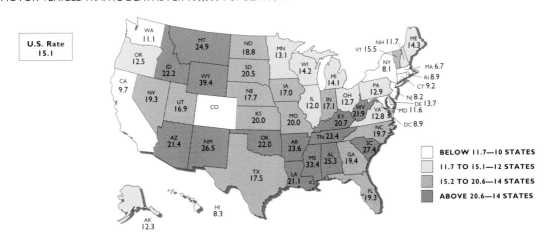

U.S. Rate
15.1

BELOW 11.7—10 STATES
11.7 TO 15.1—12 STATES
15.2 TO 20.6—14 STATES
ABOVE 20.6—14 STATES

Source: Rates estimated by National Safety Council based on data from state traffic authorities, National Center for Health Statistics, Federal Highway Administration, and the U.S. Census Bureau.

PEDESTRIANS

In 1999, there were an estimated 5,800 pedestrian deaths and 95,000 injuries in motor-vehicle accidents. About half of these deaths and injuries occur when pedestrians cross or enter streets. Walking in the roadway accounted for about 9% of pedestrian deaths and injuries, with more cases occurring while walking with traffic than against traffic.

The distribution of pedestrian deaths and injuries by action varies for persons of different ages. While crossing or entering at or between intersections was the leading type for each age group, this type varied from a low of 37.3% of the total for those aged 0 to 4 years to a high of 56.5% for those aged 65 and older (see corresponding chart).

DEATHS AND INJURIES OF PEDESTRIANS BY AGE AND ACTION, 1999

Actions		Age of Persons Killed or Injured							
	Total	0–4	5–9	10–14	15–19	20–24	25–44	45–64	65 & Over
All Actions	*100.0%*	*4.2%*	*10.0%*	*10.1%*	*11.2%*	*8.3%*	*27.4%*	*15.5%*	*13.3%*
Totals	**100.0%**	**100.0%**	**100.0%**	**100.0%**	**100.0%**	**100.0%**	**100.0%**	**100.0%**	**100.0%**
Crossing or entering at or between intersections	48.6%	37.3%	52.9%	55.3%	45.3%	45.3%	42.4%	52.7%	56.5%
Walking in roadway	8.8%	6.9%	5.9%	11.2%	12.0%	12.9%	9.1%	7.2%	6.0%
with traffic	5.7%	4.9%	4.3%	5.7%	5.7%	8.9%	6.6%	4.4%	4.5%
against traffic	3.1%	2.0%	1.6%	5.5%	6.4%	4.0%	2.5%	2.8%	1.5%
Standing (or playing) in roadway	6.4%	9.3%	4.5%	4.7%	7.7%	7.7%	8.4%	5.2%	3.4%
Pushing/working on vehicle in roadway	0.9%	0.5%	0.6%	0.0%	1.3%	1.5%	1.2%	0.7%	0.9%
Other working in roadway	2.1%	0.5%	0.2%	0.6%	0.7%	2.0%	3.9%	3.2%	1.1%
Not in roadway	2.9%	4.4%	1.6%	0.6%	3.6%	3.7%	3.0%	3.7%	2.8%
Other action	23.3%	37.3%	29.1%	21.7%	23.2%	21.0%	24.8%	20.8%	17.3%
Not stated	7.1%	3.9%	5.1%	5.9%	6.2%	5.9%	7.3%	6.6%	12.0%

Source: Based on reports from 7 state traffic authorities.

PEDESTRIAN DEATHS AND INJURIES BY AGE AND ACTION, 1999

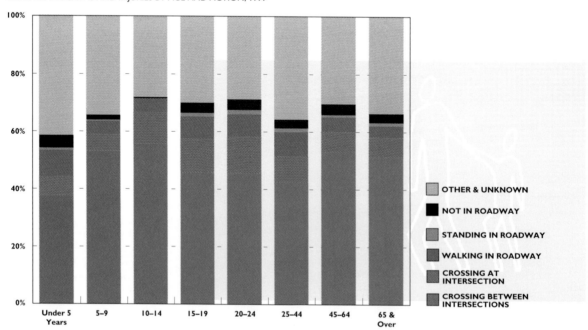

The estimated number of deaths from pedalcycle–motor-vehicle collisions increased from about 750 in 1940 to 1,200 in 1980, then declined to about 900 in 1999. Nonfatal disabling injuries were estimated to number 70,000 in 1999.

The 25-44 year age group accounted for the greatest number of pedalcycle fatalities in 1997 with 233 of the 757 total deaths. The second leading age group was 5-14 with 197 fatalities (see corresponding chart).

Deaths of pedalcycle riders not involving motor vehicles numbered 11 in 1995, 87 in 1996, and 118 in 1997, according to tabulations of National Center for Health Statistics mortality data. Emergency-room–treated injuries associated with bicycles and bicycle accessories totaled 577,621 in 1998, according to U.S. Consumer

Product Safety Commission estimates (see also page 114). Males accounted for more than 87% of all pedalcycle deaths in 1997, more than seven times the female fatalities.

The Consumer Product Safety Commission reports that bike helmet use has increased from 18% in 1991 to 50% in 1998. About 38% of adults and 69% of children under 16 reported wearing bike helmets regularly. The Bicycle Helmet Safety Institute estimates that bicycle helmets reduce the risk of all head injuries by up to 85% and reduce the risk of severe head injuries by about one third. In 1998, 15 states and over 60 localities reported having laws requiring pedalcycle helmet use.

Source: National Safety Council tabulations of National Center for Health Statistics mortality data. Rodgers, G.B., & Tinsworth, D. (1999). Bike Helmets. Consumer Product Safety Review, (4), 2-4.

PEDALCYCLE FATALITIES BY SEX AND AGE GROUP, UNITED STATES, 1997

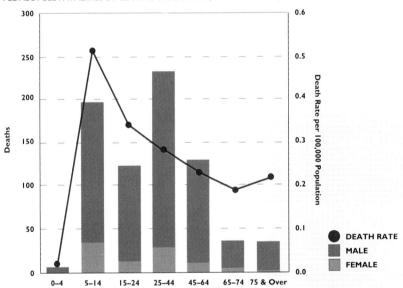

PEDALCYCLE FATALITIES BY MONTH, UNITED STATES, 1997

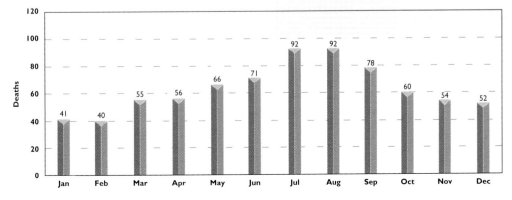

WORK ZONE DEATHS AND INJURIES

In 1998 there were 772 people killed and 37,824 people injured in work zone crashes (see table below). Compared to 1997, work zone fatalities and injuries increased 17% and 4%, respectively. Of the 772 people killed in work zones, 652 were in construction zones, 52 were in maintenance zones, 15 were in utility zones, and 53 were in an unknown type of zone.

Based on a National Safety Council survey of State Governor's Highway Safety Representatives, 40 states plus the District of Columbia reported having either work zone laws in effect or special penalties for violations in work zones such as increased/double fines as of May 2000.

PERSONS KILLED AND INJURED IN WORK ZONES, UNITED STATES, 1998

	Total	Vehicle Occupants	Pedestrians	Pedalcyclists	Other Nonmotorists
Killed	772	658	101	10	3
Injured	37,824	37,209	483	44	88

Source: National Safety Council tabulations of data from National Highway Traffic Safety Administration—1998 Fatality Analysis Reporting System (FARS) and 1998 General Estimates Systems (GES).

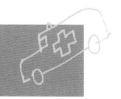

EMERGENCY VEHICLES INVOLVED IN ACCIDENTS

CRASHES INVOLVING EMERGENCY VEHICLES, UNITED STATES, 1998

	AMBULANCE		FIRE TRUCK/CAR		POLICE CAR	
	Total	Emergency Use[a]	Total	Emergency Use[a]	Total	Emergency Use[a]
Emergency vehicles in fatal crashes	25	16	17	9	83	43
Emergency vehicles in injury crashes	2,306	1,756	781	680	8,210	3,897
Emergency Vehicles in All Crashes	**4,615**	**2,683**	**3,188**	**2,421**	**24,417**	**10,205**
Emergency vehicle drivers killed	2	1	4	1	17	6
Emergency vehicle passengers killed	7	5	3	1	3	2
Occupants of OMV[b] killed	18	13	12	7	66	38
Nonmotorists killed	2	1	3	2	10	2
Total Killed in Crashes	**29**	**20**	**22**	**11**	**96**	**48**
Total Injured in Crashes	**3,274**	**2,382**	**1,035**	**834**	**12,339**	**5,714**

Source: National Safety Council tabulations of data from National Highway Traffic Safety Administration—1998 Fatality Analysis Reporting System (FARS) and 1998 General Estimates Systems (GES).
[a] Emergency lights and/or sirens in use.
[b] Other motor vehicle.

FLEET ACCIDENT RATES
BY TYPE OF VEHICLE

FLEET ACCIDENT RATES BY TYPE OF VEHICLE, 1997–1999, SUMMARIZED FROM THE NATIONAL FLEET SAFETY CONTEST

Type of Vehicle/Industry	1999			Accidents per 1,000,000 Vehicle Miles	
	No. of Fleets Reporting	No. of Vehicles	Vehicle Miles (Thousands)	1999	1997–1999
TRUCKS	**223**	**46,979**	**1,523,245**	**4.72**	**4.83**
Automobile Transporters	**18**	**6,880**	**791,243**	**4.97**	**5.02**
Truckaway	15	6,165	670,345	5.24	5.23
Driveaway	3	715	120,899	3.47	3.38
Government	**5**	**938**	**12,132**	**9.15**	**7.91**
Mail Contractors	**17**	**881**	**145,715**	**0.96**	**1.16**
Tractor-Trailers	10	735	138,928	0.91	1.11
Straight Truck	7	146	6,786	2.06	2.02
Postal Service	**90**	**4,641**	**36,414**	**13.78**	**13.91**
Intercity	5	233	844	9.48	8.06
City	9	524	5,463	14.09	10.65
Light Delivery Vehicles (LLV)	75	3,858	30,107	13.92	15.06
Trucks—Other Industries	**48**	**2,149**	**166**	**4.38**	**15.29**
Intercity	24	2,029	122,092	3.01	3.57
City	14	551	51,912	4.22	5.43
Utilities	**55**	**31,059**	**363,737**	**5.24**	**5.15**
Electric Utilities	24	20,774	233,797	4.84	4.75
Water Distribution Utilities	7	905	7,737	12.67	12.53
Communication Utilities	3	124	1,684	1.78	1.61
Gas Distribution Utilities	16	7,586	90,133	6.31	6.24
Gas Transmission Utilities	5	1,623	30,387	3.46	3.83
BUSES	**39**	**2,595**	**79,042**	**12.94**	**18.78**
Intercity Bus	**7**	**395**	**28,750**	**3.30**	**3.24**
Scheduled Route Service	6	389	28,611	3.32	3.32
School Bus	**15**	**1,196**	**16,381**	**8.36**	**9.27**
Transit Bus	**17**	**1,004**	**33,911**	**23.33**	**31.78**
CARS	**11**	**410**	**5,350**	**8.04**	**8.03**
Emergency & Medical Response	**3**	**69**	**967**	**27.91**	**24.29**
Passenger Car—Other Industries	**7**	**315**	**4,217**	**3.79**	**5.84**
Postal Service	**1**	**26**	**166**	**0.00**	**3.61**

Source: Based upon reports of National Safety Council members participating in the National Fleet Safety Contest. The data should not be interpreted as representative of the industries listed or of Council members.

Definitions
Reportable Accident—Any incident involving death, injury or property damage, regardless of preventability of the incident or the cost of the property damage.
Intercity Operation—Includes fleets that travel more than 50 miles from their terminal.
City Operation—Includes fleets that travel less than 50 miles from their terminal.

Note: The totals for Trucks, Buses and Cars may include some other industries/types of operation that have not been listed separately.

NATIONAL SAFETY COUNCIL® INJURY FACTS™ 2000 EDITION   99

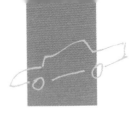

MOTOR-VEHICLE DEATHS AND RATES

MOTOR-VEHICLE DEATHS AND RATES, UNITED STATES, 1913–1999

Year	No. of Deaths	Estimated No. of Vehicles (Millions)	Estimated Vehicle Miles (Billions)	Estimated No. of Drivers (Millions)	Death Rates Per 10,000 Motor Vehicles	Per 100,000,000 Vehicle Miles	Per 100,000 Population
1913	4,200	1.3	(a)	2.0	33.38	(a)	4.4
1914	4,700	1.8	(a)	3.0	26.65	(a)	4.8
1915	6,600	2.5	(a)	3.0	26.49	(a)	6.6
1916	8,200	3.6	(a)	5.0	22.66	(a)	8.1
1917	10,200	5.1	(a)	7.0	19.93	(a)	10.0
1918	10,700	6.2	(a)	9.0	17.37	(a)	10.3
1919	11,200	7.6	(a)	12.0	14.78	(a)	10.7
1920	12,500	9.2	(a)	14.0	13.53	(a)	11.7
1921	13,900	10.5	(a)	16.0	13.25	(a)	12.9
1922	15,300	12.3	(a)	19.0	12.47	(a)	13.9
1923	18,400	15.1	85	22.0	12.18	21.65	16.5
1924	19,400	17.6	104	26.0	11.02	18.65	17.1
1925	21,900	20.1	122	30.0	10.89	17.95	19.1
1926	23,400	22.2	141	33.0	10.54	16.59	20.1
1927	25,800	23.3	158	34.0	11.07	16.33	21.8
1928	28,000	24.7	173	37.0	11.34	16.18	23.4
1929	31,200	26.7	197	40.0	11.69	15.84	25.7
1930	32,900	26.7	206	40.0	12.32	15.97	26.7
1931	33,700	26.1	216	39.0	12.91	15.60	27.2
1932	29,500	24.4	200	36.0	12.09	14.75	23.6
1933	31,363	24.2	201	35.0	12.96	15.60	25.0
1934	36,101	25.3	216	37.0	14.27	16.71	28.6
1935	36,369	26.5	229	39.0	13.72	15.88	28.6
1936	38,089	28.5	252	42.0	13.36	15.11	29.7
1937	39,643	30.1	270	44.0	13.19	14.68	30.8
1938	32,582	29.8	271	44.0	10.93	12.02	25.1
1939	32,386	31.0	285	46.0	10.44	11.35	24.7
1940	34,501	32.5	302	48.0	10.63	11.42	26.1
1941	39,969	34.9	334	52.0	11.45	11.98	30.0
1942	28,309	33.0	268	49.0	8.58	10.55	21.1
1943	23,823	30.9	208	46.0	7.71	11.44	17.8
1944	24,282	30.5	213	45.0	7.97	11.42	18.3
1945	28,076	31.0	250	46.0	9.05	11.22	21.2
1946	33,411	34.4	341	50.0	9.72	9.80	23.9
1947	32,697	37.8	371	53.0	8.64	8.82	22.8
1948	32,259	41.1	398	55.0	7.85	8.11	22.1
1949	31,701	44.7	424	59.3	7.09	7.47	21.3
1950	34,763	49.2	458	62.2	7.07	7.59	23.0
1951	36,996	51.9	491	64.4	7.13	7.53	24.1
1952	37,794	53.3	514	66.8	7.10	7.36	24.3
1953	37,956	56.3	544	69.9	6.74	6.97	24.0
1954	35,586	58.6	562	72.2	6.07	6.33	22.1
1955	38,426	62.8	606	74.7	6.12	6.34	23.4
1956	39,628	65.2	631	77.9	6.07	6.28	23.7
1957	38,702	67.6	647	79.6	5.73	5.98	22.7
1958	36,981	68.8	665	81.5	5.37	5.56	21.3
1959	37,910	72.1	700	84.5	5.26	5.41	21.5
1960	38,137	74.5	719	87.4	5.12	5.31	21.2
1961	38,091	76.4	738	88.9	4.98	5.16	20.8
1962	40,804	79.7	767	92.0	5.12	5.32	22.0
1963	43,564	83.5	805	93.7	5.22	5.41	23.1
1964	47,700	87.3	847	95.6	5.46	5.63	25.0
1965	49,163	91.8	888	99.0	5.36	5.54	25.4
1966	53,041	95.9	930	101.0	5.53	5.70	27.1
1967	52,924	98.9	962	103.2	5.35	5.50	26.8
1968	54,862	103.1	1,016	105.4	5.32	5.40	27.5
1969	55,791	107.4	1,071	108.3	5.19	5.21	27.7
1970	54,633	111.2	1,120	111.5	4.92	4.88	26.8
1971	54,381	116.3	1,186	114.4	4.68	4.57	26.3
1972	56,278	122.3	1,268	118.4	4.60	4.43	26.9
1973	55,511	129.8	1,309	121.6	4.28	4.24	26.3
1974	46,402	134.9	1,290	125.6	3.44	3.59	21.8
1975	45,853	137.9	1,330	129.8	3.33	3.45	21.3
1976	47,038	143.5	1,412	133.9	3.28	3.33	21.6

See source and footnotes on page 101.

MOTOR-VEHICLE DEATHS AND RATES, UNITED STATES, 1913–1999, Cont.

Year	No. of Deaths	Estimated No. of Vehicles (Millions)	Estimated Vehicle Miles (Billions)	Estimated No. of Drivers (Millions)	Death Rates		
					Per 10,000 Motor Vehicles	Per 100,000,000 Vehicle Miles	Per 100,000 Population
1977	49,510	148.8	1,477	138.1	3.33	3.35	22.5
1978	52,411	153.6	1,548	140.8	3.41	3.39	23.6
1979	53,524	159.6	1,529	143.3	3.35	3.50	23.8
1980	53,172	161.6	1,521	145.3	3.29	3.50	23.4
1981	51,385	164.1	1,556	147.1	3.13	3.30	22.4
1982	45,779	165.2	1,592	150.3	2.77	2.88	19.8
1983	44,452	169.4	1,657	154.2	2.62	2.68	19.0
1984	46,263	171.8	1,718	155.4	2.69	2.69	19.6
1985	45,901	177.1	1,774	156.9	2.59	2.59	19.3
1986	47,865	181.4	1,835	159.5	2.63	2.60	19.9
1987	48,290	183.9	1,924	161.8	2.63	2.51	19.9
1988	49,078	189.0	2,026	162.9	2.60	2.42	20.1
1989	47,575	191.7	2,107	165.6	2.48	2.26	19.3
1990	46,814	192.9	2,148	167.0	2.43	2.18	18.8
1991	43,536	192.5	2,172	169.0	2.26	2.00	17.3
1992	40,982	194.4	2,240	173.1	2.11	1.83	16.1
1993	41,893	198.0	2,297	173.1	2.12	1.82	16.3
1994	42,524	201.8	2,360	175.4	2.11	1.80	16.3
1995	43,363	205.3	2,423	176.6	2.11	1.79	16.5
1996	43,649	210.4	2,486	179.5	2.07	1.76	16.5
1997[b]	43,458	211.5	2,562	182.7	2.05	1.70	16.2
1998[b]	41,800	215.0	2,625	185.0	1.94	1.59	15.5
1999[c]	41,300	218.3	2,679	188.2	1.89	1.54	15.1
Changes							
1989 to 1999	−13%	+14%	+27%	+14%	−24%	−32%	−22%
1998 to 1999	−1%	+2%	+2%	+2%	−3%	−3%	−3%

Source: Deaths from National Center for Health Statistics except 1964, 1998, and 1999, which are National Safety Council estimates based on data from state traffic authorities. See Technical Appendix for comparability. Motor-vehicle registrations, mileage, and drivers estimated by Federal Highway Administration except 1999 vehicles which is a National Safety Council estimate.
[a] *Mileage data inadequate prior to 1923.*
[b] *Revised.*
[c] *Preliminary.*

MOTOR-VEHICLE DEATH RATES BY POPULATION, VEHICLES, AND MILEAGE, UNITED STATES, 1989–1999

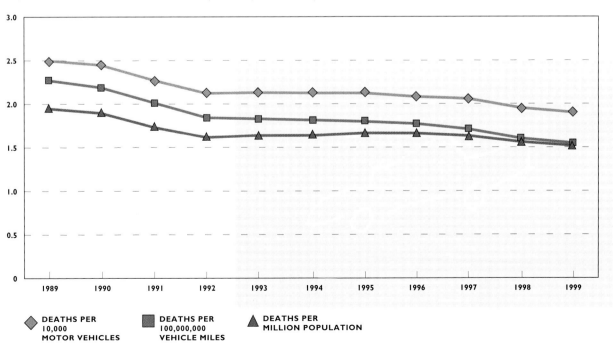

◆ DEATHS PER 10,000 MOTOR VEHICLES ■ DEATHS PER 100,000,000 VEHICLE MILES ▲ DEATHS PER MILLION POPULATION

MOTOR-VEHICLE
DEATHS BY TYPE OF ACCIDENT

MOTOR-VEHICLE DEATHS BY TYPE OF ACCIDENT, UNITED STATES, 1913–1999

Year	Total Deaths	Deaths from Collision with—							Deaths from Noncollision Accidents	Nontraffic Deaths[a]
		Pedestrians	Other Motor Vehicles	Railroad Trains	Streetcars	Pedal-cycles	Animal-Drawn Vehicle or Animal	Fixed Objects		
1913	4,200	(b)	(b)	(b)	(b)	(b)	(b)	(b)	(b)	(c)
1914	4,700	(b)	(b)	(b)	(b)	(b)	(b)	(b)	(b)	(c)
1915	6,600	(b)	(b)	(b)	(b)	(b)	(b)	(b)	(b)	(c)
1916	8,200	(b)	(b)	(b)	(b)	(b)	(b)	(b)	(b)	(c)
1917	10,200	(b)	(b)	(b)	(b)	(b)	(b)	(b)	(b)	(c)
1918	10,700	(b)	(b)	(b)	(b)	(b)	(b)	(b)	(b)	(c)
1919	11,200	(b)	(b)	(b)	(b)	(b)	(b)	(b)	(b)	(c)
1920	12,500	(b)	(b)	(b)	(b)	(b)	(b)	(b)	(b)	(c)
1921	13,900	(b)	(b)	(b)	(b)	(b)	(b)	(b)	(b)	(c)
1922	15,300	(b)	(b)	(b)	(b)	(b)	(b)	(b)	(b)	(c)
1923	18,400	(b)	(b)	(b)	(b)	(b)	(b)	(b)	(b)	(c)
1924	19,400	(b)	(b)	1,130	410	(b)	(b)	(b)	(b)	(c)
1925	21,900	(b)	(b)	1,410	560	(b)	(b)	(b)	(b)	(c)
1926	23,400	(b)	(b)	1,730	520	(b)	(b)	(b)	(b)	(c)
1927	25,800	10,820	3,430	1,830	520	(b)	(b)	(b)	(b)	(c)
1928	28,000	11,420	4,310	2,140	570	(b)	(b)	540	8,070	(c)
1929	31,200	12,250	5,400	2,050	530	(b)	(b)	620	9,380	(c)
1930	32,900	12,900	5,880	1,830	480	(b)	(b)	720	9,970	(c)
1931	33,700	13,370	6,820	1,710	440	(b)	(b)	870	9,570	(c)
1932	29,500	11,490	6,070	1,520	320	350	400	800	8,500	(c)
1933	31,363	12,840	6,470	1,437	318	400	310	900	8,680	(c)
1934	36,101	14,480	8,110	1,457	332	500	360	1,040	9,820	(c)
1935	36,369	14,350	8,750	1,587	253	450	250	1,010	9,720	(c)
1936	38,089	15,250	9,500	1,697	269	650	250	1,060	9,410	(c)
1937	39,643	15,500	10,320	1,810	264	700	200	1,160	9,690	(c)
1938	32,582	12,850	8,900	1,490	165	720	170	940	7,350	(c)
1939	32,386	12,400	8,700	1,330	150	710	200	1,000	7,900	(c)
1940	34,501	12,700	10,100	1,707	132	750	210	1,100	7,800	(c)
1941	39,969	13,550	12,500	1,840	118	910	250	1,350	9,450	(c)
1942	28,309	10,650	7,300	1,754	124	650	240	850	6,740	(c)
1943	23,823	9,900	5,300	1,448	171	450	160	700	5,690	(c)
1944	24,282	9,900	5,700	1,663	175	400	140	700	5,600	(c)
1945	28,076	11,000	7,150	1,703	163	500	130	800	6,600	(c)
1946	33,411	11,600	9,400	1,703	174	450	130	950	8,900	(c)
1947	32,697	10,450	9,900	1,736	102	550	150	1,000	8,800	(c)
1948	32,259	9,950	10,200	1,474	83	500	100	1,000	8,950	(c)
1949	31,701	8,800	10,500	1,452	56	550	140	1,100	9,100	838
1950	34,763	9,000	11,650	1,541	89	440	120	1,300	10,600	900
1951	36,996	9,150	13,100	1,573	46	390	100	1,400	11,200	966
1952	37,794	8,900	13,500	1,429	32	430	130	1,450	11,900	970
1953	37,956	8,750	13,400	1,506	26	420	120	1,500	12,200	1,026
1954	35,586	8,000	12,800	1,289	28	380	90	1,500	11,500	1,004
1955	38,426	8,200	14,500	1,490	15	410	90	1,600	12,100	989
1956	39,628	7,900	15,200	1,377	11	440	100	1,600	13,000	888
1957	38,702	7,850	15,400	1,376	13	460	80	1,700	11,800	1,016
1958	36,981	7,650	14,200	1,316	9	450	80	1,650	11,600	929
1959	37,910	7,850	14,900	1,202	6	480	70	1,600	11,800	948
1960	38,137	7,850	14,800	1,368	5	460	80	1,700	11,900	995
1961	38,091	7,650	14,700	1,267	5	490	80	1,700	12,200	1,065
1962	40,804	7,900	16,400	1,245	3	500	90	1,750	12,900	1,029
1963	43,564	8,200	17,600	1,385	10	580	80	1,900	13,800	990
1964	47,700	9,000	19,600	1,580	5	710	100	2,100	14,600	1,123
1965	49,163	8,900	20,800	1,556	5	680	120	2,200	14,900	1,113
1966	53,041	9,400	22,200	1,800	2	740	100	2,500	16,300	1,108
1967	52,924	9,400	22,000	1,620	3	750	100	2,350	16,700	1,165
1968	54,862	9,900	22,400	1,570	4	790	100	2,700	17,400	1,061
1969	55,791	10,100	23,700	1,495	2	800	100	3,900[d]	15,700[d]	1,155
1970	54,633	9,900	23,200	1,459	3	780	100	3,800	15,400	1,140
1971	54,381	9,900	23,100	1,378	2	800	100	3,800	15,300	1,015
1972	56,278	10,300	23,900	1,260	2	1,000	100	3,900	15,800	1,064
1973	55,511	10,200	23,600	1,194	2	1,000	100	3,800	15,600	1,164
1974	46,402	8,500	19,700	1,209	1	1,000	100	3,100	12,800	1,088
1975	45,853	8,400	19,550	979	1	1,000	100	3,130	12,700	1,033
1976	47,038	8,600	20,100	1,033	2	1,000	100	3,200	13,000	1,026

See source and footnotes on page 103.

MOTOR-VEHICLE DEATHS BY TYPE OF ACCIDENT, UNITED STATES, 1913–1999, Cont.

| Year | Total Deaths | Deaths from Collision with— | | | | | | | Deaths from Noncollision Accidents | Nontraffic Deaths[a] |
		Pedestrians	Other Motor Vehicles	Railroad Trains	Streetcars	Pedal-cycles	Animal-Drawn Vehicle or Animal	Fixed Objects		
1977	49,510	9,100	21,200	902	3	1,100	100	3,400	13,700	1,053
1978	52,411	9,600	22,400	986	1	1,200	100	3,600	14,500	1,074
1979	53,524	9,800	23,100	826	1	1,200	100	3,700	14,800	1,271
1980	53,172	9,700	23,000	739	1	1,200	100	3,700	14,700	1,242
1981	51,385	9,400	22,200	668	1	1,200	100	3,600	14,200	1,189
1982	45,779	8,400	19,800	554	1	1,100	100	3,200	12,600	1,066
1983	44,452	8,200	19,200	520	1	1,100	100	3,100	12,200	1,024
1984	46,263	8,500	20,000	630	0	1,100	100	3,200	12,700	1,055
1985	45,901	8,500	19,900	538	2	1,100	100	3,200	12,600	1,079
1986	47,865	8,900	20,800	574	2	1,100	100	3,300	13,100	998
1987	48,290	7,500[e]	20,700	554	1	1,000[e]	100	13,200[e]	5,200[e]	993
1988	49,078	7,700	20,900	638	2	1,000	100	13,400	5,300	1,054
1989	47,575	7,800	20,300	720	2	900	100	12,900	4,900	989
1990	46,814	7,300	19,900	623	2	900	100	13,100	4,900	987
1991	43,536	6,600	18,200	541	1	800	100	12,600	4,700	915
1992	40,982	6,300	17,600	521	2	700	100	11,700	4,100	997
1993	41,893	6,400	18,300	553	3	800	100	11,500	4,200	994
1994	42,524	6,300	18,900	549	1	800	100	11,500	4,400	1,017
1995	43,363	6,400	19,000	514	(c)	800	100	12,100	4,400	1,032
1996	43,649	6,100	19,600	373	(c)	800	100	12,100	4,600	1,127
1997[f]	43,458	5,900	19,900	371	(c)	800	100	12,000	4,400	1,118
1998[f]	41,800	5,900	18,500	400	(c)	700	100	12,000	4,200	1,000
1999[g]	41,300	5,800	18,800	300	(c)	900	100	11,100	4,300	1,000
Changes in Deaths										
1989 to 1999	−13%	−26%	−7%	−58%	—	0%	0%	−14%	−12%	+1%
1998 to 1999	−1%	−2%	+2%	−25%	—	+29%	0%	−8%	+2%	0%

Source: Total deaths from National Center for Health Statistics except 1964 and 1998-1999, which are National Safety Council estimates based on data from state traffic authorities and Federal Highway Administration. Most totals by type are estimated and may not add to the total deaths. See Technical Appendix for comparability.
[a] See definition, page 159. Nontraffic deaths are included in appropriate accident type totals in table; in 1997, 47% of the specified nontraffic deaths were pedestrians.
[b] Insufficient data for approximations.
[c] Data not available.
[d] 1969 through 1986 totals are not comparable to previous years.
[e] Procedures and benchmarks for estimating deaths for certain types of accidents were changed for the 1990 edition. Estimates for 1987 and later years are not comparable to earlier years.
[f] Revised.
[g] Preliminary.

MOTOR-VEHICLE DEATHS BY TYPE OF ACCIDENT, UNITED STATES, 1999

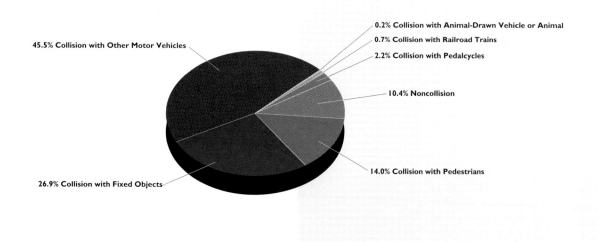

45.5% Collision with Other Motor Vehicles

26.9% Collision with Fixed Objects

0.2% Collision with Animal-Drawn Vehicle or Animal
0.7% Collision with Railroad Trains
2.2% Collision with Pedalcycles
10.4% Noncollision
14.0% Collision with Pedestrians

MOTOR-VEHICLE DEATHS BY AGE

MOTOR-VEHICLE DEATHS BY AGE, UNITED STATES, 1913–1999

Year	All Ages	Under 5 Years	5–14 Years	15–24 Years	25–44 Years	45–64 Years	65–74 Years	75 & Over[a]
1913	4,200	300	1,100	600	1,100	800	300	
1914	4,700	300	1,200	700	1,200	900	400	
1915	6,600	400	1,500	1,000	1,700	1,400	600	
1916	8,200	600	1,800	1,300	2,100	1,700	700	
1917	10,200	700	2,400	1,400	2,700	2,100	900	
1918	10,700	800	2,700	1,400	2,500	2,300	1,000	
1919	11,200	900	3,000	1,400	2,500	2,100	1,300	
1920	12,500	1,000	3,300	1,700	2,800	2,300	1,400	
1921	13,900	1,100	3,400	1,800	3,300	2,700	1,600	
1922	15,300	1,100	3,500	2,100	3,700	3,100	1,800	
1923	18,400	1,200	3,700	2,800	4,600	3,900	2,200	
1924	19,400	1,400	3,800	2,900	4,700	4,100	2,500	
1925	21,900	1,400	3,900	3,600	5,400	4,800	2,800	
1926	23,400	1,400	3,900	3,900	5,900	5,200	3,100	
1927	25,800	1,600	4,000	4,300	6,600	5,800	3,500	
1928	28,000	1,600	3,800	4,900	7,200	6,600	3,900	
1929	31,200	1,600	3,900	5,700	8,000	7,500	4,500	
1930	32,900	1,500	3,600	6,200	8,700	8,000	4,900	
1931	33,700	1,500	3,600	6,300	9,100	8,200	5,000	
1932	29,500	1,200	2,900	5,100	8,100	7,400	4,800	
1933	31,363	1,274	3,121	5,649	8,730	7,947	4,642	
1934	36,101	1,210	3,182	6,561	10,232	9,530	5,386	
1935	36,369	1,253	2,951	6,755	10,474	9,562	5,374	
1936	38,089	1,324	3,026	7,184	10,807	10,089	5,659	
1937	39,643	1,303	2,991	7,800	10,877	10,475	6,197	
1938	32,582	1,122	2,511	6,016	8,772	8,711	5,450	
1939	32,386	1,192	2,339	6,318	8,917	8,292	5,328	
1940	34,501	1,176	2,584	6,846	9,362	8,882	5,651	
1941	39,969	1,378	2,838	8,414	11,069	9,829	6,441	
1942	28,309	1,069	1,991	5,932	7,747	7,254	4,316	
1943	23,823	1,132	1,959	4,522	6,454	5,996	3,760	
1944	24,282	1,203	2,093	4,561	6,514	5,982	3,929	
1945	28,076	1,290	2,386	5,358	7,578	6,794	4,670	
1946	33,411	1,568	2,508	7,445	8,955	7,532	5,403	
1947	32,697	1,502	2,275	7,251	8,775	7,468	5,426	
1948	32,259	1,635	2,337	7,218	8,702	7,190	3,173	2,004
1949	31,701	1,667	2,158	6,772	8,892	7,073	3,116	2,023
1950	34,763	1,767	2,152	7,600	10,214	7,728	3,264	2,038
1951	36,996	1,875	2,300	7,713	11,253	8,276	3,444	2,135
1952	37,794	1,951	2,295	8,115	11,380	8,463	3,472	2,118
1953	37,956	2,019	2,368	8,169	11,302	8,318	3,508	2,271
1954	35,586	1,864	2,332	7,571	10,521	7,848	3,247	2,203
1955	38,426	1,875	2,406	8,656	11,448	8,372	3,455	2,214
1956	39,628	1,770	2,640	9,169	11,551	8,573	3,657	2,268
1957	38,702	1,785	2,604	8,667	11,230	8,545	3,560	2,311
1958	36,981	1,791	2,710	8,388	10,414	7,922	3,535	2,221
1959	37,910	1,842	2,719	8,969	10,358	8,263	3,487	2,272
1960	38,137	1,953	2,814	9,117	10,189	8,294	3,457	2,313
1961	38,091	1,891	2,802	9,088	10,212	8,267	3,467	2,364
1962	40,804	1,903	3,028	10,157	10,701	8,812	3,696	2,507
1963	43,564	1,991	3,063	11,123	11,356	9,506	3,786	2,739
1964	47,700	2,120	3,430	12,400	12,500	10,200	4,150	2,900
1965	49,163	2,059	3,526	13,395	12,595	10,509	4,077	3,002
1966	53,041	2,182	3,869	15,298	13,282	11,051	4,217	3,142
1967	52,924	2,067	3,845	15,646	12,987	10,902	4,285	3,192
1968	54,862	1,987	4,105	16,543	13,602	11,031	4,261	3,333
1969	55,791	2,077	4,045	17,443	13,868	11,012	4,210	3,136
1970	54,633	1,915	4,159	16,720	13,446	11,099	4,084	3,210
1971	54,381	1,885	4,256	17,103	13,307	10,471	4,108	3,251
1972	56,278	1,896	4,258	17,942	13,758	10,836	4,138	3,450
1973	55,511	1,998	4,124	18,032	14,013	10,216	3,892	3,236
1974	46,402	1,546	3,332	15,905	11,834	8,159	3,071	2,555
1975	45,853	1,576	3,286	15,672	11,969	7,663	3,047	2,640
1976	47,038	1,532	3,175	16,650	12,112	7,770	3,082	2,717

See source and footnotes on page 105.

MOTOR-VEHICLE DEATHS BY AGE, UNITED STATES, 1913–1999, Cont.

Year	All Ages	Under 5 Years	5–14 Years	15–24 Years	25–44 Years	45–64 Years	65–74 Years	75 & Over[a]
1977	49,510	1,472	3,142	18,092	13,031	8,000	3,060	2,713
1978	52,411	1,551	3,130	19,164	14,574	8,048	3,217	2,727
1979	53,524	1,461	2,952	19,369	15,658	8,162	3,171	2,751
1980	53,172	1,426	2,747	19,040	16,133	8,022	2,991	2,813
1981	51,385	1,256	2,575	17,363	16,447	7,818	3,090	2,836
1982	45,779	1,300	2,301	15,324	14,469	6,879	2,825	2,681
1983	44,452	1,233	2,241	14,289	14,323	6,690	2,827	2,849
1984	46,263	1,138	2,263	14,738	15,036	6,954	3,020	3,114
1985	45,901	1,195	2,319	14,277	15,034	6,885	3,014	3,177
1986	47,865	1,188	2,350	15,227	15,844	6,799	3,096	3,361
1987	48,290	1,190	2,397	14,447	16,405	7,021	3,277	3,553
1988	49,078	1,220	2,423	14,406	16,580	7,245	3,429	3,775
1989	47,575	1,221	2,266	12,941	16,571	7,287	3,465	3,824
1990	46,814	1,123	2,059	12,607	16,488	7,282	3,350	3,905
1991	43,536	1,076	2,011	11,664	15,082	6,616	3,193	3,894
1992	40,982	1,020	1,904	10,305	14,071	6,597	3,247	3,838
1993	41,893	1,081	1,963	10,500	14,283	6,711	3,116	4,239
1994	42,524	1,139	2,026	10,660	13,966	7,097	3,385	4,251
1995	43,363	1,004	2,055	10,600	14,618	7,428	3,300	4,358
1996	43,649	1,035	1,980	10,576	14,482	7,749	3,419	4,408
1997[b]	43,458	933	1,967	10,208	14,167	8,134	3,370	4,679
1998[b]	41,800	900	1,900	9,700	13,400	8,100	3,500	4,300
1999[c]	41,300	900	1,900	9,800	12,300	8,400	3,300	4,700
Changes in Deaths								
1989 to 1999	–13%	–26%	–16%	–24%	–26%	+15%	–5%	+23%
1998 to 1999	–1%	0%	0%	+1%	–8%	+4%	–6%	+9%

Source: 1913 to 1932 calculated from National Center for Health Statistics data for registration states; 1933 to 1963, 1965 to 1997 are NCHS totals. All other figures are National Safety Council estimates. See Technical Appendix for comparability.
[a] *Includes "age unknown." In 1997 these deaths numbered 22.*
[b] *Revised.*
[c] *Preliminary.*

MOTOR-VEHICLE DEATHS BY AGE, UNITED STATES, 1999

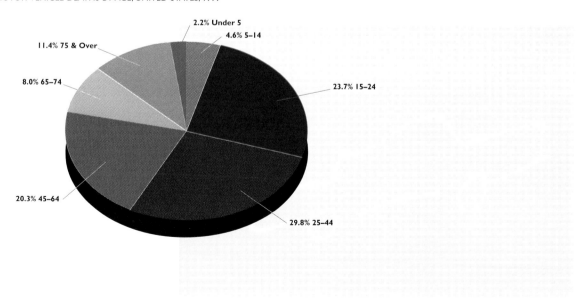

2.2% Under 5
4.6% 5–14
11.4% 75 & Over
8.0% 65–74
23.7% 15–24
20.3% 45–64
29.8% 25–44

MOTOR-VEHICLE DEATH RATES

MOTOR-VEHICLE DEATH RATES[a] BY AGE, UNITED STATES, 1913–1999

Year	All Ages	Under 5 Years	5–14 Years	15–24 Years	25–44 Years	45–64 Years	65–74 Years	75 & Over
1913	4.4	2.3	5.5	3.1	3.8	5.3	8.5	
1914	4.8	2.5	5.7	3.5	4.1	6.2	9.3	
1915	6.6	3.5	7.3	5.0	5.6	8.8	13.5	
1916	8.1	4.7	8.6	6.0	7.0	10.7	15.8	
1917	10.0	5.6	10.6	7.4	8.6	12.6	18.6	
1918	10.3	6.9	12.3	7.7	8.3	13.7	21.2	
1919	10.7	7.5	13.9	7.5	8.1	12.4	24.1	
1920	11.7	8.6	14.6	8.7	8.8	13.5	27.0	
1921	12.9	9.0	14.5	9.2	10.2	15.4	31.0	
1922	13.9	9.2	15.0	10.8	11.1	17.2	34.9	
1923	16.5	9.7	15.6	13.4	13.6	21.0	40.5	
1924	17.1	11.1	16.1	14.3	13.7	21.8	43.7	
1925	19.1	11.0	15.6	17.2	15.8	25.0	48.9	
1926	20.1	11.0	15.9	18.6	17.1	26.3	51.4	
1927	21.8	12.8	16.0	20.0	18.8	28.9	56.9	
1928	23.4	12.7	15.5	21.9	20.2	32.4	62.2	
1929	25.7	13.4	15.6	25.6	22.3	35.6	68.6	
1930	26.7	13.0	14.7	27.4	23.9	37.0	72.5	
1931	27.2	13.3	14.5	27.9	24.8	37.4	70.6	
1932	23.6	11.3	12.0	22.6	22.0	32.9	63.6	
1933	25.0	12.0	12.7	24.8	23.4	34.7	63.1	
1934	28.6	11.7	13.0	28.6	27.2	40.7	71.0	
1935	28.6	12.3	12.2	29.2	27.6	39.9	68.9	
1936	29.7	13.2	12.6	30.8	28.2	41.3	70.5	
1937	30.8	13.0	12.7	33.2	28.2	42.0	75.1	
1938	25.1	11.0	10.8	25.4	22.5	34.3	64.1	
1939	24.7	11.2	10.4	26.5	22.6	32.2	60.2	
1940	26.1	11.1	11.5	28.7	23.5	33.9	62.1	
1941	30.0	12.7	12.6	35.7	27.5	37.0	68.6	
1942	21.1	9.5	8.8	25.8	19.2	26.9	44.5	
1943	17.8	9.4	8.6	20.6	16.1	21.9	37.6	
1944	18.3	9.6	9.1	22.5	16.6	21.6	38.2	
1945	21.2	10.0	10.3	27.8	19.7	24.2	44.1	
1946	23.9	11.9	10.8	34.4	21.1	26.4	49.6	
1947	22.8	10.5	9.7	32.8	20.3	25.7	48.2	
1948	22.1	11.0	9.8	32.5	19.8	24.3	39.6	55.4
1949	21.3	10.7	9.0	30.7	19.9	23.4	37.8	53.9
1950	23.0	10.8	8.8	34.5	22.5	25.1	38.8	52.4
1951	24.1	10.9	9.2	36.0	24.7	26.5	39.5	53.0
1952	24.3	11.3	8.7	38.6	24.7	26.7	38.5	50.8
1953	24.0	11.5	8.5	39.1	24.5	25.8	37.7	52.6
1954	22.1	10.4	8.1	36.2	22.6	24.0	33.9	49.0
1955	23.4	10.2	8.0	40.9	24.5	25.2	35.1	47.1
1956	23.7	9.4	8.4	42.9	24.6	25.3	36.2	46.4
1957	22.7	9.2	8.0	39.7	23.9	24.8	34.4	45.5
1958	21.3	9.1	8.1	37.0	22.3	22.6	33.5	42.3
1959	21.5	9.1	7.9	38.2	22.2	23.2	32.3	41.8
1960	21.2	9.6	7.9	37.7	21.7	22.9	31.3	41.1
1961	20.8	9.2	7.6	36.5	21.8	22.5	30.7	40.5
1962	22.0	9.3	8.1	38.4	22.9	23.7	32.2	41.7
1963	23.1	9.8	8.0	40.0	24.3	25.2	32.6	44.3
1964	25.0	10.5	8.8	42.6	26.8	26.6	35.5	45.2
1965	25.4	10.4	8.9	44.2	27.0	27.0	34.6	45.4
1966	27.1	11.4	9.7	48.7	28.5	27.9	35.4	46.2
1967	26.8	11.2	9.5	48.4	27.8	27.1	35.6	45.4
1968	27.5	11.1	10.1	49.8	28.8	27.0	35.1	46.0
1969	27.7	12.0	9.9	50.7	29.1	26.6	34.3	42.0
1970	26.8	11.2	10.2	46.7	27.9	26.4	32.7	42.2
1971	26.3	10.9	10.5	45.7	27.4	24.7	32.4	41.3
1972	26.9	11.1	10.7	47.1	27.4	25.3	32.0	42.6
1973	26.3	11.9	10.5	46.3	27.2	23.6	29.4	39.1
1974	21.8	9.4	8.6	40.0	22.4	18.8	22.6	30.1
1975	21.3	9.8	8.6	38.7	22.1	17.5	21.9	30.1
1976	21.6	9.8	8.4	40.3	21.8	17.6	21.6	30.1

See source and footnotes on page 107.

MOTOR-VEHICLE DEATH RATES[a] BY AGE, UNITED STATES, 1913–1999, Cont.

Year	All Ages	Under 5 Years	5–14 Years	15–24 Years	25–44 Years	45–64 Years	65–74 Years	75 & Over
1977	22.5	9.5	8.5	43.3	22.7	18.1	20.9	29.3
1978	23.6	9.9	8.6	45.4	24.6	18.2	21.5	28.7
1979	23.8	9.1	8.3	45.6	25.6	18.4	20.7	28.1
1980	23.4	8.7	7.9	44.8	25.5	18.0	19.1	28.0
1981	22.4	7.4	7.5	41.1	25.2	17.6	19.4	27.5
1982	19.8	7.5	6.7	36.8	21.5	15.5	17.5	25.2
1983	19.0	7.0	6.6	34.8	20.6	15.0	17.2	26.0
1984	19.6	6.4	6.7	36.4	21.0	15.6	18.2	27.7
1985	19.3	6.7	6.9	35.7	20.5	15.4	17.9	27.5
1986	19.9	6.6	7.0	38.5	21.0	15.2	18.1	28.3
1987	19.9	6.6	7.1	37.1	21.3	15.7	18.8	29.1
1988	20.1	6.7	7.1	37.8	21.2	15.9	19.5	30.2
1989	19.3	6.6	6.5	34.6	20.8	15.9	19.4	29.8
1990	18.8	6.0	5.8	34.2	20.4	15.7	18.5	29.7
1991	17.3	5.6	5.6	32.1	18.3	14.2	17.5	28.9
1992	16.1	5.2	5.2	28.5	17.1	13.6	17.6	27.8
1993	16.3	5.5	5.3	29.1	17.3	13.5	16.7	30.0
1994	16.3	5.8	5.4	29.5	16.8	13.9	18.1	29.4
1995	16.5	5.1	5.4	29.3	17.5	14.2	17.6	29.4
1996	16.5	5.4	5.2	29.2	17.3	14.4	18.3	29.0
1997[b]	16.2	4.9	5.1	27.9	17.0	14.7	18.2	29.9
1998[b]	15.5	4.7	4.9	26.1	16.1	14.1	18.9	26.9
1999[c]	15.1	4.8	4.8	25.9	14.9	14.2	18.1	28.8
Changes in Rates								
1989 to 1999	–22%	–27%	–26%	–25%	–28%	–11%	–7%	–3%
1998 to 1999	–3%	+2%	–2%	–1%	–7%	+1%	–4%	+7%

Source: 1913 to 1932 calculated from National Center for Health Statistics data for registration states; 1933 to 1963, 1965 to 1997 are NCHS totals. All other figures are National Safety Council estimates. See Technical Appendix for comparability.
[a] Death rates are deaths per 100,000 population in each age group.
[b] Revised.
[c] Preliminary.

CHANGE IN MOTOR-VEHICLE DEATH RATES BY AGE GROUP, UNITED STATES, 1989–1999

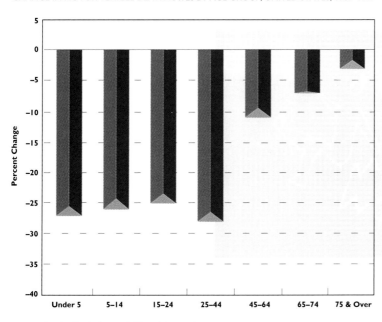

Rates based on deaths per 100,000 population in each age group.

PUBLIC

PUBLIC, 1999

Between 1912 and 1999, public unintentional-injury deaths per 100,000 population were reduced 70% from 30 to 9. In 1912, an estimated 28,000 to 30,000 persons died from public nonmotor-vehicle injuries. In 1999, with a population nearly tripled, and travel and recreational activity greatly increased, only 24,100 persons died of public unintentional injuries and 8,000,000 suffered disabling injuries. The public class excludes deaths involving motor vehicles and persons at work or at home.

The number of public unintentional-injury deaths increased by 2,700, or 13%, from the revised 1998 figure of 21,400. The death rate per 100,000 population increased from 7.9 to 8.8, or +11%.

The 1999 standardized death rate of 7.1 per 100,000 population, adjusted to the age distribution of the population in 1940, was 28% below the rate for

1950, despite an increase in deaths during the same period of 43%.

The Council adopted the Bureau of Labor Statistics' Census of Fatal Occupational Injuries count for work-related unintentional injuries retroactive to 1992 data. Because of the lower Work class total resulting from this change, several thousand unintentional-injury deaths that had been classified by the Council as work-related had to be reassigned to the Home and Public classes. For this reason, long-term historical comparisons for these three classes should be made with caution. See the Technical Appendix for an explanation of the methodological changes.

Deaths **24,100**
Disabling injuries **8,000,000**
Death rate per 100,000 population **8.8**
Costs .... **$78.4 billion**

PUBLIC DEATHS AND DEATH RATES, UNITED STATES, 1992–1999

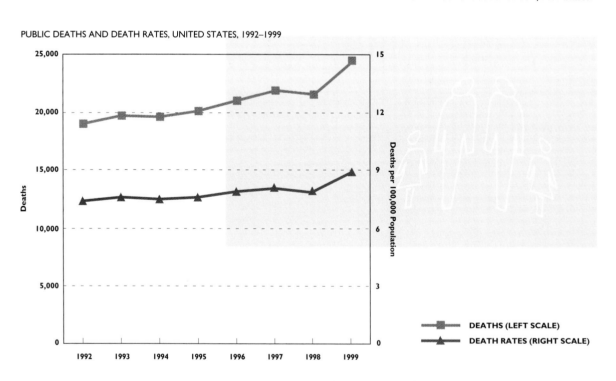

PRINCIPAL TYPES OF PUBLIC UNINTENTIONAL-INJURY DEATHS, UNITED STATES, 1950–1999

Year	Total Public	Transport[a] Total[b]	Air	Water Drowning[c]	Other	Rail[d]	Nontransport Total[b]	Falls	Drowning[c]	Firearms	Fires, Burns
1950	15,000	3,950	1,050	1,000	100	1,450	11,050	2,750	3,750	1,150	500
1955	15,500	3,600	1,300	1,000	100	950	11,900	3,200	4,300	950	450
1960	17,000	3,150	1,150	1,000[e]	100	700	13,850	3,700	4,350	1,100	750
1965	19,500	3,200	1,200	1,000	100	700	16,300	5,300	4,400	900	800
1970	23,500	3,300	1,200	1,200	100	600	20,200	5,000	5,200	900	700
1975	23,000	3,000	1,100	1,200	100	400	20,000	4,800	5,200	900	600
1979	21,000	3,100	1,300	1,100	100	400	17,900	4,400	4,400	700	600
1980	21,300	2,900	1,100	1,100	100	400	18,400	4,500	4,700	700	600
1981	19,800	2,700	1,100	900	100	400	17,100	4,300	4,100	700	600
1982	19,500	2,900	1,200	1,000	100	400	16,600	4,100	4,000	700	500
1983	19,400	2,700	1,000	1,000	100	400	16,700	4,100	4,000	700	500
1984	18,300	2,400	900	800	100	400	15,900	4,100	3,300	700	500
1985	18,800	2,500	1,000	800	100	400	16,300	4,100	3,300	600	500
1986	18,700	2,300	800	800	100	400	16,400	3,900	3,600	600	500
1987	18,400	2,300	900	700	100	400	16,100	4,000	3,200	600	500
1988	18,400	2,100	700	700	100	400	16,300	4,100	3,100	600	500
1989	18,200	2,100	800	600	100	400	16,100	4,200	3,000	600	500
1990	17,400	2,100	700	700	100	400	15,300	4,300	2,800	500	400
1991	17,600	2,100	700	600	100	500	15,500	4,500	2,800	600	400
1992	19,000	2,300	700	600	100	600	16,700	4,400	2,500	400	200
1993	19,700	2,100	600	600	100	600	17,600	4,600	2,800	400	200
1994	19,600	2,000	600	500	100	600	17,600	4,700	2,400	400	200
1995	20,100	2,100	600	600	100	500	18,000	5,000	2,800	300	200
1996	21,000	2,000	700	500	100	500	19,000	5,300	2,500	300	200
1997[f]	21,700	1,800	500	500	100	400	19,900	5,600	2,600	300	200
1998[f]	21,400	1,700	500	400	100	400	19,700	5,800	2,700	200	200
1999[g]	24,100	1,600	600	400	100	300	22,500	6,800	2,700	200	200

Source: National Safety Council estimates based on data from the National Center for Health Statistics and state vital statistics departments. The Council adopted the Bureau of Labor Statistics' Census of Fatal Occupational Injuries count for work-related unintentional injuries retroactive to 1992 data. Because of the lower Work class total resulting from this change, several thousand unintentional-injury deaths that had been classified by the Council as work-related had to be reassigned to the Home and Public classes. For this reason long-term historical comparisons for these three classes should be made with caution. See the Technical Appendix for an explanation of the methodological changes.

[a] Transport is a primary classification but each class includes deaths from falls, drowning, burns, etc., occurring in connection with each type of transport.
[b] Includes some deaths not shown separately.
[c] Nontransport drownings are included in Total drownings in the tables on pages 38–41.
[d] Includes subways and elevateds.
[e] Data for this year and subsequent years not comparable with previous years due to classification changes.
[f] Revised.
[g] Preliminary.

CHANGES IN PUBLIC UNINTENTIONAL-INJURY DEATHS AND DEATH RATES, UNITED STATES, 1998–1999

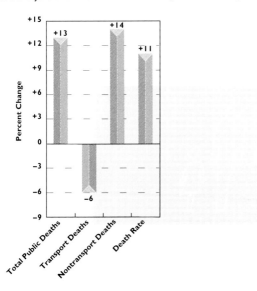

DEATHS DUE TO UNINTENTIONAL PUBLIC INJURIES, 1999

All Public

Includes deaths in public places or places used in a public way and not involving motor vehicles. Most sports, recreation, and transportation deaths are included. Excludes deaths in the course of employment.

	Total	Change from 1998	Death Rate[a]
Deaths	24,100	+13%	8.8

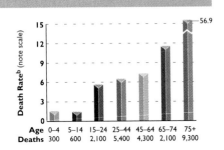

Age	0–4	5–14	15–24	25–44	45–64	65–74	75+
Deaths	300	600	2,100	5,400	4,300	2,100	9,300

Falls

Includes deaths from falls from one level to another or on the same level in public places. Excludes deaths from falls in moving vehicles.

	Total	Change from 1998	Death Rate[a]
Deaths	6,800	+17%	2.5

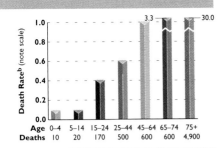

Age	0–4	5–14	15–24	25–44	45–64	65–74	75+
Deaths	10	20	170	500	600	600	4,900

Drowning

Includes drownings of persons swimming or playing in water, or falling into water, except on home premises or at work. Excludes drownings involving boats that are in water transportation.

	Total	Change from 1998	Death Rate[a]
Deaths	2,700	0%	1.0

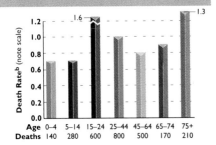

Age	0–4	5–14	15–24	25–44	45–64	65–74	75+
Deaths	140	280	600	800	500	170	210

Air Transport

Includes deaths in private flying, passengers in commercial aviation, and deaths of military personnel in the U.S. Excludes crews and persons traveling in the course of employment.

	Total	Change from 1998	Death Rate[a]
Deaths	600[c]	+20%	0.2

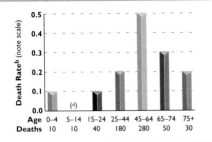

Age	0–4	5–14	15–24	25–44	45–64	65–74	75+
Deaths	10	10	40	180	280	50	30

Water Transport

Includes deaths in water transport accidents from falls, burns, etc., as well as drownings.

	Total	Change from 1998	Death Rate[a]
Deaths	500[c]	0%	0.2

See footnotes on page 113.

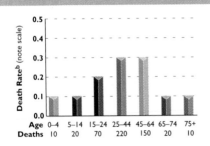

Age	0–4	5–14	15–24	25–44	45–64	65–74	75+
Deaths	10	20	70	220	150	20	10

Railroad

Includes deaths arising from railroad vehicles in motion (except those involving motor vehicles), subway and elevated trains, and persons boarding or alighting from standing trains.

	Total	Change from 1998	Death Rate[a]
Deaths	300[c]	−25%	0.1

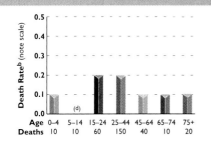

Age	0–4	5–14	15–24	25–44	45–64	65–74	75+
Deaths	10	10	60	150	40	10	20

Firearms

Includes deaths from firearms injuries in public places, including hunting injuries. Excludes deaths from explosive materials.

	Total	Change from 1998	Death Rate[a]
Deaths	200	0%	0.1

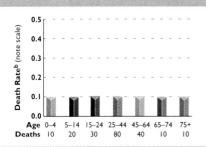

Age	0–4	5–14	15–24	25–44	45–64	65–74	75+
Deaths	10	20	30	80	40	10	10

Fires, Burns, and Deaths Associated with Fires

Includes deaths from fires, burns, and injuries in conflagrations in public places—such as asphyxiation, falls, and struck by falling objects. Excludes burns from hot objects or liquids.

	Total	Change from 1998	Death Rate[a]
Deaths	200	0%	0.1

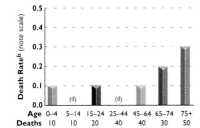

Age	0–4	5–14	15–24	25–44	45–64	65–74	75+
Deaths	10	10	20	40	40	30	50

Other Transport

Includes deaths from injuries involving pedalcycles, animal-drawn vehicles, street cars, etc., except in collision with motor vehicles. Excludes trolley buses, subways, elevateds, and scooters.

	Total	Change from 1998	Death Rate[a]
Deaths	200[c]	−33%	0.1

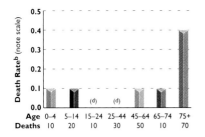

Age	0–4	5–14	15–24	25–44	45–64	65–74	75+
Deaths	10	20	10	30	50	10	70

All Other Public

Most important types included are: medical and surgical complications and misadventures, suffocation by ingestion, poisoning by solids and liquids, and excessive heat or cold.

	Total	Change from 1998	Death Rate[a]
Deaths	12,600	+17%	4.6

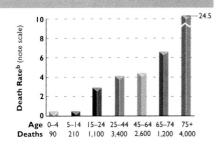

Age	0–4	5–14	15–24	25–44	45–64	65–74	75+
Deaths	90	210	1,100	3,400	2,600	1,200	4,000

[a] Deaths per 100,000 population.
[b] Deaths per 100,000 population in each age group.
[c] Excludes persons at work.
[d] Rate less than 0.05.

Basketball and bicycle riding each accounted for more than half a million emergency department visits in 1998.

SPORTS INJURIES

The table below shows estimates of injuries treated in hospital emergency departments and participants associated with various sports. Differences between the two sources in methods, coverage, classification systems, and definitions can affect comparisons among sports. Because this list of sports is not complete, because the frequency and duration of participation is not known, and because the number of participants varies greatly, no inference should be made concerning the relative hazard of these sports or rank with respect to risk of injury. In particular, it is *not* appropriate to calculate injury rates from these data.

SPORTS PARTICIPATION AND INJURIES, UNITED STATES, 1998

Sport	Participants	Injuries	Percent of Injuries by Age				
			0–4	5–14	15–24	25–64	65 & Over
Archery	4,800,000	3,110	2.8	22.7	27.5	44.7	2.4
Baseball & softball	31,500,000	312,821	2.8	37.2	26.2	33.5	0.3
Basketball	29,400,000	631,186	0.6	31.5	46.4	21.4	0.1
Bicycle riding[a]	43,500,000	577,621	7.1	55.0	15.2	20.7	2.0
Billiards, pool	32,300,000	4,942	10.8	22.5	22.9	40.1	3.6
Bowling	40,100,000	23,130	5.0	17.8	16.7	51.6	9.0
Boxing	[b]	9,183	0.0	8.6	54.4	37.0	0.0
Exercise[c]	[b]	156,497	4.0	16.4	22.8	49.4	7.4
Fishing	43,600,000	77,643	3.5	27.0	13.7	49.3	6.4
Football[d]	17,000,000	355,247	0.3	45.0	43.1	11.5	0.1
Golf	27,500,000	46,019[e]	6.4	23.0	7.5	47.8	15.2
Gymnastics	[b]	31,446[f]	3.8	77.3	16.0	2.7	0.2
Hockey, street, roller & field	[b]	14,053[g,h]	0.6	43.4	35.2	20.8	0.0
Horseback riding	[b]	64,692	1.5	20.2	15.3	61.0	2.0
Horseshoe pitching	9,600,000	2,606	11.8	20.4	5.8	56.2	5.8
Ice hockey	2,100,000	22,231[h]	0.6	35.3	37.4	26.3	0.0
Ice skating	7,800,000	33,741[i]	2.4	46.4	18.8	29.5	2.9
Martial arts	4,600,000	23,018	1.1	23.5	30.6	44.5	0.4
Mountain climbing	3,900,000	2,994	0.0	8.6	53.0	38.3	0.0
Racquetball, squash & paddleball	4,000,000	8,984	0.0	8.9	26.3	62.4	2.4
Roller skating	36,900,000	164,464[i,j]	1.2	60.9	16.7	20.7	0.5
Rugby	[b]	8,361	0.0	0.1	65.9	33.7	0.0
Scuba diving	2,600,000	1,646	4.0	0.0	16.5	79.4	0.0
Skateboarding	5,800,000	54,532	2.7	50.7	39.5	7.0	0.0
Snowmobiling	[b]	8,393	0.8	8.3	20.9	69.2	0.8
Soccer	13,200,000	169,734	0.5	45.7	37.5	16.0	0.3
Swimming	58,200,000	146,879[k]	9.7	43.1	17.1	27.0	3.0
Tennis	11,200,000	22,665	1.0	18.8	19.2	43.9	17.2
Track & field	[b]	15,560	0.0	40.9	54.6	4.4	0.0
Volleyball	14,800,000	66,191	0.1	25.2	42.6	31.7	0.3
Water skiing	7,200,000	14,487	0.0	4.7	32.9	62.0	0.4
Weight lifting	[b]	60,039	5.9	12.1	34.7	45.8	1.4
Wrestling	[b]	43,917	1.3	36.4	51.7	10.5	0.0

Source: Participants—National Sporting Goods Association (NSGA); figures include those 7 years of age or older who participated more than once per year except for bicycle riding and swimming, which include those who participated six or more times per year. Injuries—Consumer Product Safety Commission (CPSC); figures include only injuries treated in hospital emergency departments.
[a] Excludes mountain biking.
[b] Data not available.
[c] Includes exercise equipment (33,320 injuries) and exercise activity (123,177 injuries).
[d] Includes touch and tackle football.
[e] Excludes golf carts (7,887 injuries).
[f] Excludes trampolines (95,239 injuries).
[g] There were 4,581 injuries in street hockey, 4,806 in roller hockey, and 4,666 in field hockey.
[h] Excludes 42,285 injuries in hockey, unspecified.
[i] Excludes 27,481 injuries in skating, unspecified.
[j] Includes 2x2 (53,681 injuries) and in-line (110,783 injuries).
[k] Includes injuries associated with swimming, swimming pools, pool slides, diving or diving boards, and swimming pool equipment.

Football

There were six fatalities directly related to football during the 1999 football season compared to seven in 1998. All of the direct fatalities resulted from injuries to the brain. Of the six direct fatalities in 1999, four were associated with high school football, one with college football, and one with sandlot football. In 1998, six of the seven direct fatalities were associated with high school football and one was associated with college football. There were also twelve indirect fatalities (caused by systemic failure as a result of exertion while participating in football activities or by a complication) recorded in 1999, four more than in 1998. Eleven indirect fatalities were associated with high school football and one was associated with sandlot football.

Source: Mueller, F.O., & Diehl, J.L. (2000). Annual Survey of Football Injury Research, 1931–1999. Overland Park, KS: National Collegiate Athletic Association.

Other Sports

In 1999, the U.S. Parachute Association reported 27 fatalities out of an estimated 3.4 million jumps, while the U.S. Hang Gliding Association reported six deaths. According to National Safety Council estimates, there were 1,500 swimming fatalities in 1999. The Hunter Education Association recorded 93 fatal and 926 nonfatal hunting injuries in 1999 in the United States. The National Ski Areas Association reported 33 skier and 6 snowboarder fatalities during the 1998–1999 season.

Recreational Boating

Deaths associated with recreational boating numbered 815 in the United States and its territories in 1998 according to data from the United States Coast Guard. Florida and California experienced the greatest number of deaths with 73 and 56, respectively, followed by Texas with 46 and Alaska with 38. Alcohol was found to be involved in 217 (27%) of recreational boating deaths. Coast Guard estimates found that persons with a blood alcohol concentration (BAC) of .10 percent are more than 10 times as likely to be killed in a boating accident than boaters with a BAC of zero.

In 1998 there were a record high 4,612 reported injuries and approximately 8,061 reported boating accidents, although both of these figures are probably underreported. There were 574 drowning deaths in 1998. Approximately 80% of victims in fatal boating accidents were not wearing life jackets. The Coast Guard estimates that life jackets could have saved about 509 of the boaters who drowned in 1998. The property damage due to recreational boating accidents is estimated at more than $31 million in 1998. There were a total of 12,565,930 numbered recreational vessels in the United States and its territories in 1998, with the number varying significantly by state.

The tables below show recreational boating accidents, fatalities, and fatalities due to drowning by accident type and also types of recreational boats involved in accidents in 1998.

RECREATIONAL BOATING ACCIDENTS, FATALITIES, AND FATALITIES DUE TO DROWNING BY ACCIDENT TYPE, UNITED STATES AND TERRITORIES, 1998

Accident Type	Reported Accidents	Drowning Deaths	Total Fatalities
Total U.S.	**8,061**	**574**	**815**
Collision with Vessel	2,837	16	112
Collision with Fixed Object	833	33	60
Falls Overboard	662	198	234
Capsizing	569	216	243
Skier Mishap	497	6	17
Grounding	472	1	11
Flooding/Swamping	439	57	60
Fall in Boat	343	5	7
Sinking	243	19	20
Fire/Explosion (Fuel)	202	1	4
Collision with Floating Object	172	6	11
Struck Submerged Object	165	3	4
Struck by Boat	142	0	7
Fire/Explosion (Other than Fuel)	110	1	1
Struck by Motor/Propeller	101	0	1
Other casualty; Unknown	274	12	23

TYPES OF RECREATIONAL BOATS IN ACCIDENTS, 1998

Type of Boat	Reported Boats in Accidents	Reported Fatalities	Reported Injuries
Total U.S.	**11,368**	**815**	**4,612**
Open Motorboat	4,368	441	1,973
Personal Watercraft	3,607	78	1,743
Cabin Motorboat	1,477	53	405
Auxiliary Sail	381	7	56
Pontoon	224	12	73
Canoe/Kayak	167	115	80
Sail (only)	131	8	34
Houseboat	147	2	17
Rowboat	82	44	39
Inflatable	50	19	33
Other/Unknown	734	36	159

Source: United States Coast Guard

WEATHER

Floods/Flash Floods

There have been 6,523 deaths associated with floods in the United States since 1940, averaging 111 deaths per year according to the National Climatic Data Center (NCDC). In 1998, there were 133 flood related fatalities, 16 more than 1997 and 22 more than the annual national average. Texas and California had the largest number of deaths in 1998, with 41 and 17 respectively. Flood deaths outnumbered both lightning and tornado deaths in 1998.

Lightning

Deaths due to lightning in the United States totaled 44 in 1998, 2 more than 1997, according to the NCDC. June and August had the greatest number of deaths, with 12, followed by July (6), and May (3). Florida ranked the highest in both lightning deaths with 8 (18%) and injuries with 47 (17%). The average number of lightning deaths per year was 89 during the last 39 years.

Tornadoes

According to the NCDC, there were a record high 1,424 reported tornadoes in the United States in 1998 resulting in 1,869 injuries and 130 deaths. The number

of tornadoes was significantly above the annual average of 821 from 1950-1998. Tornado deaths were also above the annual average of 87. Florida, Alabama, and Georgia accounted for 95 of the 130 deaths (73%). Florida and Georgia had the greatest number of injuries with 309 (17%) and 291 (16%), respectively.

Excessive Heat

According to the Morbidity and Mortality Weekly Report (MMWR), there was an annual average of 371 deaths in the United States attributed to "excessive heat exposure" between 1979 and 1997. During these years, a total of 7,046 deaths were brought on by heat exposure. The average annual rate of death caused by excessive heat was 1.5 per million population for those years. The number of fatalities ranged from a low of 148 in 1979 to the high of 1,700 in 1980. Arizona and Missouri had the highest rate of heat-related deaths due to weather conditions with four per million population. Arkansas and Kansas followed with a rate of three per million.

Source: National Safety Council tabulation of National Climatic Data Center data.
Adcock, M.P., Bines, W.H., & Smith, F.W. (2000, June 2). Heat-related illnesses, deaths, and risk factors—Cincinnati and Dayton, Ohio, 1999 and United States, 1979-1997. Morbidity and Mortality Weekly Report, 49 (21), 470-473.

STORM DEATHS BY TYPE AND YEAR, 1989–1998

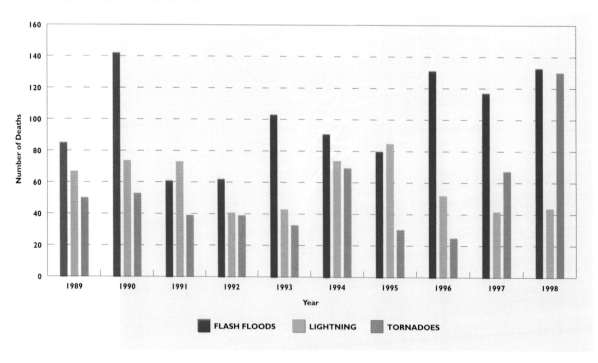

Unintentional firearm-related deaths fell 36% in 1997 from its 1993 high.

Firearm-related deaths from unintentional, intentional, and undetermined causes totaled 32,166 in 1997 (see table below), a decrease of 4.7% from 1996. Another 270 deaths occurred during legal intervention. Suicides accounted for nearly 55% of firearms deaths, about 41% were homicides, and more than 3% were unintentional deaths. Males dominate all categories of firearms deaths and accounted for more than 85% of the total.

The number of homicide deaths by firearms decreased 3% from 1988 to 1997 and has decreased each of the last four years. The number of unintentional firearms deaths has decreased steadily over the past 4 years, decreasing nearly 36% in 1997 from its 1993 high.

According to a 1995 study, ratios of nonfatal firearm-related injuries to deaths are relatively high for accidents, about 12.8 nonfatal injuries for each death. The ratios for homicides and suicides are much lower, about 3.3 nonfatal injuries per death for homicides and 0.3 for suicides.

Source: National Safety Council tabulation of National Center for Health Statistics data; Annest, J.L., Mercy, J.A., Gibson, D.R., & Ryan, G.W. (1995). National estimates of nonfatal firearm-related injuries. Journal of the American Medical Association, 273 (22), 1749-1754.

DEATHS INVOLVING FIREARMS, BY AGE AND SEX, UNITED STATES, 1997

Type & Sex	All Ages	Under 5 Years	5–14 Years	15–19 Years	20–24 Years	25–44 Years	45–64 Years	65–74 Years	75 & Over
Total Firearm Deaths[a]	**32,166**	**84**	**545**	**3,576**	**4,536**	**12,688**	**6,221**	**2,198**	**2,318**
Male	27,499	46	419	3,162	4,091	10,598	5,178	1,903	2,102
Female	4,667	38	126	414	445	2,090	1,043	295	216
Unintentional	**981**	**20**	**122**	**164**	**136**	**295**	**154**	**51**	**39**
Male	856	11	107	159	123	252	127	43	34
Female	125	9	15	5	13	43	27	8	5
Suicides	**17,566**	**0**	**127**	**1,135**	**1,452**	**6,331**	**4,506**	**1,906**	**2,109**
Male	15,194	0	99	975	1,309	5,317	3,823	1,694	1,977
Female	2,372	0	28	160	143	1,014	683	212	132
Homicides	**13,252**	**62**	**284**	**2,216**	**2,894**	**5,923**	**1,505**	**224**	**144**
Male	11,147	34	203	1,973	2,613	4,922	1,180	151	71
Female	2,105	28	81	243	281	1,001	325	73	73
Undetermined[b]	**367**	**2**	**12**	**61**	**54**	**139**	**56**	**17**	**26**
Male	302	1	10	55	46	107	48	15	20
Female	65	1	2	6	8	32	8	2	6

[a] *Excludes firearm deaths from legal intervention. These deaths totaled 270 in 1997.*
[b] *Undetermined means the intentionality of the deaths (unintentional, suicide, homicide) was not determined.*

FIREARMS DEATHS BY INTENTIONALITY AND YEAR, UNITED STATES, 1988–1997

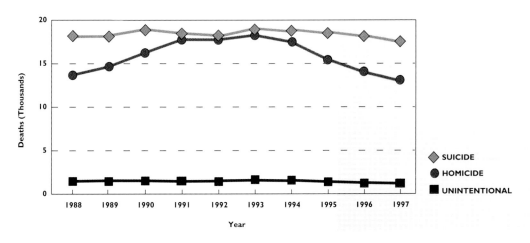

TRANSPORTATION ACCIDENT COMPARISONS

Passenger transportation comparisons account for about one-fourth of all unintentional-injury deaths. But the risk of death to the passenger, expressed on a per mile basis, varies greatly by transportation mode. Automobile travel presents the greatest risk; air, rail, and bus travel have much lower death rates. The tables below show the latest information on passenger transportation deaths and death rates.

Passenger Automobiles and Taxis

Automobile occupants account for about 60% of all highway vehicle occupant deaths, and automobiles represent about 59% of the total vehicle miles of highway travel. The automobile statistics shown in the tables below represent all passenger car usage, both intercity and local.

Buses

Intercity buses carried 358 million passengers and transit buses carried 5.5 billion passengers in 1998. Passenger mileage data for school buses in 1998 was not available (see pages 90–91 for data on school bus fatalities and injuries).

Railroad Passenger Trains

In 1998, Amtrak accounted for about 40% of the railroad passenger miles. Railroads carried about 386 million passengers in 1998 and had 4 passenger deaths that year.

Scheduled Airlines

There were no passenger deaths in 1998 on scheduled service. Domestic certified airlines carried 561 million passengers in 1998.

TRANSPORTATION ACCIDENT DEATH RATES, UNITED STATES, 1996–1998

Kind of Transportation	1998			1996–1998 Average Death Rate
	Passenger Deaths	Passenger Miles (Billions)	Deaths per 100,000,000 Passenger Miles	
Passenger automobiles[a]	21,099	2,457.9	0.86	0.91
Buses[b]	26[c]	52.5	0.05	0.03
Transit buses	2	20.8	0.01	0.01
Intercity buses	11	31.7	0.03	0.02
Railroad passenger trains[d]	4	13.4	0.03	0.06
Scheduled airlines[e]	0	484.4	0.00	0.03

Source: Automobile and bus passenger deaths—Fatality Analysis Reporting System data. Railroad passenger deaths—Federal Railroad Administration. Airline passenger deaths—National Transportation Safety Board. Passenger miles for intercity buses, railroad, and airlines—Wilson, R.A. (2000). Transportation in America, 17th edition. Washington, DC: Eno Transportation Foundation, Inc. Passenger miles for transit buses—American Public Transit Association. All other figures—National Safety Council estimates.

[a] Includes taxi passengers. Drivers of passenger automobiles are considered passengers.
[b] Figures do not include school buses.
[c] Deaths include other and unknown bus types.
[d] Includes commutation.
[e] Includes large airlines and scheduled commuter airlines; excludes cargo service. Rates exclude suicide/sabotage deaths.

PASSENGER DEATHS AND DEATH RATES, UNITED STATES, 1988–1998

Year	Passenger Cars & Taxis		Buses[a]		Railroad Passenger Trains		Scheduled Airlines	
	Deaths	Rate[b]	Deaths	Rate[b]	Deaths	Rate[b]	Deaths	Rate[b]
1988	25,614	1.19	10	0.02	2	0.02	272	0.01[c]
1989	24,871	1.12	17	0.04	8	0.06	284	0.09
1990	23,924	0.99	16	0.04	3	0.02	11	0.003
1991	22,215	0.91	16	0.04	8	0.06	100	0.03
1992	21,257	0.83	17	0.04	3	0.02	38	0.01
1993	21,414	0.86	9	0.02	58	0.45	19	0.01
1994	21,813	0.91	13	0.03	5	0.04	245	0.06
1995	22,288	0.97	16	0.03	0	0.00	159	0.04
1996	22,359	0.96	10	0.02	12	0.09	329	0.08
1997	21,920	0.92	4	0.01	6	0.05	42	0.01
1998	21,099	0.86	26	0.05	4	0.03	0	0.00

Source: See table above.
[a] Figures do not include school buses.
[b] Deaths per 100,000,000 passenger miles.
[c] Rate excludes 243 deaths due to sabotage.

PASSENGER[a] DEATH RATES, UNITED STATES, 1996–1998

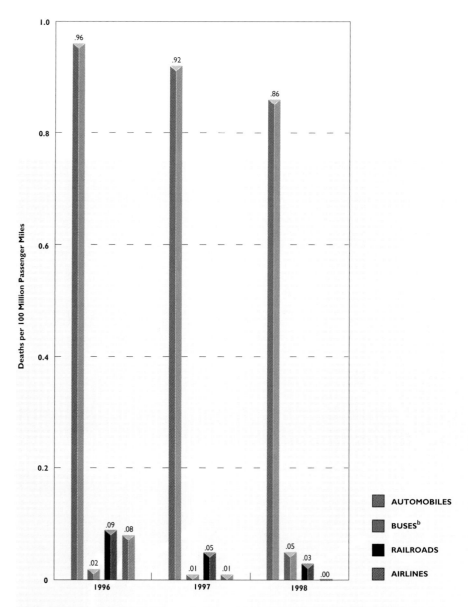

[a]Drivers of passenger automobiles are considered passengers.
[b]Figures do not include school buses.

AVIATION

Worldwide passenger deaths in scheduled air service totaled 487 in 1999, according to the International Civil Aviation Organization, a specialized United Nations agency with 185 member states. The death rate per 100 million passenger miles in 1999 was 0.03.

Aircraft accidents involving a passenger fatality totaled 19. The death rate dropped from .06 in 1998 to .03 in 1999. Passenger deaths per year averaged 766 for the last 10 years.

WORLDWIDE SCHEDULED AIR SERVICE ACCIDENTS, DEATHS, AND DEATH RATES, 1980–1999

Year	Aircraft Accidents[a]	Passenger Deaths	Death Rate[b]	Year	Aircraft Accidents[a]	Passenger Deaths	Death Rate[b]
1980	21	734	0.13	1990	23	473	0.05
1981	22	365	0.06	1991	24	518	0.05
1982	25	762	0.13	1992	24	978	0.09
1983	21	817	0.13	1993	31	806	0.07
1984	16	218	0.03	1994	23	962	0.08
1985	25	1,037	0.14	1995	20	541	0.04
1986	19	427	0.05	1996	21	1,125	0.08
1987	23	889	0.10	1997	25	867	0.05
1988	26	712	0.08	1998[c]	20	904	0.06
1989	29	879	0.09	1999[d]	19	487	0.03

Source: International Civil Aviation Organization. Figures exclude the USSR up to 1992 and the Commonwealth of Independent States thereafter.
[a] *Involving a passenger fatality.*
[b] *Passenger deaths per 100 million passenger miles.*
[c] *Revised.*
[d] *Preliminary.*

U.S. CIVIL AVIATION ACCIDENTS, DEATHS, AND DEATH RATES, 1995–1999

				Accident Rates			
	Accidents			Per 100,000 Flight-Hours		Per Million Aircraft-Miles	
Year	Total	Fatal	Deaths[a]	Total	Fatal	Total	Fatal
Large Airlines[b]							
1995	34	2	166	0.266	0.016	0.0064	0.0004
1996	32	3	342	0.247	0.023	0.0059	0.0006
1997	44	3	3	0.292	0.020	0.0069	0.0005
1998	43	1	1	0.270	0.006	0.0068	0.0002
1999	48	2	12	0.291	0.012	0.0075	0.0003
Commuter Airlines[b]							
1995	12	2	9	0.457	0.076	0.0218	0.0036
1996	11	1	14	0.399	0.036	0.0186	0.0017
1997	16	5	46	1.628	0.509	0.0636	0.0199
1998	8	0	0	2.261	—	0.1576	—
1999	13	5	12	4.833	1.859	0.3095	0.1190
On-Demand Air Taxis[b]							
1995	75	24	52	4.39	1.41	—	—
1996	90	29	63	4.44	1.43	—	—
1997	82	15	39	3.64	0.67	—	—
1998	77	18	48	3.03	0.71	—	—
1999	76	12	38	2.71	0.43	—	—
General Aviation[b]							
1995	2,053	412	734	8.23	1.64	—	—
1996	1,908	360	632	7.67	1.45	—	—
1997	1,853	353	643	7.28	1.39	—	—
1998	1,909	365	623	7.12	1.36	—	—
1999	1,908	342	628	7.05	1.26	—	—

Source: National Transportation Safety Board: 1999 preliminary, 1995–1998 revised; exposure data for rates from Federal Aviation Administration.
[a] *Includes passengers, crew members, and others.*
[b] *Civil aviation accident statistics collected by the National Transportation Safety Board are classified according to the Federal air regulations under which the flights were made. The classifications are (1) large airlines operating scheduled service under Title 14, Code of Federal Regulations, part 121 (14 CFR 121); (2) commuter carriers operating scheduled service under 14 CFR 135; (3) unscheduled, "on-demand" air taxis under 14 CFR 135; and (4) "general aviation," which includes accidents involving aircraft flown under rules other than 14 CFR 121 and 14 CFR 135. Suicide/sabotage is included in accident and fatality totals but excluded from rates. Not shown in the table is nonscheduled air carrier operations under 14 CFR 121 which experienced no accidents and no fatalities in 1999. Since 1997, Large Airlines includes aircraft with 10 or more seats, formerly operated as commuter carriers under 14 CFR 135.*

DEATHS AND INJURIES IN RAILROAD ACCIDENTS AND INCIDENTS, UNITED STATES, 1990–1999

Year	Casualties Not at Grade Crossings	All Casualties					
		Total	Passengers on Trains[a]	Employees on Duty		Other Non-trespassers[a]	Trespassers
				Number	Rate[b]		
Deaths							
1990	599	1,297	3	40	0.014	551	700
1991	586	1,194	8	35	0.013	484	663
1992	591	1,170	3	34	0.013	475	646
1993	653	1,279	58	47	0.018	489	675
1994	611	1,226	5	31	0.012	505	682
1995	567	1,146	0	34	0.013	443	660
1996	551	1,039	12	33	0.013	365	620
1997	602	1,063	6	37	0.015	362	646
1998	577	1,008	4	27	0.010	324	644
1999	530	932	14	31	0.012	302	572
Nonfatal Injuries							
1990	22,736	25,143	473	20,970	7.58	2,339	793
1991	21,374	23,468	382	19,626	7.40	2,110	769
1992	19,408	21,383	411	17,755	6.87	1,909	772
1993	17,284	19,121	559	15,363	5.91	1,856	733
1994	14,851	16,812	497	13,080	5.04	1,913	764
1995	12,546	14,440	573	10,777	4.22	1,869	700
1996	10,948	12,558	513	9,199	3.65	1,660	750
1997	10,227	11,767	601	8,295	3.29	1,517	728
1998	10,156	11,459	535	8,398	3.26	1,201	677
1999	10,304	11,700	481	8,622	3.38	1,307	650

Source: Federal Railroad Administration. Includes train accidents, train incidents, and non-train incidents at both public and private grade crossings.
[a] Federal Railroad Administration definitions: "Persons on or getting on or off passenger-carrying trains under conditions not constituting trespass are designated as 'passengers on trains.' Other persons lawfully on railroad premises in connection with their journeys by railroads are designated 'other nontrespassers.'"
[b] The rates are the number of deaths or injuries per 200,000 hours worked. Because of differences in definitions, the injury rates are not comparable with those for other industries shown elsewhere in Injury Facts™.

RAIL-HIGHWAY PUBLIC GRADE-CROSSING DEATHS AND INJURIES, UNITED STATES, 1990–1999

Year	Deaths				Nonfatal Injuries			
	Total	Motor-Vehicle	Pedestrian	Other	Total	Motor-Vehicle	Pedestrian	Other
1990	698	614	60	24	2,407	2,332	28	47
1991	608	535	52	21	2,094	2,029	30	35
1992	579	506	49	24	1,975	1,891	31	53
1993	626	554	48	24	1,837	1,760	28	49
1994	615	542	50	23	1,961	1,885	30	46
1995	579	508	47	24	1,894	1,825	28	41
1996	488	415	60	13	1,610	1,545	31	34
1997	461	419	38	4	1,540	1,494	33	13
1998	431	369	50	12	1,303	1,257	33	13
1999	402	345	45	12	1,396	1,338	35	23

Source: Federal Railroad Administration data for public and private grade-crossing accidents.

HOME AND FARM

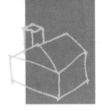

HOME, 1999

Between 1912 and 1999, unintentional home injury deaths per 100,000 population were reduced 61% from 28 to 11. In 1912, when there were 21 million households, an estimated 26,000 to 28,000 persons were killed by unintentional home injuries. In 1999, with more than 102 million households and the population nearly tripled, home deaths numbered only 28,800.

The injury total of 6,900,000 means that 1 person in 40 in the United States was disabled one full day or more by unintentional injuries received in the home in 1999. Disabling injuries are more numerous in the home than in the workplace and in motor-vehicle crashes combined.

The National Health Interview Survey indicates that about 17,189,000 episodes of home injuries occurred in 1996 (the latest year available). This means that about 1 person in 15 incurred a home injury requiring

medical attention or resulting in one-half day or more of restricted activity. Approximately 147,676,000 days of restricted activity and 45,064,000 days of bed disability resulted from injuries in and around the home. See page 20 for definitions and numerical differences between National Health Interview Survey and National Safety Council figures.

The Council adopted the Bureau of Labor Statistics' Census of Fatal Occupational Injuries count for work-related unintentional injuries retroactive to 1992 data. Because of the lower Work class total resulting from this change, several thousand unintentional-injury deaths that had been classified by the Council as work-related had to be reassigned to the Home and Public classes. For this reason long-term historical comparisons for these three classes should be made with caution. See the Technical Appendix for an explanation of the methodological changes.

Deaths	**28,800**
Disabling injuries	**6,900,000**
Death rate per 100,000 population	**10.6**
Costs	**$101.7 billion**

HOME DEATHS AND DEATH RATES, UNITED STATES, 1992–1999

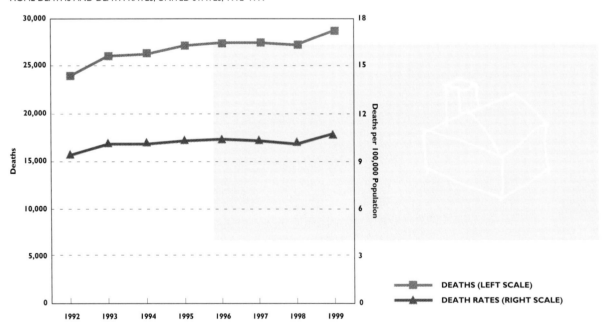

PRINCIPAL TYPES OF HOME UNINTENTIONAL-INJURY DEATHS, UNITED STATES, 1950–1999

Year	Total Home	Falls	Fires, Burns[a]	Suffocation Ing. Obj.	Suffocation Mech.	Drowning	Poison (Solid, Liquid)	Poison (Gas, Vapor)	Firearms	Other
1950	29,000	14,800	5,000	(b)	1,600	(b)	1,300	1,250	950	4,100
1955	28,500	14,100	5,400	(b)	1,250	(b)	1,150	900	1,100	4,600
1960	28,000	12,300	6,350	1,850	1,500	(b)	1,350	900	1,200	2,550
1965	28,500	11,700	6,100	1,300c	1,200	(b)	1,700	1,100	1,300	4,100c
1970	27,000	9,700	5,600	1,800c	1,100c	(b)	3,000	1,100	1,400c	3,300c
1975	25,000	8,000	5,000	1,800	800	(b)	3,700	1,000	1,300	3,400
1979	22,500	7,100	4,900	2,000	500	(b)	2,500	900	1,100	3,500
1980	22,800	7,100	4,800	2,000	500	(b)	2,500	700	1,100	4,100d
1981	21,700	6,800	4,700	2,000	500	(b)	2,600	800	1,000	3,300
1982	21,200	6,500	4,300	2,100	600	(b)	2,700	800	1,000	3,200
1983	21,200	6,500	4,100	2,200	600	(b)	2,700	800	900	3,400
1984	21,200	6,400	4,100	2,300	600	(b)	3,000	700	900	3,200
1985	21,600	6,500	4,000	2,400	600	(b)	3,200	700	900	3,300
1986	21,700	6,100	4,000	2,500	600	(b)	3,700	600	800	3,400
1987	21,400	6,300	3,900	2,500	600	(b)	3,500	600	800	3,200
1988	22,700	6,600	4,100	2,600	600	(b)	4,300	500	800	3,200
1989	22,500	6,600	3,900	2,500	600	(b)	4,400	600	800	3,100
1990	21,500	6,700	3,400	2,300	600	(b)	4,000	500	800	3,200
1991	22,100	6,900	3,400	2,200	700	(b)	4,500	500	800	3,100
1992	24,000	7,700	3,700	1,500	700	900	4,800	400	1,000	3,300
1993	26,100	7,900	3,700	1,700	700	900	6,000	500	1,100	3,600
1994	26,300	8,100	3,700	1,600	800	900	6,300	500	900	3,500
1995	27,200	8,400	3,500	1,500	800	900	6,600	400	900	4,200
1996	27,500	9,000	3,500	1,500	800	900	6,800	500	800	3,700
1997e	27,700	9,100	3,200	1,500	800	900	7,400	400	700	3,500
1998e	27,300	9,600	2,700	1,600	600	1,000	7,100	400	600	3,700
1999f	28,800	9,600	2,800	1,400	700	800	8,300	300	500	4,400

Source: National Safety Council estimates based on data from National Center for Health Statistics and state vital statistics departments. The Council adopted the Bureau of Labor Statistics' Census of Fatal Occupational Injuries count for work-related unintentional injuries retroactive to 1992 data. Because of the lower Work class total resulting from this change, several thousand unintentional-injury deaths that had been classified by the Council as work-related had to be reassigned to the Home and Public classes. For this reason long-term historical comparisons for these three classes should be made with caution. See the Technical Appendix for an explanation of the methodological changes.
a Includes deaths resulting from conflagration, regardless of nature of injury.
b Included in Other.
c Data for this year and subsequent years not comparable with previous years due to classification changes.
d Includes about 1,000 excessive heat deaths due to summer heat wave.
e Revised.
f Preliminary.

PRINCIPAL TYPES OF HOME UNINTENTIONAL-INJURY DEATHS, UNITED STATES, 1999

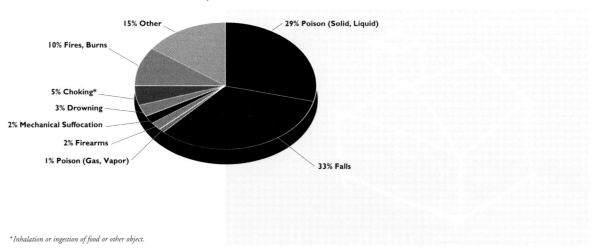

Inhalation or ingestion of food or other object.

DEATHS DUE TO UNINTENTIONAL HOME INJURIES, 1999

TYPE OF EVENT AND AGE OF VICTIM

All Home
Includes deaths in the home and on home premises of occupants, guests, and trespassers. Also includes hired household workers but excludes other persons working on home premises.

	Total	Change from 1998	Death Rate[a]
Deaths	28,800	+5%	10.6

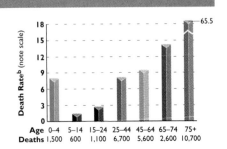

Falls
Includes deaths from falls from one level to another or on the same level in the home or on home premises.

	Total	Change from 1998	Death Rate[a]
Deaths	9,600	0%	3.5

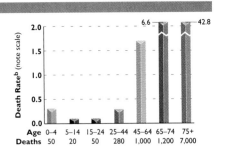

Poisoning by Solids and Liquids
Includes deaths from drugs, medicines, mushrooms, and shellfish, as well as commonly recognized poisons. Excludes poisonings from spoiled foods, salmonella, etc., which are classified as disease deaths.

	Total	Change from 1998	Death Rate[a]
Deaths	8,300	+17%	3.0

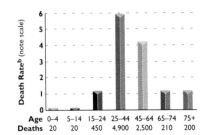

Fires, Burns, and Deaths Associated with Fires
Includes deaths from fires, burns, and injuries in conflagrations in the home—such as asphyxiation, falls, and struck by falling objects. Excludes burns from hot objects or liquids.

	Total	Change from 1998	Death Rate[a]
Deaths	2,800	+4%	1.0

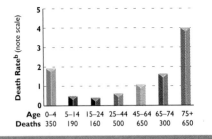

Suffocation by Ingested Object
Includes deaths from unintentional ingestion or inhalation of objects or food resulting in the obstruction of respiratory passages.

	Total	Change from 1998	Death Rate[a]
Deaths	1,400	−13%	0.5

See footnotes on page 127.

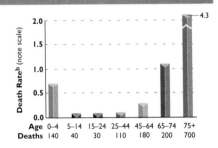

Drowning

Includes drownings of persons in or on home premises—such as in swimming pools and bathtubs. Excludes drowning in floods and other cataclysms.

	Total	Change from 1998	Death Rate[a]
Deaths	800	–20%	0.3

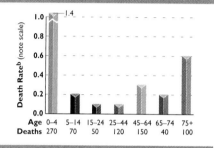

Age	0–4	5–14	15–24	25–44	45–64	65–74	75+
Deaths	270	70	50	120	150	40	100

Mechanical Suffocation

Includes deaths from smothering by bedclothes, thin plastic materials, etc.; suffocation by cave-ins or confinement in closed spaces; and mechanical strangulation.

	Total	Change from 1998	Death Rate[a]
Deaths	700	+17%	0.3

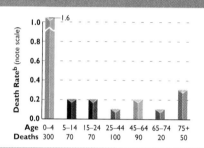

Age	0–4	5–14	15–24	25–44	45–64	65–74	75+
Deaths	300	70	70	100	90	20	50

Firearms

Includes firearms injuries in or on home premises—such as while cleaning or playing with guns. Excludes deaths from explosive materials.

	Total	Change from 1998	Death Rate[a]
Deaths	500	–17%	0.2

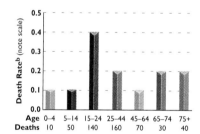

Age	0–4	5–14	15–24	25–44	45–64	65–74	75+
Deaths	10	50	140	160	70	30	40

Poisoning by Gases and Vapors

Principally carbon monoxide due to incomplete combustion, involving cooking stoves, heating equipment, and standing motor vehicles. Gas poisonings in conflagrations are classified as fire deaths.

	Total	Change from 1998	Death Rate[a]
Deaths	300	–25%	0.1

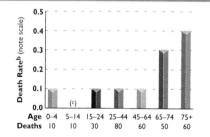

Age	0–4	5–14	15–24	25–44	45–64	65–74	75+
Deaths	10	10	30	80	60	50	60

All Other Home

Most important types included are electric current; hot substances, corrosive liquids, and steam; and explosive materials.

	Total	Change from 1998	Death Rate[a]
Deaths	4,400	+19%	1.6

[a] Deaths per 100,000 population.
[b] Deaths per 100,000 population in each age group.
[c] Death rate less than 0.05.

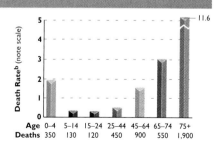

Age	0–4	5–14	15–24	25–44	45–64	65–74	75+
Deaths	350	130	120	450	900	550	1,900

UNINTENTIONAL POISONINGS

Deaths from unintentional solid and liquid poisoning increased approximately 8% from 8,872 in 1996 to 9,587 in 1997, the latest year for which detailed tabulations are available. Deaths attributed to local anesthetics and other drugs acting on the central and autonomic nervous system, including cocaine, decreased by about 5%, from 1,411 fatalities in 1996 to 1,336 in 1997.

Over the last 30 years, the number and circumstances of deaths from unintentional solid and liquid poisoning have changed greatly. Since 1967, the death rate per 100,000 population has nearly tripled from 1.3 to 3.6 in 1997. The 25 to 44 year age group had the greatest increase in death rate, from 1.9 in 1966 to 7.1 in

1997. The death rate for the 0 to 4 year age group has fallen dramatically, from 1.8 in 1967 to 0.1 in 1997.

Due to classification system changes, death figures by type of poisoning are only comparable since 1979. The number of deaths from drugs, medicaments, and biologicals has increased steadily since 1979, while the number of deaths from other solid and liquid poisonings, including household chemicals, has decreased.

Total human poisoning exposure cases reported, both fatal and nonfatal, were estimated to be 2.3 million in 1997, according to the American Association of Poison Control Centers.

UNINTENTIONAL POISONING DEATHS BY TYPE AND AGE, UNITED STATES, 1997

Type of Poisoning	All Ages	Under 5 Years	5–14 Years	15–24 Years	25–44 Years	45–64 Years	65 Years & Over
Total Poisoning by Solids and Liquids, E850-E866	**9,587**	**22**	**19**	**658**	**5,972**	**2,349**	**567**
Rate (deaths per 100,000 population)	3.6	0.1	0.1	1.8	7.1	4.2	1.7
Male	7,176	17	10	523	4,627	1,741	258
Female	2,411	5	9	135	1,345	608	309
Drugs, medicaments, biologicals, E850-E858	**9,099**	**11**	**16**	**613**	**5,775**	**2,179**	**505**
Male	6,809	10	7	485	4,476	1,612	219
Female	2,290	1	9	128	1,299	567	286
Analgesics, antipyretics, antirheumatics, E850	2,813	3	8	226	1,766	742	68
Opiates, related narcotics, E850.0	2,377	2	3	197	1,546	602	27
Salicylates (incl. aspirin), E850.1	27	1	0	0	10	8	8
Other, unspecified analgesics, antipyretics, antirheumatics, E850.2-E850.5, E850.8, E850.9	409	0	5	29	210	132	33
Barbiturates, E851	24	0	0	0	11	9	4
Other sedatives, hypnotics, E852	9	0	0	0	3	6	0
Tranquilizers, E853	94	0	1	3	45	39	6
Other psychotropic agents, E854	393	0	2	31	240	111	9
Other drugs acting on central and autonomic nervous system (incl. local anesthetics), E855	1,336	0	0	85	894	326	31
Antibiotics, E856	48	0	0	3	7	12	26
Anti-infectives, E857	8	0	0	0	2	1	5
Other drugs, E858	4,374	8	5	265	2,807	933	356
Cardiovascular drugs, E858.3	195	0	0	0	2	15	178
Gastrointestinal drugs, E858.4	1	0	0	1	0	0	0
Other, unspecified drugs, E858.0-E858.2, E858.5-E858.9	4,178	8	5	264	2,805	918	178
Other solids and liquids, E860-E866	**488**	**11**	**3**	**45**	**197**	**170**	**62**
Male	367	7	3	38	151	129	39
Female	121	4	0	7	46	41	23
Alcohol, E860	342	1	0	23	158	136	24
Cleansing, polishing agents, disinfectants, paints, varnishes, E861	14	2	0	1	3	4	4
Petroleum products, other solvents and their vapors, E862	46	2	0	12	17	9	6
Agricultural, horticultural chemical, pharmaceutical preparations, E863	12	0	0	2	5	2	3
Corrosives, caustics, E864	8	4	0	0	1	0	3
Foodstuffs, poisonous plants, E865	11	0	0	3	5	2	1
Other, unspecified solids and liquids, E866	55	2	3	4	8	17	21
Total Poisoning by Gases and Vapors, E867-E869	**576**	**17**	**23**	**72**	**199**	**137**	**128**
Rate (deaths per 100,000 population)	0.2	0.1	0.1	0.2	0.2	0.2	0.4
Male	446	11	12	62	173	112	76
Female	130	6	11	10	26	25	52
Gas distributed by pipeline, E867	13	0	0	1	2	3	7
Other utility gas, other carbon monoxide, E868	459	9	17	57	162	121	93
Other gases and vapors, E869	104	8	6	14	35	13	28

Source: National Safety Council tabulations of National Center for Health Statistics mortality data. See pages 38–41 for earlier year totals and rates; see Technical Appendix for comparability.

An estimated 11,000 people were treated in emergency rooms for suspected non-fire carbon monoxide poisoning in 1997.

CARBON MONOXIDE POISONING

Carbon monoxide (CO) is a colorless, odorless, and poisonous gas that is a byproduct of incomplete combustion of fuels such as natural or liquefied propane (LP) gas, oil, wood, or coal. Totals for unintentional deaths or injuries due to carbon monoxide poisoning are difficult to estimate because of instances such as suicide, structure fire, and automobile crashes. Examiners may be unable to run tests because of the nature of the death, or carbon monoxide poisoning may simply be overlooked in favor of a more obvious cause of death.

Between 1991 and 1995, the total number of unintentional non-fire CO poisoning deaths, including both deaths associated with consumer products and deaths associated with motor-vehicle exhaust, averaged about 560 annually, according to the Consumer Product Safety Commission (CPSC). About 340 of these deaths (60%) were attributed to motor-vehicle exhaust each year. The remaining 220 yearly deaths were associated with various consumer products. (See the table below.) Most non-fire CO related deaths took place in the home (66%) compared to campers/tents (14%) and automobiles (7%). The remaining 13% of the fatalities were categorized as unknown or other place.

For non-fatal incidents occurring from 1993 through 1997, the CPSC estimates that 32% of victims of non-fire CO poisonings are between the ages of 25 and 44 years old. About 21% of the victims are 5–14 years

old, while children under 5 account for 15% of non-fire poisonings. Persons 45–64 years, 15–24 years, and older than 64 years were estimated to account for 14%, 13%, and 6% of non-fire CO poisonings, respectively.

Carbon monoxide poisoning can also be a potential danger in the workplace. Occupational fatalities caused by unintentional CO poisoning made up about 5% of all unintentional CO fatalities between 1992 and 1996. The Bureau of Labor Statistics (BLS) estimates that there were 867 non-fatal poisonings requiring time away from work and 32 fatal poisonings (including motor-vehicle exhaust) in private industry in the United States in 1992. From 1992 through 1997 the services industry (which includes vehicle repair facilities) accounted for the largest share (25%) of workplace CO-related fatalities. Manufacturing accounted for about 14.9% of CO-related fatalities compared to construction and agriculture, which accounted for 14.2% of CO-related fatalities each. Other industries accounted for a substantially lower proportion of carbon monoxide-related deaths. Among them were retail trade (7.4%), public administration (6.1%), transportation (4.7%), mining (3.4%), wholesale trade (2.7%), and finance (2.7%). Industries categorized as nonclassifiable were the site of 4.7% of industrial CO-related deaths.

Sources: Ault, K. L. (1998, September). Non-fire Carbon Monoxide Deaths and Injuries Associated with the Use of Consumer Products: Annual Estimates. Bethesda, MD: U.S. Consumer Product Safety Commission. Janicak, C. A. (1998). Job Fatalities Due to Unintentional Carbon Monoxide Poisoning, 1992-96. Compensation and Working Conditions, 3, 26–28.

ESTIMATED NON-FIRE CARBON MONOXIDE POISONING DEATHS BY TYPE OF CONSUMER PRODUCT REPORTED, 1991–1995

Consumer Product	Average Percent	1991	1992	1993	1994	1995
Total Deaths	100%	250	211	214	223	201
Heating Systems	74%	186	139	152	177	159
Unspecified Gas Heating	19%	53	24	44	59	26
LP Gas Heating	17%	35	43	27	35	51
Natural Gas Heating	11%	34	22	14	24	31
Coal/Wood Heating	3%	8	9	7	6	6
Kerosene/Oil Heating	4%	17	6	10	9	5
Heating Systems, Not Specified	19%	39	35	50	44	40
Charcoal Grills	10%	25	27	27	15	14
Gas Water Heaters	4%	13	6	11	7	5
Camp Stoves, Lanterns	6%	10	17	10	12	15
Gas Ranges, Ovens	4%	14	13	6	9	5
Other Appliances	2%	3	9	7	3	3

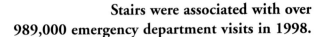

**Stairs were associated with over
989,000 emergency department visits in 1998.**

INJURIES ASSOCIATED
WITH CONSUMER PRODUCTS

The following list of items found in and around the home was selected from the U.S. Consumer Product Safety Commission's National Electronic Injury Surveillance System (NEISS) for 1998. The NEISS estimates are calculated from a statistically representative sample of hospitals in the United States. Injury totals represent estimates of the number of hospital emergency department-treated cases nationwide associated with various products. However, product involvement may or may not be the cause of the injury.

ESTIMATED HOSPITAL EMERGENCY DEPARTMENT VISITS RELATED TO SELECTED CONSUMER PRODUCTS, 1998
(excluding chemicals and most sports or sports equipment; see also page 114)

Description	Injuries[a]
Home Workshop Equipment	
Saws (hand or power)	98,707
Hammers	42,426
Power grinders, buffers & polishers	17,818
Drills	17,199
Welding & soldering equipment	16,771
Packaging and Containers, Household	
Household containers & packaging	202,252
Bottles and jars	87,201
Bags	28,273
Housewares	
Knives	454,246
Tableware and flatware (excluding knives)	122,306
Waste containers, trash baskets, etc.	31,608
Cookware, bowls and canisters	31,288
Scissors	30,819
Manual cleaning equipment (excl. buckets)	17,419
Home Furnishings, Fixtures, and Accessories	
Beds	437,980
Tables, n.e.c.[b]	316,733
Chairs	286,020
Bathtubs and showers	181,837
Ladders	157,219
Sofas, couches, davenports, divans, etc.	124,258
Rugs and carpets	117,588
Other furniture[c]	68,271
Toilets	48,964
Misc. decorating items	32,355
Benches	26,670
Sinks	23,711
Electric lighting equipment	23,335
Mirrors or mirror glass	22,367
Stools	17,502
Home Structures and Construction Materials	
Stairs or steps	989,977
Floors or flooring materials	986,093
Other doors[d]	342,302
Ceilings and walls	251,722
Household cabinets, racks & shelves	242,078
Nails, screws, tacks or bolts	183,068
Windows	143,138
Porches, balconies, open-side floors	138,123
Fences or fence posts	124,202
House repair and construction materials	83,493
Door sills or frames	42,984
Glass doors	40,721

Description	Injuries[a]
Poles	39,876
Handrails, railings or banisters	39,136
Counters or countertops	37,823
Fireplaces	18,419
Cabinet or door hardware	18,262
Ramps or landings	16,811
General Household Appliances	
Refrigerators	30,163
Ranges	27,467
Irons	17,329
Heating, Cooling, and Ventilating Equipment	
Pipes (excluding smoking pipes)	28,497
Fans	18,120
Home Communication and Entertainment Equipment	
Televisions	39,388
Sound recording and reproducing equipment	22,096
Telephones or telephone accessories	16,758
Personal Use Items	
Jewelry	61,977
Razors and shavers	38,238
Coins	28,570
Daywear	26,453
Hair grooming equipment & accessories	22,134
Other clothing[e]	20,189
Luggage	15,975
Yard and Garden Equipment	
Lawn mowers	76,337
Pruning, trimming & edging equipment	39,651
Chainsaws	33,158
Other unpowered garden tools[f]	23,439
Sports and Recreation Equipment	
Trampolines	95,239
Swings or swing sets	81,984
Swimming pools	81,079
Monkey bars or other playground climbing equipment	78,219
All-terrain vehicles	73,900
Skateboards	54,532
Slides or sliding boards	49,540
Other playground equipment[g]	27,799
Go-carts	19,649
Bleachers	19,161
BB's or pellets	17,356
Grills	16,167

Source: U.S. Consumer Product Safety Commission, National Electronic Injury Surveillance System, Product Summary Report, All Products, CY1998. Not all product categories are shown. Products were selected for high injury frequency.
[a] *Estimated number of product-related injuries in the United States and territories that were treated in hospital emergency departments.*
[b] *Excludes baby changing and television tables or stands.*
[c] *Includes cabinets, racks, shelves, desks, bureaus, chests, buffets, etc.*
[d] *Excludes glass doors and garage doors.*
[e] *Excludes costumes, masks, daywear, footwear, nightwear, and outerwear.*
[f] *Includes cultivators, hoes, pitchforks, rakes, shovels, spades, and trowels.*
[g] *Excludes monkey bars, seesaws, slides and swings.*
n.e.c. = not elsewhere classified.

In 1997, 15 of 16 homes in the United States had at least one smoke alarm.

According to the National Fire Protection Association (NFPA), homes with smoke alarms (operational or otherwise) usually have a death rate that is 40–50% lower than the rate for homes that have no alarms. In one and two family dwellings, only 16% of fire deaths from 1988 to 1997 resulted from fires where a smoke alarm sounded. During this time 39% of apartment fire deaths occurred under these conditions. Overall, 20% of home fire fatalities in this time period resulted from fires that triggered a functioning smoke alarm.

In 1992 the U.S. Consumer Product Safety Commission surveyed households to investigate how many homes have smoke alarms as well as to determine what percentage of them are functioning. Of the homes containing at least one smoke alarm, one of every five had no functioning smoke alarms. The total of homes without smoke alarms and homes with only non-functioning smoke alarms make up approximately 25% of all U.S. households.

In 1983, a study for the International Association of Fire Chiefs Foundations investigated 314 fires in which smoke alarms failed to sound. The results showed that 69% of failures were due to a disconnected power source, a dead battery, or a missing battery; while 12% of the failures were due to improper installation; and 11% were due to improper placement of the alarm. Routine monthly testing of household smoke alarms

is usually adequate protection from alarm dysfunction. However, in 1982 studies showed that 60% of those surveyed said they did not test as often as once a month. Furthermore, 16% of the respondents said they never tested their alarms.

One of the largest reasons for disconnected or missing power sources in smoke alarms is the frequency of nuisance alarms. In a survey conducted for the NFPA, 39% of the respondents with smoke alarms claimed that one had sounded at least once in the last 12 months. An overwhelming majority (90%) of nuisance alarms were attributed to two causes. Cooking fumes or heat caused 73% of the false alarms, while 16% reported the sounding alarm was caused by a low battery. Frequent nuisance alarms make many home owners impervious to the alarm's danger signal. In fact, the respondents who reported an alarm within the past 12 months were asked for their first thought after hearing the sound. Forty percent said that food had burned, 11% were annoyed at what they assumed to be a nuisance alarm, 10% had no concern because they claimed they knew what caused the alarm, 9% wondered how to turn off the alarm, 8% assumed the alarm had a low battery, and a mere 7% thought there was a fire and that they should get out.

Source: Ahrens, M. (2000, January). U.S. experience with smoke alarms and other fire alarms. Quincy, MA: National Fire Protection Association.

FIRE DEATH RATES IN HOMES BY ALARM PRESENCE, U.S., 1980–1997

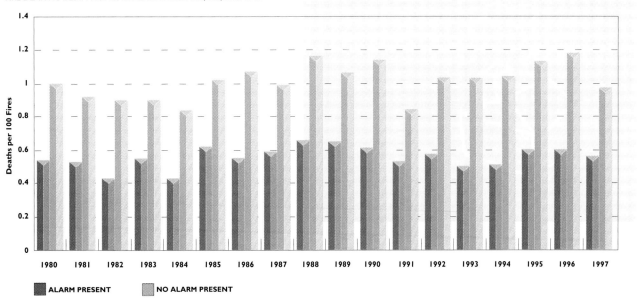

■ ALARM PRESENT   ■ NO ALARM PRESENT

AGRICULTURAL WORK FATALITIES

Nearly 6,000 people were killed as a result of agriculture-related injuries from 1992 through 1998, an average of over 830 persons each year. Production of crops and livestock had the highest death totals for this time period with 2,702 and 1,228, respectively. The chart below provides 7-year totals of state-by-state data for the five sectors of the agriculture industry.

FATAL OCCUPATIONAL INJURIES IN AGRICULTURE BY STATE, 1992–1998

State	Total	Agricultural Production of Crops	Agricultural Production of Livestock	Agricultural Services	Forestry	Fishing, Hunting, and Trapping
Total	5,820	2,702	1,228	1,134	95	511
Alabama	73	22	16	20	7	—
Alaska	144	—	—	—	—	144
Arizona	45	15	9	20	—	—
Arkansas	61	26	9	24	—	—
California	469	155	56	219	—	37
Colorado	100	44	34	21	—	—
Connecticut	23	—	—	14	—	—
Delaware	11	—	—	5	—	—
Florida	238	79	14	116	—	26
Georgia	118	52	15	40	7	—
Hawaii	22	—	—	—	—	15
Idaho	79	39	16	15	5	—
Illinois	227	128	29	34	—	—
Indiana	145	114	12	19	—	—
Iowa	194	178	8	8	—	—
Kansas	162	96	58	8	—	—
Kentucky	258	223	14	18	—	—
Louisiana	92	28	9	27	—	25
Maine	34	—	5	—	—	24
Maryland	46	22	—	15	—	—
Massachusetts	72	6	—	20	—	42
Michigan	104	56	19	22	—	—
Minnesota	178	68	38	8	—	—
Mississippi	94	52	12	22	—	8
Missouri	184	109	57	15	—	—
Montana	96	41	52	—	—	—
Nebraska	141	115	16	10	—	—
Nevada	17	—	7	5	—	—
New Hampshire	6	—	—	—	—	—
New Jersey	44	8	7	22	—	7
New Mexico	34	15	15	—	—	—
New York	197	44	112	32	—	5
North Carolina	196	89	26	51	6	24
North Dakota	82	69	11	—	—	—
Ohio	184	130	17	36	—	—
Oklahoma	76	19	17	13	—	—
Oregon	92	30	8	13	16	25
Pennsylvania	233	152	45	28	8	—
Rhode Island	9	—	—	—	—	7
South Carolina	55	19	6	18	—	8
South Dakota	85	65	17	—	—	—
Tennessee	230	152	53	20	—	5
Texas	305	66	101	92	—	43
Utah	38	6	23	6	—	—
Vermont	10	—	8	—	—	—
Virginia	118	66	22	23	—	5
Washington	129	59	13	24	—	30
West Virginia	16	8	—	—	—	—
Wisconsin	212	12	191	8	—	—
Wyoming	35	7	20	—	—	—

Source: U.S. Department of Labor, Bureau of Labor Statistics, Census of Fatal Occupational Injuries.
Dash (—) indicates data not available or data that do not meet publication criteria.
Totals for major categories may include subcategories not shown separately.

TRACTOR FATALITY RATES ON THE FARM

Overturns have the highest fatality rate for unintentional injuries involving tractors that occur on the farm, according to reports from 22 states covering about 41% of the farm tractors in the United States. In 1998, overturns accounted for 52% of all on-the-farm fatalities reported, with an annual rate of 4.3 deaths per 100,000 tractors.

For all tractor fatalities combined, projecting the overall rate of 8.2 deaths per 100,000 tractors in this sample to the nation's more than 3.8 million tractors yields an estimated 317 tractor-related deaths on the farm nationwide in 1998.

TRACTOR FATALITY RATES ON THE FARM BY TYPE OF EVENT, UNITED STATES, 1988–1998

| Year | Deaths per 100,000 Tractors | | | | | Percent of Deaths | | | | |
	All Types	Overturns	Run Over	Power Takeoff	Other	Total	Overturns	Run Over	Power Takeoff	Other
1988	8.6	3.7	2.4	0.6	1.7	100%	44	29	7	20
1989	7.2	4.0	1.1	0.2	2.0	100%	55	15	2	28
1990	9.9	5.1	3.3	0.3	1.2	100%	52	33	3	12
1991	9.2	4.3	2.7	0.4	1.7	100%	47	30	4	19
1992	6.8	3.6	1.7	0.2	1.3	100%	53	25	3	19
1993	7.5	4.1	1.7	0.3	1.3	100%	55	23	4	18
1994	8.2	4.3	2.2	0.3	1.5	100%	52	26	4	18
1995	10.0	5.5	2.7	0.3	1.6	100%	55	27	2	16
1996	6.6	3.4	1.6	0.1	1.6	100%	52	24	1	24
1997	6.5	3.4	1.7	0.4	1.0	100%	52	26	6	16
1998[a]	8.2	4.3	2.0	0.4	1.6	100%	52	24	5	19

Source: Deaths based on reports provided by state agricultural safety specialists; tractors based on National Safety Council tabulations of U.S. Census of Agriculture data, 1997.
[a] *Tractor fatality rates for 1998 are based on data provided by 22 states, which may not be the same states that reported data in prior years.*

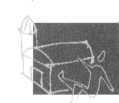

DEATHS ON FARMS

The table below shows deaths from unintentional injuries that occurred on farms to all persons, primarily farm residents, but includes others such as nonresident workers, hunters, and visitors. Excluded are farm home deaths, transport deaths, and deaths of farm residents that occurred off farm property. Tabulations are understated as not all death certificates indicate the place of occurrence.

DEATHS FROM NONTRANSPORT UNINTENTIONAL INJURIES ON FARMS BY TYPE,
UNITED STATES, 1987–1997 (EXCLUDING FARM HOME DEATHS)

Year	All Types[a]	Machinery	Drowning	Firearms	Falls	Struck by Object	Fires, Burns	Electric Current	Animals	Poisoning	Suffocation	Lightning
1987	945	458	94	43	56	88	23	40	44	12	22	10
1988	831	405	78	46	58	76	17	26	28	8	23	12
1989	770	354	101	52	42	57	4	16	35	28	22	7
1990	779	403	61	42	48	67	9	26	31	13	28	10
1991	743	379	59	45	54	65	15	19	30	5	17	7
1992	726	363	59	38	35	61	15	12	49	15	26	2
1993	793	387	49	43	60	64	11	19	42	15	32	8
1994	705	342	51	34	54	75	17	12	25	13	25	6
1995	679	316	50	30	58	58	20	15	27	14	21	5
1996	677	295	50	32	55	63	21	13	46	10	34	3
1997[b]	690	313	77	31	66	49	9	8	40	18	27	5

Source: National Safety Council tabulations of National Center for Health Statistics mortality data.
[a] *Includes some deaths not shown separately.*
[b] *Latest official figures.*

ENVIRONMENTAL HEALTH

ENVIRONMENTAL HEALTH FACTS

While we are used to thinking of "injuries" and "accidents" as unintentional, preventable, physical traumas like falls or car crashes, we often overlook the deaths and harm to health that come from environmental causes.

Here are some areas where personal behavior, corporate behavior, and public policy choices actually can make a difference in reducing unintentional death, disease, and injury.

Lung Cancer. In 1998, there were an estimated 171,500 new cases of lung cancer (14% of all cancer diagnosed) and 161,100 deaths from it. The biggest risk factor is cigarette smoking, a lifestyle choice with a preventable cause. Several environmental factors are also known to be risks: radon, environmental tobacco smoke, asbestos, and certain occupational and medical exposures. Radon is estimated to account for 10% of all lung cancer deaths, which was about 15,000 deaths in 1998[a]. There are about 2,000-3,000 new cases of malignant mesothelioma a year in the United States, and asbestos exposure is the main risk factor for this kind of lung cancer[b].

Environmental Tobacco Smoke. The U.S. Environmental Protection Agency has estimated that environmental tobacco smoke (ETS)—secondhand smoke breathed in by non-smokers—causes about 3,000 deaths from lung cancer annually. EPA's position is simple: "Secondhand smoke is a preventable health risk." According to the EPA, an estimated 150,000 to 300,000 children under 18 months of age get pneumonia or bronchitis from breathing secondhand tobacco smoke. Secondhand smoke is a risk factor for the development of asthma in children and worsens the condition of up to one million asthmatic children.

Skin Cancer. There are roughly one million cases a year of skin cancer in the United States. Most are basal cell or squamous cell cancers, which are highly curable. A more serious kind, melanoma, was expected to be diagnosed in approximately 41,600 people in 1998. Of the estimated 9,200 skin cancer deaths in 1998, about 7,300 were from melanoma. Fair skin and exposure to

the ultraviolet rays in sunlight are major risk factors. Exposure to sunlight can be limited through lifestyle choices (hats, sunglasses, sunscreen, long sleeves, etc.). Scientists believe depletion of the stratospheric ozone layer is increasing people's ultraviolet exposure, although this is hard to measure[c].

Lead Poisoning. In 1994, the last year for which data are available, 393,000 children ages 1–5 were estimated to have blood lead levels above 15 µg/dL, and 59,000 to have levels above 25 µg/dL. Untreated, lead poisoning causes harmful effects on children's learning and behavior, and neurological disorders, which in their most acute form are fatal. Lead poisoning disproportionately affects children, nonwhites, and poor people.

Food, Water, Air. At least 200 distinct diseases can be transmitted through food. In the United States, the Centers for Disease Control and Prevention (CDC) estimates incidence of foodborne illness at 76 million cases per year, resulting in 325,000 hospitalizations and 5,000 deaths per year[d]. During 1995–96, the last period for which CDC reported on surveillance of waterborne disease, at least 2,567 people became ill from drinking water and 9,129 became ill from recreational water exposure[e]. In 1996, asthma caused over 5,500 deaths in the United States. Some 15 million Americans have asthma; about 5 million of them are children (it is the most common chronic disease of childhood). The incidence of asthma has more than doubled in the past two decades. In 1996, there were about 15 million outpatient visits, 445,000 hospitalizations, 1.2 million emergency room visits, and 10 million missed school days, resulting in an estimated health care cost of $14 billion for 1996.

[a] Lubin, J.H., Boice, J.D. Jr., Edling, C., Hornung, R.W., Howe, G.R., Kunz, E., Kusiak, R.A., Morrison, H.I., Radford, E.P., Samet, J.M., Tirmarche, M., Woodward, A., Yao, S.Z., & Pierce, D.A. (1995). Lung Cancer in Radon-Exposed Miners and Estimation of Risk From Indoor Exposure. Journal of the National Cancer Institute, 87, 817–826.
[b] American Cancer Society. (2000). Mesothelioma FAQ [On-line]. Available: http://www.cancer.org/cancerinfo/load_cont.asp?ct=29&st=fq.
[c] National Cancer Society. (2000) [On-line]. Available: http://www.cancer.org/statistics/cff98/selectedcancers.html.
[d] Mead, P.S., Slutsker, L., Dietz, V. et al. (1999). Food-Related Illness and Death in the United States. Emerging Infectious Diseases, 5(5).
[e] Levy, D.A., Bens, M.S., Craun, G.F., Calderon, R.L., & Herwaldt, B.L. (1998). Surveillance for Waterborne-Disease Outbreaks—United States, 1995–1996. Atlanta, GA: Centers for Disease Control and Prevention.

Worldwide, waterborne disease is still one of the major problems in public health. A century ago in the United States, waterborne diseases like cholera and typhoid were common causes of sickness and death. Today, since most of the United States population benefits from modern sewage treatment and drinking water purification, diarrheal diseases like cholera and typhoid are exceedingly rare. However, diarrheal diseases (which are mostly waterborne) were the sixth highest cause of death in 1998 among all nations belonging to the World Health Organization[a].

Estimating all cases of waterborne disease in the United States is difficult. Not everyone who gets sick goes to a doctor or clinic. Not every case of gastroenteritis is diagnosed as being caused by a specific germ, and even then the source of the germ may remain unknown. Federal agencies and state epidemiologists maintain a surveillance system for waterborne disease. However, according to the Centers for Disease Control and Prevention (CDC), "Not all WBDOs (waterborne disease outbreaks) are recognized, investigated, and reported to CDC or EPA, and the extent to which WBDOs are unrecognized and underreported is unknown[b]."

In one outbreak in one year alone (an outbreak of cryptosporidiosis in Milwaukee in 1993), a confirmed waterborne disease was estimated to have sickened some 403,000 people and killed 111. Various studies of waterborne disease in the United States have estimated the annual incidence of sickness at anywhere from 230,000 to 7.1 million, and the annual deaths from 50 to 1,200. The truth may lie in between, and it certainly varies from year to year.

Most cases of waterborne disease are probably preventable. The most common route of transmission involves the contamination of a water body by bacteria or viruses from the feces of an infected person or animal—and the subsequent drinking of that contaminated water, its use with food, or even recreational contact like swimming. Communities in the United States have made significant advances in sewage treatment and drinking water purification since the enactment of the Clean Water Act of 1972 and the Safe Drinking Water Act of 1974.

[a] *World Health Organization. (1999). Leading causes of mortality and burden of disease, estimates for 1998. World Health Report 1999. Geneva, Switzerland: Author.*
[b] *Centers for Disease Control and Prevention. (2000). Surveillance for Waterborne-disease Outbreaks, United States, 1997–1998. Morbidity and Mortality Weekly Report, 49, No. SS–4, 2.*

WATERBORNE-DISEASE OUTBREAKS ASSOCIATED WITH DRINKING WATER, BY DISEASE-CAUSING AGENT, WATER SYSTEM, WATER SOURCE, AND DEFICIENCY—UNITED STATES, 1997–1998

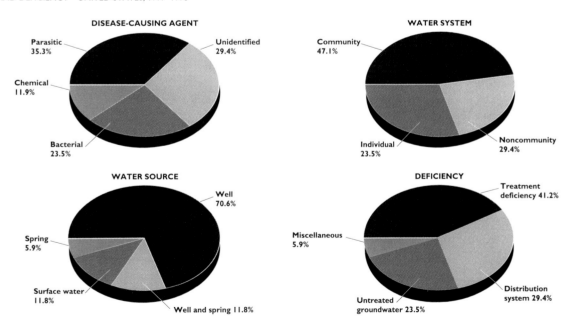

FOODBORNE ILLNESS

Foodborne diseases cause approximately 76 million illnesses, 325,000 hospitalizations, and 5,000 deaths in the United States every year, according to the latest estimates from the Centers for Disease Control and Prevention (CDC)[a]. The estimated annual cost of foodborne diseases in the United States is $5 to $6 billion in direct medical costs and lost productivity, according to the National Institute of Allergy and Infectious Diseases[b].

Although meticulous care goes into such estimates, foodborne diseases often go untreated and unreported. The causative pathogen is known in only about 14 million (18%) of the illnesses and 1,800 (36%) of the deaths from foodborne disease, according to CDC estimates. Over 200 known diseases can be transmitted by food, but they are underreported. Many people with foodborne gastroenteritis never seek medical attention,

and many times medical professionals overlook such illnesses. CDC estimates that 38 cases of salmonella poisoning occur for every one that is diagnosed and reported[c]. Some foodborne diseases can also be transmitted by water or human contact. In many cases, the cycle of transmission involves all of these, or the living animals and plants we eat. Many of the microbes that worry health authorities today were not even recognized as causing foodborne disease two decades ago.

Foodborne disease is highly preventable most of the time. These diseases are noticeable because they often occur in outbreaks affecting a number of people at the same time—people who have all eaten from a food source contaminated by the same pathogen. Such contamination can usually be prevented by proper sanitation and food-handling procedures.

[a] Mead, P.S., Slutsker, L., Dietz, V., McCaig, L.F., Bresee, J.S., Shapiro, C., Griffin, P.M., & Tauxe, R.V. (1999). Emerging Infectious Diseases. Synopses: Food-Related Illness and Death in the United States (Vol. 5, No. 5). Atlanta, GA: Centers for Disease Control and Prevention.
[b] Office of Communications and Public Liaison, National Institute of Allergy and Infectious Diseases. (1998, March). Fact Sheet: Foodborne Diseases. Bethesda, MD: National Institutes of Health.
[c] Centers for Disease Control and Prevention. (2000). Disease Information: Foodborne Infections [On-line]. Available:
http://www.cdc.gov/ncidod/dbmd/diseaseinfo/foodborneinfections_g.htm#howdiagnosed

ESTIMATED ILLNESSES, HOSPITALIZATIONS, AND DEATHS CAUSED BY KNOWN FOODBORNE PATHOGENS, UNITED STATES, 1997

Disease or Agent	Illnesses		Hospitalizations		Deaths	
	Foodborne	% of Total	Foodborne	% of Total	Foodborne	% of Total
Total	13,814,924	100.0	60,854	100.0	1,809	100.0
Bacterial	4,175,565	30.2	36,466	59.9	1,297	71.7
E. coli	173,107	1.3	2,785	4.5	78	4.3
Salmonella	1,342,532	9.7	16,102	26.4	556	30.7
Parasitic	357,190	2.6	3,219	5.3	383	21.2
Toxoplasma gondil	112,500	0.8	2,500	4.1	375	20.7
Viral	9,282,170	67.2	121,167	34.8	129	7.1
Norwalk-like viruses	9,200,000	66.6	20,000	32.9	124	6.9
Hepatitis A	4,170	0.0	90	0.9	4	0.2

Source: See footnote "a" in text.

It may not be possible to count the exact number of people in the United States who are killed or injured by air pollution, but the estimates are telling. Lung disease is a major cause of death and disability in the United States. Of course, the leading causes of death are heart attack, cancer, and stroke (together they account for almost 62% of deaths). But the Center for Disease Control and Prevention (CDC) statistics put chronic obstructive pulmonary diseases (4.7% of all deaths) slightly ahead of unintentional injuries and adverse effects (4.1%) as a cause of death, and right behind that is another group of lung diseases, pneumonia and influenza (3.7%)[a]. "Chronic obstructive pulmonary disease" usually refers to a combination of emphysema and chronic bronchitis, the most important cause of which is smoking. Lung diseases have an array of causes and complicating factors—but air pollution is clearly one of them. Air pollution makes the struggle to breathe that much harder for people with these life-threatening diseases.

The landmark Clean Air Act of 1970 required EPA to set primary National Ambient Air Quality Standards (NAAQS), scientifically based benchmark levels of air pollution which, if achieved, would be protective of public health. EPA has set primary NAAQS for six pollutants, called criteria pollutants—ozone (smog), particulates (soot) [designated PM10 in the graph below], carbon monoxide [CO], lead [Pb], nitrogen dioxide [NO_2], and sulfur dioxide [SO_2]. Nationwide, more than 102,000,000 people in 1999 lived in areas that in some way failed to meet these basic healthy-air standards[b].

[a] *Hoyert, D.L., Kochanek, K.D., & Murphy, S.L. (1999). Deaths: Final data for 1997 (National Vital Statistics Reports, 47(19)). Hyattsville, MD: National Center for Health Statistics.*
[b] *U.S. Environmental Protection Agency, Office of Air Quality Planning and Standards. USA Air Quality Nonattainment Areas. http://www.epa.gov/airs/nonattn.html.*

NATIONAL LONG-TERM AIR QUALITY TRENDS, UNITED STATES, 1989–1998

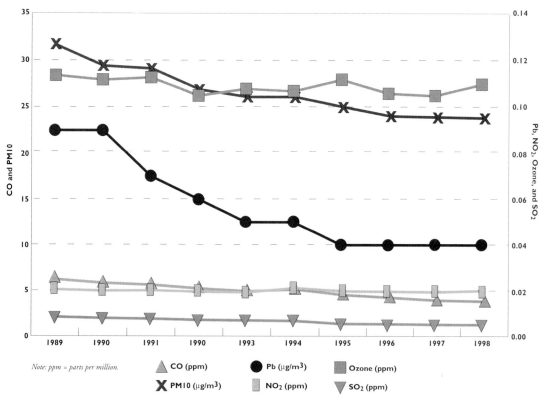

RADON

Radon is a colorless, odorless radioactive gas formed by the natural radioactive decay of uranium in rock, soil, and water. It occurs naturally at low levels in all 50 states. Once produced, radon moves through the ground to the air and ground water.

Radon from rock and soil can seep through cracks and openings in the walls and floors of buildings, where it can collect and concentrate. The gas decays into radioactive particles that can get trapped in people's lungs when they breathe. As they break down further, these particles release small bursts of energy. This can damage lung tissue and lead to an increased chance of lung cancer over the course of a lifetime.

The Surgeon General has warned that radon is the second leading cause of lung cancer in the United States. Only smoking causes more cases. The risk to smokers who breathe elevated levels of radon is especially high.

In 1998, the National Academy of Sciences released the Biological Effects of Ionizing Radiation (BEIR VI) Report, "The Health Effects of Exposure to Indoor Radon." The study reviewed and evaluated data from many prior studies and drew conclusions. It fully supports estimates by EPA that radon causes about 15,000 lung cancer deaths per year. Though some people debate the number of deaths, radon's importance as a cause of lung cancer is widely agreed on.

Nearly 1 out of every 15 homes has a radon level EPA considers to be elevated—4 picocuries per liter (pCi/L) or greater. The U.S. average radon-in-air level in single-family homes is 1.3 pCi/L. Because most people spend as much as 90% of their time indoors, indoor exposure to radon is an important concern.

Fortunately, people can test their homes for radon inexpensively. If radon levels are elevated, the problem can usually be remedied by sealing cracks in basements and using fans to change the air pressure difference between soil and building. The cost for fixing an existing home rarely exceeds $2,500 and the cost for making a new home radon-resistant is often less than one-quarter of that.

The graphic below shows 1999 estimates of unintentional injury deaths alongside a 1995 estimate of lung cancer deaths caused by radon. Time discrepancy, differences in estimation technique, and difference in the nature of the cause of death can affect comparisons among categories. The purpose of the graphic is to illustrate that radon exposure is a valid threat. However, no inference should be made concerning the relative risk of the potential hazards shown below.

RADON DEATHS VERSUS OTHER UNINTENTIONAL INJURIES

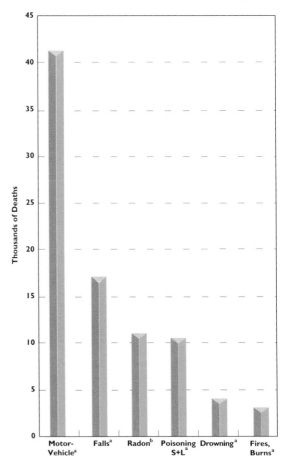

Source: Committee on Health Risks of Exposure to Radon. (1999). Health Effects of Exposure to Radon. Washington DC: National Academy Press.
[a] 1999 National Safety Council estimates.
[b] Estimated number of lung cancer deaths in 1995 caused by radon in persons who have never smoked.

Asthma is an inflammatory condition of the lungs in which the small air tubes swell and produce more mucus, and the muscles around them tighten—making breathing difficult. It is a chronic, episodic disease that often affects people most of their lives. If a person has asthma, many different things can trigger attacks. They include preventable allergens and environmental pollutants like sulfur dioxide, dust mites, cockroaches, animal dander, tobacco smoke, and mold. Mild attacks may subside naturally then reoccur. Medication can relieve or prevent attacks. Severe attacks, unless treated quickly, can be fatal.

By some estimates, the incidence of asthma has more than doubled in the past two decades, and the highest incidence is among poor, urban, and minority populations. Mortality rates are higher among older age groups, but the growth of incidence is higher among younger age groups.

The details that follow show the significant impact of asthma:

• Asthma caused 5,434 deaths in 1997, the latest year for which U.S. data are available[a]. This is an increase from 2,598 in 1979, an increase of almost 109%[b].

• CDC[c] estimated that 17,299,000 people in the United States had asthma in 1998.

• More than 4.8 million children under age 18 suffer from asthma[d].

• Asthma is the ninth leading cause of hospitalization nationally[c].

• Asthma was the first-listed diagnosis in 468,000 hospital admissions in the United States in 1993[d].

• Asthma caused more than 1,867,000 visits to emergency rooms in 1995[d].

• The number of visits to doctors' offices for asthma or for treatment related to asthma more than doubled between 1975 and 1993–95—from 4.6 million to 10.4 million[e].

• From 1980 to 1994, the prevalence of self-reported asthma in the United States increased by 75%[c]. The reasons for this increase are not clearly understood.

• Asthma costs the United States an estimated $11.3 billion annually. That includes $7.5 billion in direct healthcare costs and $3.8 billion in indirect costs from lost productivity[b]. The "lost productivity" includes 10 million lost schooldays.

• Asthma is 26% more prevalent in African-American children than in Caucasian children[d].

[a] Centers for Disease Control and Prevention. (1999). Number of deaths from 72 selected causes, States, 1997 (Table 10). National Vital Statistics Reports, 47(19), 53.
[b] American Lung Association, Epidemiology & Statistics Unit. (2000, Feb.). Trends in asthma morbidity and mortality. Cites National Center for Health Statistics, Annual Summary of Vital Statistics, 1979-1997. [On-line]. Available: http://www.lungusa.org/data/asthma/part1.pdfs
[c] Centers for Disease Control and Prevention. (1998). Forecasted State-Specific Estimates of Self-Reported Asthma Prevalence—United States, 1998. Morbidity and Mortality Weekly, 47, 1022-1025.
[d] American Academy of Allergy, Asthma & Immunology. Fast Facts: Statistics on Asthma [On-line]. Available: http://www.aaaai.org/public/fastfacts/statistics.stm
[e] Centers for Disease Control and Prevention. (1998). Surveillance for Asthma—United States, 1960–1995 (Table 3). Morbidity and Mortality, 47:SS-1.

ASTHMA PREVALENCE BY RACE, 1982–1996

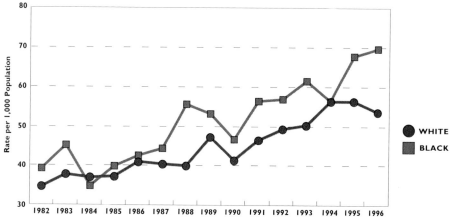

Source: National Center for Health Statistics: National Health Interview Survey, 1982–1996.

STATE DATA

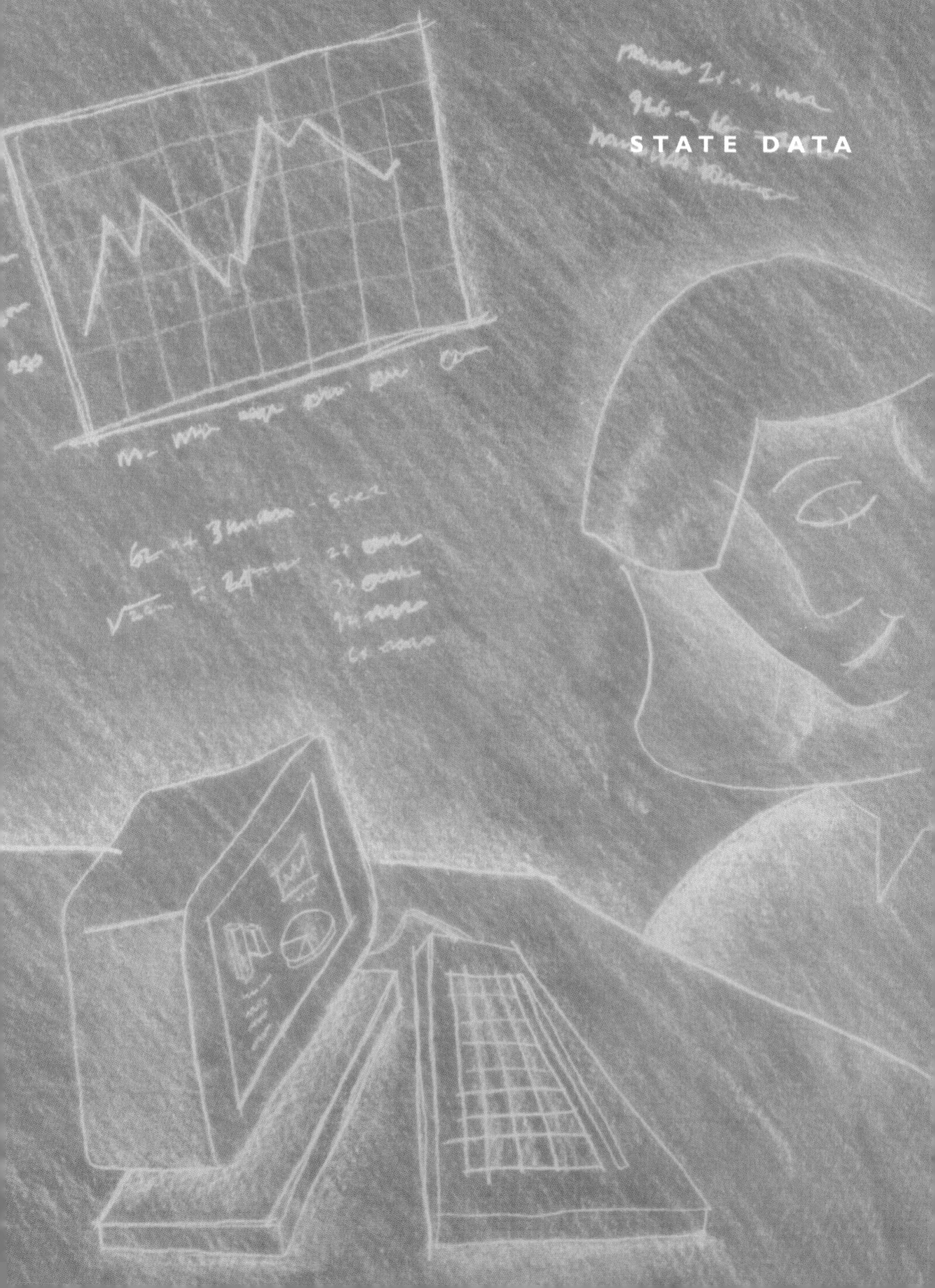

STATE DATA

Death rates for unintentional injuries can vary greatly from state to state and from one type of injury to the next. The graph on page 145 gives statistical information for selected types of unintentional-injury deaths. The colored diamond locates the median death rate for each type of unintentional injury. To determine the median, the state death rates are arranged in order from least to greatest. The median value is simply the center value on the arranged list. Motor-vehicle deaths had the highest median value (18.4 per 100,000 population) while air transportation had the lowest (0.2).

The colored triangles above and below the median diamond represent the range of death rates throughout the states. The bottom triangle represents the lowest death rate (minimum) for each type of unintentional-injury death while the top triangle represents the highest (maximum) of the death rates. The lower white triangle is representative of the 1st quartile death rate, meaning that 25% of the states reported a death rate lower than this rate. The upper white triangle represents the rate for the 3rd quartile, meaning that 75% of the states reported a death rate lower than this rate. The difference between the 3rd and 1st quartile rates is called the interquartile range. If the interquartile range is short, then most of the rates are clustered near the median. If the interquartile range is large, then the rates vary more from state to state.

The table on page 146 consists of a three-year state-by-state comparison of unintentional-injury deaths and death rates for 1997, 1996, and 1995. Rates of unintentional-injury deaths remained fairly consistent for each state over the three-year span. Illinois and Wyoming showed the most dramatic decreases in death rates. The rate for Illinois dropped from 32.2 in 1995 to 26.4 in 1997 while unintentional-injury death rates in Wyoming fell from 59.7 in 1995 to 54.0 in 1997. The most dramatic increases in rates were in Montana, which rose from 46.3 in 1995 to 55.5 in 1997, and Mississippi, whose rate increased from 53.3 in 1996 to 57.5 in 1997.

In 1997, deaths caused by unintentional injuries ranked fifth among all causes of death with 95,644 deaths. Motor-vehicle deaths accounted for more than 45% of unintentional-injury deaths (43,458), followed by falls (15,447), solid and liquid poisoning (9,587), drowning (4,051), and fires and burns (3,490). Of the 50 states and Washington, D.C., New Mexico had the highest unintentional-injury death rate with 62.6 deaths per 100,000 population. Massachusetts had the lowest death rate of 20.7 unintentional-injury deaths per 100,000 population. The highest rates of deaths due to motor-vehicle crashes occurred in Mississippi (32.7), Montana (30.8), New Mexico (29.2), Alabama (28.0), and Wyoming (27.7). The states with the lowest motor-vehicle death rates were Massachusetts (7.9), Rhode Island (9.2), New Jersey (10.1), Connecticut (10.3), and Illinois (10.5).

STATE DEATH RATES BY TYPE OF EVENT, UNITED STATES, 1997

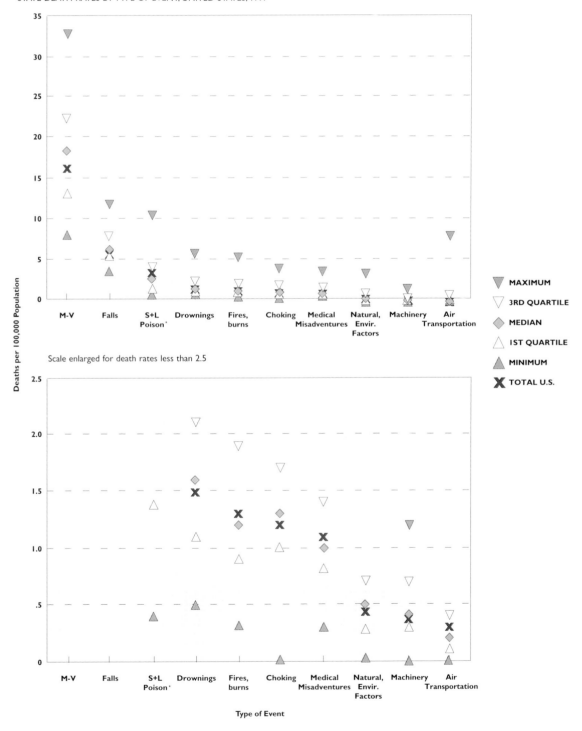

Scale enlarged for death rates less than 2.5

Type of Event

* Solid and liquid poisoning.

UNINTENTIONAL-INJURY DEATHS BY STATE, UNITED STATES, 1995–1997

State	Deaths[a]			Death Rate[c]		
	1997[b]	1996	1995	1997	1996	1995
Total U.S.	**95,644**	**94,948**	**93,320**	**35.7**	**35.8**	**35.5**
Alabama	2,255	2,187	2,269	52.2	51.2	53.4
Alaska	286	325	372	47.0	53.5	61.7
Arizona	2,192	2,178	2,079	48.2	49.2	48.3
Arkansas	1,262	1,209	1,184	50.0	48.2	47.7
California	8,897	9,368	9,103	27.6	29.4	28.8
Colorado	1,476	1,452	1,524	37.9	40.0	40.7
Connecticut	980	996	1,058	30.0	30.4	32.4
Delaware	286	249	264	38.9	34.3	38.9
Dist. of Columbia	260	246	245	49.2	45.3	44.2
Florida	5,640	5,557	5,533	38.4	38.6	39.0
Georgia	3,091	3,010	2,928	41.3	40.9	40.6
Hawaii	365	403	337	30.7	34.0	28.5
Idaho	575	562	537	47.5	47.3	46.1
Illinois	3,176	3,436	3,799	26.4	29.0	32.2
Indiana	2,077	2,110	2,167	35.4	36.1	37.3
Iowa	1,060	1,059	1,115	37.1	37.1	39.2
Kansas	959	1,006	948	36.7	39.1	37.0
Kentucky	1,757	1,735	1,714	45.0	44.7	44.1
Louisiana	1,957	1,845	1,862	45.0	42.4	42.9
Maine	444	410	415	35.7	33.0	33.5
Maryland	1,326	1,363	1,369	26.0	26.9	27.2
Massachusetts	1,269	1,256	1,197	20.8	20.6	19.7
Michigan	3,081	3,006	3,056	31.5	31.3	32.0
Minnesota	1,681	1,621	1,646	35.9	34.8	35.7
Mississippi	1,570	1,448	1,574	57.5	53.3	58.4
Missouri	2,562	2,495	2,454	47.4	46.6	46.1
Montana	487	438	403	55.5	49.8	46.3
Nebraska	669	670	601	40.4	40.6	36.6
Nevada	722	693	617	43.1	43.2	40.2
New Hampshire	334	292	276	28.5	25.1	24.0
New Jersey	2,268	2,225	2,193	28.2	27.9	27.6
New Mexico	1,076	1,035	988	62.5	60.4	58.5
New York	4,803	4,706	4,867	26.5	25.9	26.7
North Carolina	3,128	3,197	3,021	42.1	43.7	42.0
North Dakota	274	247	240	42.8	38.4	37.4
Ohio	3,388	3,292	3,206	30.2	29.5	28.8
Oklahoma	1,600	1,526	1,402	48.3	46.2	42.8
Oregon	1,342	1,375	1,388	41.4	42.9	44.1
Pennsylvania	4,819	4,378	4,295	40.1	36.3	35.7
Rhode Island	227	211	211	23.0	21.3	21.3
South Carolina	1,708	1,687	1,646	45.1	45.6	44.9
South Dakota	311	365	340	42.6	49.9	46.6
Tennessee	2,847	2,872	2,718	52.9	54.0	51.8
Texas	7,148	7,290	6,445	36.9	38.1	34.3
Utah	734	663	669	35.5	33.2	34.1
Vermont	220	203	209	37.4	34.5	35.7
Virginia	2,279	2,220	2,167	33.9	33.3	33.6
Washington	1,865	1,890	1,823	33.3	34.2	33.5
West Virginia	797	793	731	43.9	43.4	40.1
Wisconsin	1,855	1,873	1,829	35.7	36.3	35.7
Wyoming	259	275	286	54.0	57.2	59.7

Source: National Safety Council estimates based on data from National Center for Health Statistics and U.S. Bureau of the Census. See Technical Appendix for comparability.
[a] *Deaths for each state are by place of occurrence. All death totals exclude nonresident aliens (1997–718 deaths, 1996–718 deaths, 1995–554 deaths).*
[b] *Latest official figures.*
[c] *Rates are deaths per 100,000 population.*

UNINTENTIONAL-INJURY DEATHS BY STATE

The following series of charts is a state-by-state ranking of deaths due to unintentional injuries (U-I). The first line of each section gives the total number of unintentional-injury deaths, the rate of unintentional injury deaths per 100,000 population, and the rank of unintentional-injury deaths among all causes of death. The following lines list the five leading types of unintentional-injury deaths along with the total and rate for each type.

TOTAL UNITED STATES

Rank	Cause	Deaths	Rate
5	All U-I	95,644	35.7
1	Motor-vehicle	43,458	16.2
2	Falls	15,447	5.8
3	S+L Poison[a]	9,587	3.6
4	Drowning[b]	4,051	1.5
5	Fires, burns	3,490	1.3

ALABAMA

Rank	Cause	Deaths	Rate
4	All U-I	2,255	52.2
1	Motor-vehicle	1,211	28.0
2	Falls	200	4.6
3	Fires, burns	117	2.7
4	Choking[c]	104	2.4
5	Drowning[b]	97	2.2

ALASKA

Rank	Cause	Deaths	Rate
3	All U-I	286	47.0
1	Motor-vehicle	85	13.9
2	Air transportation	47	7.7
3	Drowning[b]	34	5.6
4	S+L Poison[a]	26	4.3
5	Falls	22	3.6

ARIZONA

Rank	Cause	Deaths	Rate
5	All U-I	2,192	48.2
1	Motor-vehicle	971	21.3
2	Falls	350	7.7
3	S+L Poison[a]	316	6.9
4	Drowning[b]	100	2.2
5	Natural, envir. factors	64	1.4

ARKANSAS

Rank	Cause	Deaths	Rate
4	All U-I	1,262	50.0
1	Motor-vehicle	692	27.4
2	Falls	143	5.7
3	Drowning[b]	66	2.6
4	Fires, burns	57	2.3
5	Choking[c]	46	1.8
5	Natural, envir. factors	46	1.8

CALIFORNIA

Rank	Cause	Deaths	Rate
6	All U-I	8,897	27.6
1	Motor-vehicle	3,749	11.6
2	S+L Poison[a]	1,794	5.6
3	Falls	1,169	3.6
4	Drowning[b]	481	1.5
5	Fires, burns	245	0.8

COLORADO

Rank	Cause	Deaths	Rate
5	All U-I	1,476	37.9
1	Motor-vehicle	648	16.7
2	Falls	294	7.6
3	S+L Poison[a]	117	3.0
4	Drowning[b]	52	1.3
5	Choking[c]	48	1.2

CONNECTICUT

Rank	Cause	Deaths	Rate
6	All U-I	980	30.0
1	Motor-vehicle	337	10.3
2	Falls	184	5.6
3	S+L Poison[a]	168	5.1
4	Medical misadventures[d]	72	2.2
5	Choking[c]	54	1.7

DELAWARE

Rank	Cause	Deaths	Rate
5	All U-I	286	38.9
1	Motor-vehicle	142	19.3
2	S+L Poison[a]	39	5.3
3	Falls	38	5.2
4	Choking[c]	13	1.8
5	Drowning[b]	8	1.1

DISTRICT OF COLUMBIA

Rank	Cause	Deaths	Rate
4	All U-I	260	49.2
1	Motor-vehicle	87	16.5
2	Falls	47	8.9
3	Fires, burns	27	5.1
4	S+L Poison[a]	26	4.9
5	Choking[c]	20	3.8

FLORIDA

Rank	Cause	Deaths	Rate
5	All U-I	5,640	38.4
1	Motor-vehicle	2,840	19.3
2	Falls	811	5.5
3	S+L Poison[a]	543	3.7
4	Drowning[b]	401	2.7
5	Choking[c]	191	1.3

GEORGIA

Rank	Cause	Deaths	Rate
4	All U-I	3,091	41.3
1	Motor-vehicle	1,618	21.6
2	Falls	429	5.7
3	S+L Poison[a]	195	2.6
4	Drowning[b]	141	1.9
5	Fires, burns	115	1.5

HAWAII

Rank	Cause	Deaths	Rate
4	All U-I	365	30.7
1	Motor-vehicle	138	11.6
2	Falls	58	4.9
2	Drowning[b]	58	4.9
4	S+L Poison[a]	35	2.9
5	Choking[c]	21	1.8

IDAHO

Rank	Cause	Deaths	Rate
4	All U-I	575	47.5
1	Motor-vehicle	283	23.4
2	Falls	77	6.4
3	Drowning[b]	37	3.1
4	S+L Poison[a]	28	2.3
5	Air transportation	21	1.7

ILLINOIS

Rank	Cause	Deaths	Rate
6	All U-I	3,176	26.4
1	Motor-vehicle	1,261	10.5
2	Falls	525	4.4
3	S+L Poison[a]	418	3.5
4	Fires, burns	150	1.2
5	Choking[c]	131	1.1

INDIANA

Rank	Cause	Deaths	Rate
5	All U-I	2,077	35.4
1	Motor-vehicle	960	16.3
2	Falls	345	5.9
3	Medical misadventures[d]	122	2.1
4	Choking[c]	87	1.5
5	Drowning[b]	81	1.4

IOWA

Rank	Cause	Deaths	Rate
6	All U-I	1,060	37.2
1	Motor-vehicle	484	17.0
2	Falls	292	10.2
3	Choking[c]	44	1.5
4	S+L Poison[a]	29	1.0
5	Fires, burns	24	0.8

KANSAS

Rank	Cause	Deaths	Rate
5	All U-I	959	36.7
1	Motor-vehicle	487	18.6
2	Falls	171	6.5
3	Choking[c]	49	1.9
4	Fires, burns	39	1.5
5	S+L Poison[a]	38	1.5

See page 149 for footnotes.

KENTUCKY

Rank	Cause	Deaths	Rate
5	All U-I	1,757	45.0
1	Motor-vehicle	845	21.6
2	Falls	281	7.2
3	S+L Poison[a]	98	2.5
4	Fire	73	1.9
5	Choking[c]	61	1.6

LOUISIANA

Rank	Cause	Deaths	Rate
4	All U-I	1,957	45.0
1	Motor-vehicle	963	22.1
2	Falls	233	5.4
3	Drowning[b]	136	3.1
4	S+L Poison[a]	125	2.9
5	Fires, burns	84	1.9

MAINE

Rank	Cause	Deaths	Rate
5	All U-I	444	35.7
1	Motor-vehicle	201	16.1
2	Falls	100	8.0
3	Drowning[b]	24	1.9
3	S+L Poison[a]	24	1.9
5	Medical misadventures[d]	17	1.4

MARYLAND

Rank	Cause	Deaths	Rate
7	All U-I	1,326	26.0
1	Motor-vehicle	627	12.3
2	Falls	227	4.5
3	Medical misadventures[d]	90	1.8
4	Fires, burns	58	1.1
4	Choking[c]	58	1.1

MASSACHUSETTS

Rank	Cause	Deaths	Rate
7	All U-I	1,269	20.7
1	Motor-vehicle	486	7.9
2	Falls	372	6.1
3	Choking[c]	83	1.4
4	Drowning[b]	54	0.9
5	Fires, burns	53	0.9

MICHIGAN

Rank	Cause	Deaths	Rate
5	All U-I	3,081	31.5
1	Motor-vehicle	1,472	15.0
2	Falls	532	5.4
3	S+L Poison[a]	197	2.0
4	Fires, burns	141	1.4
5	Drowning[b]	101	1.0

MINNESOTA

Rank	Cause	Deaths	Rate
4	All U-I	1,681	35.9
1	Motor-vehicle	565	12.1
2	Falls	527	11.2
3	S+L Poison[a]	75	1.6
4	Drowning[b]	69	1.5
5	Medical misadventures[d]	53	1.1

MISSISSIPPI

Rank	Cause	Deaths	Rate
4	All U-I	1,570	57.5
1	Motor-vehicle	892	32.7
2	Falls	184	6.7
3	Fires, burns	106	3.9
4	Drowning[b]	69	2.5
5	Choking[c]	64	2.3

MISSOURI

Rank	Cause	Deaths	Rate
5	All U-I	2,562	47.4
1	Motor-vehicle	1,276	23.6
2	Falls	426	7.9
3	S+L Poison[a]	135	2.5
4	Fires, burns	119	2.2
5	Drowning[b]	93	1.7

MONTANA

Rank	Cause	Deaths	Rate
5	All U-I	487	55.4
1	Motor-vehicle	270	30.7
2	Falls	83	9.4
3	Drowning[b]	25	2.8
4	Air transportation	22	2.5
5	Natural, envir. factors	11	1.3

NEBRASKA

Rank	Cause	Deaths	Rate
5	All U-I	669	40.4
1	Motor-vehicle	305	18.4
2	Falls	159	9.6
3	Medical misadventures[d]	24	1.4
4	Choking[c]	23	1.4
5	S+L Poison[a]	18	1.1

NEVADA

Rank	Cause	Deaths	Rate
5	All U-I	722	43.1
1	Motor-vehicle	400	23.9
2	S+L Poison[a]	92	5.5
3	Falls	70	4.2
4	Drowning[b]	26	1.6
5	Fires, burns	20	1.2

NEW HAMPSHIRE

Rank	Cause	Deaths	Rate
5	All U-I	334	28.5
1	Motor-vehicle	143	12.2
2	Falls	67	5.7
3	S+L Poison[a]	26	2.2
4	Drowning[b]	13	1.1
4	Medical misadventures[d]	13	1.1

NEW JERSEY

Rank	Cause	Deaths	Rate
7	All U-I	2,268	28.2
1	Motor-vehicle	814	10.1
2	S+L Poison[a]	475	5.9
3	Falls	339	4.2
4	Fires, burns	90	1.1
5	Choking[c]	84	1.0

NEW MEXICO

Rank	Cause	Deaths	Rate
3	All U-I	1,076	62.6
1	Motor-vehicle	503	29.2
2	S+L Poison[a]	178	10.3
3	Falls	122	7.1
4	Natural, envir. factors	48	2.8
5	Medical misadventures[d]	39	2.3

NEW YORK

Rank	Cause	Deaths	Rate
6	All U-I	4,803	26.5
1	Motor-vehicle	1,719	9.5
2	S+L Poison[a]	974	5.4
3	Falls	901	5.0
4	Fires, burns	246	1.4
5	Medical misadventures[d]	171	0.9

NORTH CAROLINA

Rank	Cause	Deaths	Rate
5	All U-I	3,128	42.1
1	Motor-vehicle	1,588	21.4
2	Falls	452	6.1
3	S+L Poison[a]	224	3.0
4	Choking[c]	127	1.7
5	Drowning[b]	113	1.5
5	Medical misadventures[d]	113	1.5

NORTH DAKOTA

Rank	Cause	Deaths	Rate
4	All U-I	274	42.7
1	Motor-vehicle	126	19.7
2	Falls	75	11.7
3	Drowning[b]	11	1.7
4	Natural, envir. factors	9	1.4
5	Machinery	7	1.1

OHIO

Rank	Cause	Deaths	Rate
6	All U-I	3,388	30.2
1	Motor-vehicle	1,407	12.5
2	Falls	665	5.9
3	S+L Poison[a]	245	2.2
4	Choking[c]	166	1.5
5	Medical misadventures[d]	136	1.2

OKLAHOMA

Rank	Cause	Deaths	Rate
5	All U-I	1,600	48.3
1	Motor-vehicle	852	25.7
2	Falls	227	6.9
3	S+L Poison[a]	89	2.7
4	Fires, burns	68	2.1
5	Drowning[b]	65	2.0

OREGON

Rank	Cause	Deaths	Rate
5	All U-I	1,342	41.4
1	Motor-vehicle	566	17.5
2	Falls	260	8.0
3	S+L Poison[a]	170	5.2
4	Drowning[b]	79	2.4
5	Fires, burns	40	1.2

See page 149 for footnotes.

PENNSYLVANIA

Rank	Cause	Deaths	Rate
5	All U-I	4,819	40.1
1	Motor-vehicle	1,648	13.7
2	Falls	894	7.4
3	S+L Poison[a]	782	6.5
4	Medical misadventures[d]	304	2.5
5	Fires, burns	234	1.9

RHODE ISLAND

Rank	Cause	Deaths	Rate
7	All U-I	227	23.0
1	Motor-vehicle	91	9.2
2	Falls	55	5.6
3	Drowning[b]	11	1.1
3	Choking[c]	11	1.1
5	Fires, burns	9	0.9
5	Medical misadventures[d]	9	0.9

SOUTH CAROLINA

Rank	Cause	Deaths	Rate
4	All U-I	1,708	45.1
1	Motor-vehicle	917	24.2
2	Falls	165	4.4
3	S+L Poison[a]	113	3.0
4	Drowning[b]	88	2.3
5	Choking[c]	86	2.3

SOUTH DAKOTA

Rank	Cause	Deaths	Rate
5	All U-I	311	42.6
1	Motor-vehicle	155	21.2
2	Falls	81	11.1
3	Drowning[b]	15	2.1
4	S+L Poison[a]	9	1.2
4	Natural, envir. factors	9	1.2

TENNESSEE

Rank	Cause	Deaths	Rate
4	All U-I	2,847	52.9
1	Motor-vehicle	1,445	26.9
2	Falls	364	6.8
3	S+L Poison[a]	166	3.1
4	Fires, burns	122	2.3
5	Choking[c]	106	2.0

TEXAS

Rank	Cause	Deaths	Rate
4	All U-I	7,148	36.9
1	Motor-vehicle	3,736	19.3
2	Falls	869	4.5
3	S+L Poison[a]	656	3.4
4	Drowning[b]	354	1.8
5	Choking[c]	191	1.0

UTAH

Rank	Cause	Deaths	Rate
4	All U-I	734	35.5
1	Motor-vehicle	403	19.5
2	Falls	111	5.4
3	Medical misadventures[d]	29	1.4
4	Drowning[b]	28	1.4
5	Choking[c]	19	0.9

VERMONT

Rank	Cause	Deaths	Rate
5	All U-I	220	37.4
1	Motor-vehicle	86	14.6
2	Falls	52	8.8
3	Fires, burns	12	2.0
4	Choking[c]	11	1.9
5	Drowning[b]	7	1.2
5	S+L Poison[a]	7	1.2
5	Medical misadventures[d]	7	1.2

VIRGINIA

Rank	Cause	Deaths	Rate
5	All U-I	2,279	33.9
1	Motor-vehicle	962	14.3
2	Falls	374	5.6
3	S+L Poison[a]	207	3.1
4	Medical misadventures[d]	113	1.7
5	Choking[c]	96	1.4

WASHINGTON

Rank	Cause	Deaths	Rate
5	All U-I	1,865	33.3
1	Motor-vehicle	704	12.6
2	Falls	367	6.5
3	S+L Poison[a]	306	5.5
4	Drowning[b]	116	2.1
5	Fires, burns	42	0.7
5	Choking[c]	42	0.7

WEST VIRGINIA

Rank	Cause	Deaths	Rate
5	All U-I	797	43.9
1	Motor-vehicle	406	22.4
2	Falls	110	6.1
3	Choking[c]	39	2.1
4	Fires, burns	34	1.9
5	Drowning[b]	33	1.8

WISCONSIN

Rank	Cause	Deaths	Rate
5	All U-I	1,855	35.7
1	Motor-vehicle	759	14.6
2	Falls	509	9.8
3	S+L Poison[a]	92	1.8
4	Drowning[b]	73	1.4
5	Choking[c]	60	1.2

WYOMING

Rank	Cause	Deaths	Rate
3	All U-I	259	54.0
1	Motor-vehicle	133	27.7
2	Falls	39	8.1
3	Natural, envir. factors	15	3.1
4	Drowning[b]	12	2.5
5	S+L Poison[a]	9	1.9

[a] Solid and liquid poison.
[b] Includes drowning in transport.
[c] Inhalation or ingestion of food or other objects.
[d] Medical and surgical complications and misadventures.

TECHNICAL APPENDIX
OTHER SOURCES
GLOSSARY
INDEX

TECHNICAL APPENDIX

This appendix gives a brief explanation of some of the sources and methods used by the National Safety Council (NSC) Research and Statistics Department in preparing the estimates of deaths, injuries, and costs presented in this book. Because many of the estimates depend on death certificate data provided by the states or the National Center for Health Statistics (NCHS), it begins with a brief introduction to the certification and classification of deaths.

Certification and classification. The medical certification of death involves entering information on the death certificate about the disease or condition directly leading to death, antecedent causes, and other significant conditions. The death certificate is then registered with the appropriate authority and a nosologist assigns a code for the underlying cause of death. The underlying cause is defined as "(a) the disease or injury which initiated the train of morbid events leading directly to death, or (b) the circumstances of the accident or violence which produced the fatal injury" (World Health Organization [WHO], 1977). Deaths are classified and coded on the basis of a WHO standard, the *Manual of the International Statistical Classification of Diseases, Injuries, and Causes of Death,* commonly known as the International Classification of Diseases, or ICD (WHO, 1977). For deaths due to injury and poisoning, the ICD provides a system of "external cause" codes, or E-codes, to which the underlying cause of death is assigned. (See pages 16–17 of *Injury Facts*™ for a condensed list of E-codes.)

Comparability across ICD revisions. The ICD is revised each decade and these revisions can affect comparability from year to year. The sixth revision (1948) substantially expanded the list of external causes and provided for classifying the place of occurrence. Changes in the classification procedures for the sixth revision as well as the seventh (1958) and eighth (1968) revisions classified as diseases some deaths previously classified as injuries. The eighth revision also expanded and reorganized some external cause sections. The ninth revision (1979) provides more detail on the agency involved, the victim's activity, and the place of occurrence. Specific external cause categories affected by the revisions are noted in the historical tables. The tenth revision was adopted

in the United States in 1999.

Beginning with 1970 data, tabulations published by the NCHS no longer include deaths of nonresident aliens. In 1997, there were 648 such unintentional-injury deaths, of which 332 were motor-vehicle related.

Fatality estimates. The Council uses four classes to categorize unintentional injuries: Motor-Vehicle, Work, Home, and Public. Each class represents an environment and an intervention route for injury prevention through a responsible authority such as a police department, an employer, a home owner, or public health department.

Motor vehicle. The Motor-Vehicle class can be identified by the underlying cause of death (ICD codes E810–E825).

Work. The National Safety Council has adopted the Bureau of Labor Statistics' Census of Fatal Occupational Injuries (CFOI) figure, beginning with the 1992 data year, as the authoritative count of unintentional work-related deaths. The CFOI system is described in detail in Toscano and Windau (1994).

The 2-Way Split. After subtracting the Motor-Vehicle and Work figures from the unintentional-injury total (ICD codes E800–E949), the remainder belong to the Home and Public classes. The Home class can be identified by the "place of occurrence" subclassification (code .0) used with most nontransport deaths; the Public class is the remainder. Missing "place of occurrence" information, however, prevents the direct determination of the Home and Public class totals. Because of this, the Council allocates nonmotor-vehicle, nonwork deaths into the Home and Public classes based on the external cause, age group, and cases with specified "place of occurrence." This procedure, known as the 2-Way Split, uses the most recent death certificate data available from the NCHS and the CFOI data for the same calendar year. For each E-code group and age group combination, the Motor-Vehicle (ICD E810–E825) and Work (CFOI) deaths are subtracted and the remainder, including those with "place of occurrence" unspecified, are allocated to Home and Public in the same proportion as those with "place of occurrence" specified.

The table on page 157 shows the ICD-9 E-codes and CFOI event codes for the most common causes of unintentional-injury death. The CFOI event codes (BLS, 1992) do not match exactly with ICD-9 E-codes, so there is some error in the allocation of deaths among the classes.

State reporting system. The Council operates a reporting system through which about 25 states send monthly tabulations of unintentional-injury death data by age group, class, and type of event or industry. This is known as the Accidental Death Summary reporting system. These data are used to make current year estimates based on the most recent 2-Way Split and CFOI data, and to update monthly estimates published in *Injury Facts*^TM.

Linking up to current year. The benchmark data published by NCHS are usually two years old and the CFOI data are usually one year old. The link-relative technique is used to make current year estimates from these data using the state vital statistics data. This method assumes that the change in deaths from one year to the next in states reporting for both years reflects the change in deaths for the entire nation. The ratio is calculated and multiplied times the benchmark figure resulting in an estimate for the next year. It may be necessary to repeat the process, depending on the reference year of the benchmark. For example, the 1997 NCHS and CFOI data were used this year for a 2-Way Split and state data were used to make estimates for 1998 and 1999 Home and Public classes using the link-relative technique. CFOI data for 1998 were also available so it was necessary only to make 1999 Work estimates.

Revisions of prior years. When the figures for a given year are published by NCHS, the 2-Way Split based on those figures and the CFOI become the final estimate of unintentional-injury deaths by class, age group, and type of event or industry. Subsequent years are revised by repeating the link-relative process described above. For example, in this edition of *Injury Facts*^TM, the 1997 NCHS and CFOI data were used to produce final esti-

mates using the 2-Way Split, the 1998 estimates were revised using more complete state data and 1998 CFOI figures, and the new 1999 estimates were made with the state data available in the spring of 2000.

Nonfatal injury estimates. The Council uses the concept of "disabling injury" to define the kinds of injuries included in its estimates. See page 20 for the definition of disabling injury and the National Health Interview Survey (NHIS) injury definitions.

Injury to death ratios. There is no national injury surveillance system that provides disabling injury estimates on a current basis. The National Health Interview Survey, a household survey conducted by the NCHS (see page 20), produces national estimates using its own definition of injury, but the data are not published until well after the reference year (Adams, Hendershot, & Marano, 1999). For this reason, the Council uses injury-to-death ratios to estimate nonfatal disabling injuries for the current year. Complete documentation of the background and new procedure, effective with the 1993 edition, may be found in Landes, Ginsburg, Hoskin, and Miller (1990).

The ratios, one for each class, are a 3-year moving average of the NHIS injury data and the corresponding Council estimates of deaths. Because the NHIS does not use the Council's definition of disabling injury, the NHIS data are adjusted to approximate the disabling concept. The adjustment involves counting only injuries that result in two or more days of restricted activity. (The NHIS counts only whole days of restricted activity even though the definition is stated in terms of half days. One day counted includes from one-half day up to one and one-half days of actual restriction. Two days counted includes from one and one-half up to two and one-half.)

Comparability over time. Even though the injury-to-death ratios are updated each time a new NHIS is released, the resulting estimates are not direct measures of nonfatal injuries and should not be compared with prior years.

Population sources. All population figures used in computing rates are taken from various reports in the P-25 series published by the Bureau of the Census, U.S. Department of Commerce. *Resident* population is used for computing rates.

Costs (pp. 4–7). The procedures for estimating the economic losses due to fatal and nonfatal unintentional injuries were extensively revised for the 1993 edition of *Accident Facts*®. New components were added, new benchmarks adopted, and a new discount rate assumed. All of these changes resulted in significantly higher cost estimates. For this reason, it must be re-emphasized that the cost estimates should not be compared to those in earlier editions of the book.

The Council's general philosophy underlying its cost estimates is that the figures represent income not received or expenses incurred because of fatal and non-fatal unintentional injuries. Stated this way, the Council's cost estimates are a measure of the economic impact of unintentional injuries and may be compared to other economic measures such as gross domestic product, per capita income, or personal consumption expenditures. (See page 79 and "lost quality of life" [p. 155] for a discussion of injury costs for cost-benefit analysis.)

The general approach followed was to identify a benchmark unit cost for each component, adjust the benchmark to the current year using an appropriate inflator, estimate the number of cases to which the component applied, and compute the product. Where possible, benchmarks were obtained for each class: Motor-Vehicle, Work, Home, and Public.

Wage and productivity losses include the value of wages, fringe benefits, and household production for all classes, and travel delay for the Motor-Vehicle class.

For fatalities, the present value of after-tax wages, fringe benefits, and household production was computed using the human capital method. The procedure incorporates data on life expectancy from the NCHS life tables, employment likelihood from the Bureau of Labor Statistics household survey, and mean earnings from the Bureau of the Census money income survey.

The discount rate used was 4%, reduced from 6% used in earlier years. The present value obtained is highly sensitive to the discount rate; the lower the rate, the greater the present value.

For permanent partial disabilities, an average of 17% of earning power is lost (Berkowitz & Burton, 1987). The incidence of permanent disabilities, adjusted to remove intentional injuries, was computed from data on hospitalized cases from the National Hospital Discharge Survey (NHDS) and nonhospitalized cases from the National Health Interview Survey and National Council on Compensation Insurance data on probabilities of disability by nature of injury and part of body injured.

For temporary disabilities, an average daily wage, fringe benefit, and household production loss was calculated and this was multiplied by the number of days of restricted activity from the NHIS.

Travel delay costs were obtained from the Council's estimates of the number of fatal, injury, and property-damage crashes and an average delay cost per crash from Miller et al. (1991).

Medical expenses, including ambulance and helicopter transport costs, were estimated for fatalities, hospitalized cases, and nonhospitalized cases in each class.

The incidence of hospitalized cases was derived from the NHDS data adjusted to eliminate intentional injuries. Average length of stay was benchmarked from Miller, Pindus, Douglass, and Rossman (1993b) and adjusted to estimate lifetime length of stay. The cost per hospital day was benchmarked to the National Medical Expenditure Survey (NMES).

Nonhospitalized cases were estimated by taking the difference between total NHIS injuries and hospitalized cases. Average cost per case was based on NMES data adjusted for inflation and lifetime costs.

Medical cost of fatalities was benchmarked to data from the National Council on Compensation Insurance (1989) to which was added the cost of a premature funeral and coroner costs (Miller et al., 1991).

Cost per ambulance transport was benchmarked to NMES data and cost per helicopter transport was benchmarked to data in Miller et al. (1993a). The number of cases transported was based on data from Rice and MacKenzie (1989) and the National Electronic Injury Surveillance System.

Administrative expenses include the administrative cost of private and public insurance, which represents the cost of having insurance, and police and legal costs.

The administrative cost of motor-vehicle insurance was the difference between premiums earned (adjusted to remove fire, theft, and casualty premiums) and pure losses incurred, based on data from A. M. Best. Workers' compensation insurance administration was based on A. M. Best data for private carriers and regression estimates using Social Security Administration data for state funds and the self-insured. Administrative costs of public insurance (mainly Medicaid and Medicare) amount to about 4% of the medical expenses paid by public insurance, which were determined from Rice and MacKenzie (1989) and Hensler et al. (1991).

Average police costs for motor-vehicle crashes were taken from Miller et al. (1991) and multiplied by the Council's estimates of the number of fatal, injury and property-damage crashes.

Legal expenses include court costs, and plaintiff's and defendant's time and expenses. Hensler et al. (1991) provided data on the proportion of injured persons who hire a lawyer, file a claim, and get compensation. Kakalik and Pace (1986) provided data on costs per case.

Fire losses were based on data published by the National Fire Protection Association in the *NFPA Journal*. The allocation into the classes was based on the property use for structure fires and other NFPA data for nonstructure fires.

Motor-vehicle damage costs were benchmarked to Blincoe and Faigin (1992) and multiplied by the Council's estimates of crash incidence.

Employer costs for work injuries is an estimate of the productivity costs incurred by employers. It assumes each fatality or permanent injury resulted in 4 person-months of disruption, serious injuries 1 person-month, and minor to moderate injuries 2 person-days. All injuries to nonworkers were assumed to involve 2 days of worker productivity loss. Average hourly earnings for supervisors and nonsupervisory workers were computed and then multiplied by the incidence and hours lost per case. Property damage and production delays (except motor-vehicle related) are not included in the estimates but can be substantial.

Lost quality of life is the difference between the value of a statistical fatality or statistical injury and the value of after-tax wages, fringe benefits, and household production. Because this does not represent real income not received or expenses incurred, it is not included in the total economic cost figure. If included, the resulting *comprehensive costs* can be used in cost-benefit analysis because the total costs then represent the maximum amount society should spend to prevent a statistical death or injury.

Work deaths and injuries (p. 44). The method for estimating total work-related deaths and injuries is discussed above. The breakdown of deaths by industry division for the current year is obtained from the CFOI and state Accidental Death Summary figures using the link-relative technique (also discussed above).

The estimate of nonfatal disabling injuries by industry division is made by multiplying the estimate of employment for each industry division by the BLS estimate of the incidence rate of cases involving days away from work for each division (e.g., BLS, 1999) and then adjusting the results so that they add to the work-injury total previously established. The "private sector" average incidence rate is used for the government division, which is not covered in the BLS survey.

Employment. The employment estimates for 1992 to the present were changed for the 1998 edition. Estimates for these years in prior editions are not comparable. The total employment figure used by the Council represents the number of persons in the civilian labor force, aged

16 and older, who were wage or salary workers, self-employed, or unpaid family workers, plus active duty military personnel resident in the U.S. The total employment estimate is a combination of three figures—total civilian employment from the Current Population Survey (CPS) as published in *Employment and Earnings,* plus the difference between total resident population and total civilian population, which represents active duty military personnel.

Employment by industry division is obtained from an unpublished Bureau of Labor Statistics table titled "Employed and experienced unemployed persons by detailed industry and class of worker, Annual Average [year] (based on CPS)."

Time lost (p. 47) is the product of the number of cases and the average time lost per case. Deaths average 150 workdays lost in the current year and 5,850 in future years; permanent disabilities involve 75 and 565 days lost in current and future years, respectively; temporary disabilities involve 17 days lost in the current year only. Off-the-job injuries to workers are assumed to result in similar lost time.

Off-the-job (p. 50) deaths and injuries are estimated by assuming that employed persons incur injuries at the same rate as the entire population.

NSC v. BLS rates by industry. Occupational injury and illness incidence rates on pages 62–65 are compiled from data submitted by Council members that choose to participate in the Council's *Occupational Safety/Health Award Program.* The data are obtained from OSHA logs and the rates are computed using the OSHA incidence rate formula (see page 57). Because participation is voluntary, the resulting incidence rates are not representative of the industries or of Council members.

The Bureau of Labor Statistics rates on pages 56–61 are compiled through a nationwide random sample of establishments (BLS, 1999). The sample is selected to be representative of all private employers in the United States.

The Council's rates may be useful in goal-setting because they are generally lower than the BLS rates and may represent the average rate of the establishments with "better" safety programs. The BLS rates should be used, however, to determine where an establishment stands with respect to the true average for an industry.

Motor-Vehicle section (pp. 74–107). Estimates of miles traveled, registered vehicles, and licensed drivers are published by the Federal Highway Administration in *Highway Statistics* and *Traffic Volume Trends.*

In addition to the death certificate data from NCHS and state registrars, the Council receives annual summary reports of traffic crash characteristics from about 15 states. Most national estimates are made using various ratios and percent distributions from the state crash data.

Beginning with the 1998 edition of *Accident Facts*[®], national estimates of crashes by manner of collision (p. 78) and motor vehicles involved in crashes by type of vehicle (p. 88) are made using the percent changes from the previous year to the current year as reported by the states. This percent change is then applied to benchmark figures obtained from the National Highway Traffic Safety Administration (NHTSA), Fatality Analysis Reporting System (FARS), and General Estimates System (GES) data for the previous year, which yields the current year estimates. These current year estimates are then adjusted to add to the Council's overall number of deaths, injuries and fatal, injury, and property-damage-only crashes that are listed on page 74. Because of these changes, comparisons to previous years should not be made.

Fleet accident rates (p. 99) represents the experience of motor fleets that participated in the Council's National Fleet Safety Contest. For the purposes of the contest all death and injury accidents were included as well as *all* accidents (preventable or not preventable) resulting in property damage except when the vehicle was properly parked. Because of the nature of the reporting system, these accident rates cannot be considered representative of the national experience of motor fleets.

REFERENCES

Adams, P.F., Hendershot, G.E., & Marano, M.A. (1999). Current estimates from the National Health Interview Survey, 1996. Vital and Health Statistics 10(200). Hyattsville, MD: National Center for Health Statistics.

Berkowitz, M., & Burton, J.F., Jr. (1987). Permanent Disability Benefits in Workers' Compensation. Kalamazoo, MI: W.E. Upjohn Institute for Employment Research.

Blincoe, L.J., & Faigin, B.M. (1992). Economic Cost of Motor Vehicle Crashes, 1990. Springfield, VA: National Technical Information Service.

Bureau of Labor Statistics [BLS]. (1992). Occupational Injury & Illness Classification Manual. Itasca, IL: National Safety Council.

Bureau of Labor Statistics [BLS]. (1999, December 16). Workplace Injuries and Illnesses in 1998. Press release USDL-99-358.

Hensler, D.R., Marquis, M.S., Abrahamse, A.F., Berry, S.H., Ebener, P.A., Lewis, E.D., Lind, E.A., MacCoun, R.J., Manning, W.G., Rogowski, J.A., & Vaiana, M.E. (1991). Compensation for Accidental Injuries in the United States. Santa Monica, CA: The RAND Corporation.

Kakalik, J.S., & Pace, N. (1986). Costs and Compensation Paid in Tort Litigation. R-3391-ICJ. Santa Monica, CA: The RAND Corporation.

Landes, S.R., Ginsburg, K.M., Hoskin, A.F., & Miller, T.A. (1990). Estimating Nonfatal Injuries. Itasca, IL: Statistics Department, National Safety Council.

Miller, T., Viner, J., Rossman, S., Pindus, N., Gellert, W., Douglass, J., Dillingham, A., & Blomquist, G. (1991). The Costs of Highway Crashes. Springfield, VA: National Technical Information Service.

Miller, T.R., Brigham, P.A., Cohen, M.A., Douglass, J.B., Galbraith, M.S., Lestina, D.C., Nelkin, V.S., Pindus, N.M., & Smith-Regojo, P. (1993a). Estimating the costs to society of cigarette fire injuries. Report to Congress in Response to the Fire Safe Cigarette Act of 1990. Washington, DC: U.S. Consumer Product Safety Commission.

Miller, T.R., Pindus, N.M., Douglass, J.B., & Rossman, S.B. (1993b). Nonfatal Injury Incidence, Costs, and Consequences: A Data Book. Washington, DC: The Urban Institute Press.

Rice, D.P., & MacKenzie, E.J. (1989). Cost of Injury in the United States: A Report to Congress. Atlanta, GA: Centers for Disease Control and Prevention.

Toscano, G., & Windau, J. (1994). The changing character of fatal work injuries. Monthly Labor Review, 117(10), 17-28.

World Health Organization. (1977). Manual of the International Statistical Classification of Diseases, Injuries, and Causes of Death. Geneva, Switzerland: Author.

SELECTED UNINTENTIONAL-INJURY CODE GROUPINGS

Manner of Injury	ICD-9 E-Codes[a]	OI&ICM[b] Event Codes
Air transport accident	E840-E845	46
Drowning	E910	381
Falls	E880-E888	1
Firearms	E922	0220, 0222, 0229 with source = 911[c]
Fires and burns	E890-E899	51
Mechanical suffocation	E913	383, 384, 389
Motor-vehicle accident	E810-E825	41, 42, 43
Poisoning by gases and vapors	E867-E869	341
Poisoning by solids & liquids	E850-58, E860-66	344
Railway accident	E800-E807	44
Suffocation by ingestion	E911-E912	382
Water transport accident	E830-E838	45

Source: National Safety Council.
[a] International Classification of Diseases, 9th Revision, external cause codes, WHO (1977).
[b] Occupational Injury & Illness Classification Manual, BLS (1992).
[c] Struck by flying object where the source of injury was a bullet.

OTHER SOURCES

The following organizations may be useful for obtaining more current data or more detailed information on various subjects in *Injury Facts*™.

Visit the National Safety Council's web site at www.nsc.org for links to these and other sources.

Federal Highway Administration
400 7th Street, SW, Washington, DC 20590
(202) 366-0660   www.fhwa.dot.gov

Federal Railroad Administration
400 7th Street, SW, Washington, DC 20590
(202) 366-2760   www.fra.dot.gov

Insurance Information Institute
110 William Street, New York, NY 10038
(212) 669-9200   www.iii.org

Insurance Institute for Highway Safety
1005 N. Glebe Road, Suite 800, Arlington, VA 22201
(703) 247-1500   www.highwaysafety.org

International Hunter Education Association
P.O. Box 490, Wellington, CO 80549-0490
(970) 568-7954   www.ihea.com

International Labour Office
4, rue des Morillons
CH-1211 Geneva 22
Switzerland
Phone: +41-22-799-6111
Fax: +41-22-798-8685   www.ilo.org

Mine Safety and Health Administration
Health & Safety Analysis Center
Division of Mining Information
P.O. Box 25367, Denver, CO 80225
(303) 231-5445   www.msha.gov

Motorcycle Safety Foundation
2 Jenner St., Suite 150, Irvine, CA 92718-3812
(714) 727-3227   www.msf-usa.org

National Academy of Social Insurance
1776 Massachusetts Avenue, NW, Suite 615
Washington, DC 20036-1904
(202) 452-8097   www.nasi.org

National Center for Health Statistics
6525 Belcrest Road, Hyattsville, MD 20782
(301) 458-4636   www.cdc.gov/nchs

National Center for Injury Prevention and Control
Office of Communication Resources
4770 Buford Hwy., NE, Mail Stop K65, Atlanta, GA 30341-3724
(770) 488-1506   www.cdc.gov/ncipc

National Clearinghouse for Alcohol and Drug Information
P.O. Box 2345, Rockville, MD 20847-2345
(301) 468-2600 or 1-800-729-6686   www.health.org

National Collegiate Athletic Association
6201 College Boulevard, Overland Park, KS 66211-2422
(913) 339-1906   www.ncaa.org

National Council on Compensation Insurance
750 Park of Commerce Drive, Boca Raton, FL 33487
1-800-NCCI-123 (1-800-622-4123)   www.ncci.com

National Fire Protection Association
P.O. Box 9101, Batterymarch Park, Quincy, MA 02269-0910
(617) 770-3000 or 1-800-344-3555   www.nfpa.org

National Head Injury Foundation
1776 Massachusetts Ave., NW, Suite 100, Washington, DC 20036
(202) 296-6443

National Highway Traffic Safety Administration
400 7th Street, SW, Washington, DC 20590
(202) 366-0123 or 1-800-424-9393   www.nhtsa.dot.gov

National Center for Statistics and Analysis (NRD-31)
400 7th Street, SW, Washington, DC 20590
(202) 366-1470 or 1-800-934-8517

National Institute for Occupational Safety and Health
Clearinghouse for Occupational Safety and Health Information
4676 Columbia Parkway, Cincinnati, OH 45226
1-800-356-4674   www.cdc.gov/niosh

National Spinal Cord Injury Association
600 W. Cummings Park, Suite 2000, Woburn, MA 01801
1-800-962-9629 (Hotline) or (617) 935-2722   www.spinalcord.org

National Sporting Goods Association
1699 Wall Street, Mt. Prospect, IL 60056-5780
(847) 439-4000

National Transportation Safety Board
490 L'Enfant Plaza East, SW, Washington, DC 20594
(202) 382-6735   www.ntsb.gov

Prevent Blindness America
500 E. Remington Road, Schaumburg, IL 60173
(847) 843-2020   www.preventblindness.org

Transportation Research Board
2101 Constitution Avenue, NW, Washington, DC 20418
(202) 334-2935   www.nas.edu/trb

U.S. Coast Guard
2100 2nd Street, SW, Washington, DC 20593-0001
(202) 267-2229   www.uscgboating.org

U.S. Consumer Product Safety Commission
National Injury Information Clearinghouse
4330 East West Highway, Washington, DC 20207
(301) 504-0424   www.cpsc.gov

U.S. Department of Commerce
Bureau of the Census, Public Information Office
Washington, DC 20233-8200
(301) 457-2794   www.census.gov

U.S. Department of Labor
Bureau of Labor Statistics
2 Massachusetts Ave., NE, Washington, DC 20212
(202) 691-7828   stats.bls.gov/oshhome.htm

OSHA Office of Statistics, Room N-3507
200 Constitution Ave., NW, Washington, DC 20210
(202) 693-1702

World Health Organization
20, ave. Appia
CH-1211 Geneva 27
Switzerland
Phone: +41-22-791-2111
Fax: +41-22-791-0746   www.who.int

Accident is that occurrence in a sequence of events that produces unintended injury, death or property damage. *Accident* refers to the event, not the result of the event (see *unintentional injury*).

Cases without lost workdays are cases that do not involve lost workdays but result in medical treatment other than first aid, restriction of work or motion, loss of consciousness, transfer to another job, or diagnosis of occupational illness.

Death from accident is a death that occurs within one year of the accident.

Disabling injury is an injury causing death, permanent disability, or any degree of temporary total disability beyond the day of the injury.

Fatal accident is an accident that results in one or more deaths within one year.

Home is a dwelling and its premises within the property lines including single-family dwellings and apartment houses, duplex dwellings, boarding and rooming houses and seasonal cottages. Excluded from Home are barracks, dormitories, and resident institutions.

Incidence rate, as defined by OSHA, is the number of occupational injuries and/or illnesses or lost workdays per 100 full-time employees. See formula on page 57.

Injury is physical harm or damage to the body resulting from an exchange, usually acute, of mechanical, chemical, thermal, or other environmental energy that exceeds the body's tolerance.

Lost workdays are those days on which, because of occupational injury or illness, the employee was away from work or limited to restricted work activity. *Days away from work* are those days on which the employee would have worked but could not. *Days of restricted work* activity are those days on which the employee was assigned to a temporary job, worked at a permanent job less than full time, or worked at a permanent job but could not perform all duties normally connected with it. The number of lost workdays (consecutive or not) does not include the day of injury or onset of illness or any days on which the employee would not have worked even though able to work.

Lost workday cases are cases that involve days away from work, days of restricted work activity, or both.

Motor vehicle is any mechanically or electrically powered device not operated on rails, upon which or by which any person or property may be transported upon a land highway. The load on a motor vehicle or trailer attached to it is considered part of the vehicle. Tractors and motorized machinery are included while self-propelled in transit or used for transportation. *Nonmotor vehicle* is any road vehicle other than a motor vehicle, such as a bicycle or animal-drawn vehicle, **except** a coaster wagon, child's sled, child's tricycle, child's carriage, and similar means of transportation; persons using these latter means of transportation are considered pedestrians.

Motor-vehicle accident is an unstabilized situation that includes at least one harmful event (injury or property damage) involving a motor vehicle in transport (in motion, in readiness for motion, or on a roadway but not parked in a designated parking area) that does not result from discharge of a firearm or explosive device and does not directly result from a cataclysm. [See Committee on Motor Vehicle Traffic Accident Classification (1997), *Manual on Classification of Motor Vehicle Traffic Accidents*, ANSI D16.1-1996, Itasca, IL: National Safety Council.]

Motor-vehicle traffic accident is a motor-vehicle accident that occurs on a trafficway—a way or place, any part of which is open to the use of the public for the purposes of vehicular traffic. *Motor-vehicle nontraffic accident* is any motor-vehicle accident that occurs entirely in any place other than a trafficway.

Nonfatal injury accident is an accident in which at least one person is injured and no injury results in death.

Occupational illness is any abnormal condition or disorder other than one resulting from an occupational injury caused by exposure to environmental factors associated with employment. It includes acute and chronic illnesses or diseases that may be caused by inhalation, absorption, ingestion, or direct contact. See also page 57.

Occupational injury is any injury such as a cut, fracture, sprain, amputation, etc., which results from a work accident or from a single instantaneous exposure in the work environment. See also page 57.

Pedalcycle is a vehicle propelled by human power and operated solely by pedals; excludes mopeds.

Pedestrian is any person involved in a motor-vehicle accident who is not in or upon a motor vehicle or nonmotor vehicle. Includes persons injured while using a coaster wagon, child's tricycle, roller skates, etc. Excludes persons boarding, alighting, jumping, or falling from a motor vehicle in transport who are considered occupants of the vehicle.

Permanent disability (or permanent impairment) includes any degree of permanent nonfatal injury. It includes any injury that results in the loss or complete loss of use of any part of the body or in any permanent impairment of functions of the body or a part thereof.

Property-damage accident is an accident that results in property damage but in which no person is injured.

Public accident is any accident other than motor-vehicle that occurs in the public use of any premises. Includes deaths in recreation (swimming, hunting, etc.), in transportation (except motor-vehicle, public buildings, etc.), and from widespread natural disasters even though some may have happened on home premises. Excludes accidents to persons in the course of gainful employment.

Source of injury is the principal object such as tool, machine, or equipment involved in the accident and is usually the object inflicting injury or property damage. Also called agency or agent.

Temporary total disability is an injury that does not result in death or permanent disability but that renders the injured person unable to perform regular duties or activities on one or more full calendar days after the day of the injury.

Total cases include all work-related deaths and illnesses and those work-related injuries that result in loss of consciousness, restriction of work or motion, transfer to another job, or require medical treatment other than first aid.

Unintentional injury is the preferred term for accidental injury in the public health community. It refers to the *result* of an accident.

Work hours are the total number of hours worked by all employees. They are usually compiled for various levels, such as an establishment, a company, or an industry. A work hour is the equivalent of one employee working one hour.

Work injuries (including occupational illnesses) are those that arise out of and in the course of gainful employment regardless of where the accident or exposure occurs. Excluded are work injuries to private household workers and injuries occurring in connection with farm chores that are classified as home injuries.

Workers are all persons gainfully employed, including owners, managers, other paid employees, the self-employed, and unpaid family workers but excluding private household workers.

Work/Motor-vehicle duplication includes *work injuries* that occur in *motor-vehicle accidents* (see definitions for work injuries and motor-vehicle accident on this page).

INDEX